Arrested Dev

Arrested Development

Pop Culture and the Erosion of Adulthood

Andrew Calcutt

CASSELL

London and Washington

Cassell
Wellington House
125 Strand
London WC2R 0BB

PO Box 605
Herndon
VA 20172–0605

First published in 1998

British Library Cataloguing-in-Publication Data
A catalogue record for this book is available from the British Library.

Library of Congress Cataloging-in-Publication Data
Calcutt, Andrew
    Arrested development : pop culture and the erosion of adulthood /
Andrew Calcutt.
        p. cm.
    Includes bibliographical references and index.
    ISBN 0-304-33955-5
    1. Popular culture—United States—Psychological aspects.
2. Adulthood—United States—Psychological aspects. 3. Victims—
United States. 4. Personality and culture—United States.
5. Subculture—United States—History—20th century. I. Title.
E169.04.C35 1998
306—dc21   97-34288
                                                                   CIP

ISBN 0-304-33955-5

Typeset by BookEns Ltd, Royston, Herts.
Printed and bound in Great Britain by Biddles Ltd, Guildford and King's Lynn.

Contents

Preface   vii

Introduction   Safe   1

Chapter 1   Alienation   23

Chapter 2   Now   49

Chapter 3   The Child   78

Chapter 4   Vulnerable   107

Chapter 5   Madness   123

Chapter 6   Spirit   149

Chapter 7   Irony   166

Chapter 8   Wiggas   190

Chapter 9   Limits   207

Chapter 10   The End of Adulthood?   233

Index   255

Preface

'There's nothing left to rebel against.' These words, spoken to me by a student in media and communications, prompted me to question my assumptions about the counterculture, and my own limited participation in it. Until recently I had always assumed that in my largely unsuccessful career as a musician and record producer I must somehow have failed to live up to the requirements of the counterculture; either I did not take enough drugs, or have enough sexual partners, or I never threw a television set into the hotel swimming-pool. But this student's remark, which was made in the context of a discussion about the relative lack of rebelliousness in today's society, prompted me to wonder whether in fact it was the counterculture which had failed me, by being too limited, too facile and not really 'counter'.

This book is the end result of that line of thought. It is not meant to be an indictment of the counterculture as the root cause of either my personal failings or the ills of society. However, it does suggest that the tradition which goes back fifty years to Existential Paris, bebop jazz and the first motorcycle gangs represents not so much the capacity to rebel, but the tendency to limit our capacity as human beings and to pretend to ourselves that this is what constitutes rebellion. Moreover, it is my suggestion that the sense of limits which was the founding principle of the counterculture has now crossed over not only into pop culture but also into politics. This means that pop and politics now share the same language of diminished humanity – a communal experience which has catalysed what is generally known as 'victim culture', and now facilitates the further negation of our human potential.

Again this is not to say that the counterculture *caused* today's victim culture, but rather to suggest that the latter could not exist in its present form without the former.

I should add that, when I mentioned to a couple of academic

colleagues that I was writing a book about the identification with children as a largely postwar phenomenon, they both replied along the lines that 'you can find it [infantilization] much further back than that'. As indeed you can, if you look hard enough. But that is exactly my point. Yes, the Romantic Imagination was ever obsessed with childhood innocence. But Romanticism was always a minority interest, until something akin to the Romantic Imagination became part of our mental make-up in the period after the Second World War. Furthermore, if you look at the creative work of the previous two centuries, you will find that literature which focuses on the child is far outweighed by the literature of leaving childhood behind and moving into new adult territory, as in the plethora of novels which are usually described as 'rites of passage'.

I maintain that this long-established balance has only recently been reversed, with an unprecedented number of authors and artists now suggesting that the only passage worth making is not onwards to adulthood and heroism (how quaint!) but backwards to childhood (how authentic, allegedly, and emotionally satisfying). To my mind, therefore, infantilism is not completely new, but its significance in today's society is entirely unprecedented.

Andrew Calcutt
Walthamstow, London
June 1997

To Alka, Cora and the memory of my mother . . .
. . . and to Mick Hume, the magazine editor with *cojones*

Safe

By celebrating an idea of ourselves as vulnerable and childlike, pop culture has contributed to the development of a society obsessed by safety.

'It makes you like yourself and other people.' Speaking on BBC1's *Kilroy*[1] in a debate prompted by the death of Leah Betts (the Essex student who died in November 1995 after taking an Ecstasy tablet on her eighteenth birthday), an unnamed E-user explained that she would continue taking the drug because of the unique sense of warmth and security which she derived from it.

Likewise the singer Brian Harvey, in a widely reported statement (later retracted) which got him sacked from his band East 17 (he was subsequently reinstated), praised the drug for 'increasing the love' and promoting a sense of well-being among people who have taken it.

Most of the chroniclers of Ecstasy and the rave culture associated with it stress the feelings of warmth and mutual reassurance to be gained from the E experience. In a column in the *Observer*, Joan Smith likened rave culture to having safe sex with thousands of people at the same time.[2] Writing about the effects of Ecstasy, the novelist Thomas Pynchon noted the relaxation and relief arising from the temporary disconnection of the 'circuits of the brain which mediate alarm, fear, flight, fight, lust and territorial paranoia'.[3] In *Ecstasy: The MDMA Story* Bruce Eisner also described it as a chemical comforter:

> *It is a room in which both your inner experience and your relations with others seem magically transformed. You feel really good about yourself and your life. At the same time, everyone who comes into this room seems more*

lovable. You find your thoughts flowing, turning into words that previously were blocked by fear and inhibition.[4]

The American cyber-journalist and essayist Douglas Rushkoff, who has been described as the Tom Wolfe of the New Edge, explains that Ecstasy is attractive to many young people because it 'creates a loving ego resiliency in which no personal problem seems too big or scary. This is why it has become popular in the younger gay and alternative lifestyle communities, where identity crises are commonplace.'[5]

In *Heaven's Promise*, probably the first novel about the E scene, Paolo Hewitt has his 'on one' protagonist feel 'a camaraderie for every smiling herbert I passed' and 'a surge of real companionship'.[6] In *Altered State*, an account of Ecstasy culture and Acid House, the British writer and editor Matthew Collin chronicled 'spontaneous acts of kindness, of expressions of unconditional love, like the whole club singing Happy Birthday'.[7] In a postscript to *Storming Heaven: LSD and the American Dream* Jay Stevens described Ecstasy as 'an empathy drug'. It is 'the perfect domestic psychedelic' which encourages users to 'become more loving' in that it 'eliminates the affect of the past, like fear'.[8]

The aspect of the E experience most frequently cited by its advocates is that the drug induces a wonderful feeling of safety and security. Ecstasy appears to function as the antidote to the prevailing atmosphere of risk and anxiety, in which growing numbers of people have come to feel permanently vulnerable and to define themselves as potential victims. The prospect of temporary respite from this overheated and overbearing risk-consciousness seems to be the main motivation for taking E.

The desire for safety on the part of those who advocate Ecstasy mirrors the demand for safety-consciousness on the part of those who warn against it. This means that in an important sense the discussion about the merits or dangers of Ecstasy is a non-debate. There is no divide between those whose priority is safety and those who might describe themselves as risk-takers or think of themselves as cultural adventurers. The non-debate about Ecstasy is the first discussion about the recreational use of illegal drugs in which all sides are using the same word as their touchstone. The magic word is: safety. The anti-drugs lobby warn that E can never be safe, and that large numbers of people will become victims of the drug unless its use is immediately curtailed. Their opponents claim that Ecstasy can be safe under the right conditions, and recommend it on the grounds that it releases us from the perceived threat of victimization.

Noticeable by its absence is the traditional contest of ideologies, with one side insisting that the law on drugs must be obeyed whatever its merits, and the other side declaring that drugs might be unsafe but it is up to the individual to decide whether he or she wants to take a risk. Both sides have abandoned their traditional vocabulary in favour of a new language of personal safety.

The consensus around the notion of safety was summed up in the *New Statesman* by its (then) editor Steve Platt, who wrote, 'It is time to end the "war on drugs" and start thinking about minimising the risks.'[9] The editor of this traditional political magazine was clearly thinking along the same safety-first lines as the managers of the Liverpool nightclub Cream, who began to deploy doctors in the house to look after overheated ravers, in a move which *The Face* subsequently described as 'a decision to make that world safe not sorry'.[10]

The privilege accorded to safety is even more forcefully expressed whenever sex is discussed. In the 1990s, you can have any sexuality you like, as long as it is safe. The irony is that the contemporary emphasis on sexual relations as one of the defining aspects of our lives may have well emerged in preference to the perceived risks of public life and ideological contestation. Sex and the preoccupation with it have functioned as a refuge from the difficulty of trying to deal with wider society. But once safety has been introduced into the body politic, it seems we can never get enough of it. Likewise the recent enthusiasm for cybersex was predicated on the assumption that it was safe, i.e. it did not involve the exchange of bodily fluids. But the notion of a digitized sexual playground where safety need not be a consideration was immediately replaced by the consensus that any kind of sexual contact, whether meat to meat or mouse to mouse, must be made safe.

Safety: the ultimate high

If everyone is indeed preoccupied with safety, then this decade truly deserves to be known as 'the nervous nineties'. And if, as E fans seem to be suggesting, safety is now the ultimate high, then surely we are living through a low point of human endeavour.

This is the decade which has diminished the meaning of ecstasy (once an experience associated with the awesome and the infinite) to the point where it entails nothing more extravagant than cosy feelings of closeness, empathy and a temporary lapse in risk-consciousness. No wonder Marek Kohn, a leading commentator on drugs and lifestyle, was prompted to say that 'the E culture is remarkable in its banality'.[11] Comparing the E-induced feeling of love to an anorexic's belief that she is fat, newspaper columnist Charlotte Raven agreed that E makes you 'smug'.[12]

Drug culture was not always so 'banal' or 'smug'. In the 1960s Dr Timothy Leary's acid-driven 'politics of ecstasy' entailed an abortive attempt to transcend the ego. For the safety-conscious ravers of the 1990s, however, the special joy of E is that it allows the user to 'take your ego with you'. It seems to soothe today's fragile psyche in the same way that the infant Linus draws comfort from his security blanket in the *Peanuts* strip cartoon. Even former *Face* editor Sheryl Garratt, who is generally sympathetic to club culture, had to admit that 'ecstasy over amphetamines' means 'escapism over anger'.[13]

Snapshot: Stay safe

It was in Liverpool 8 that I first heard 'safe' used as a word with which to sign off a conversation. This was in the late 1980s, when, as a campaigning journalist, I was trying to draw attention to the plight of black youth in what outsiders referred to as 'Toxteth' (locals always preferred 'Liverpool 8'), who were the victims of a style of policing more readily associated with the townships of South Africa under apartheid. I wrote a number of articles in collaboration with a local hero by the name of Delroy Burris. As I left his house at night, with a half-finished typescript in my bag, he would say to me 'stay safe', or just 'safe'. The threatening figures from whom Burris exhorted me to 'stay safe' were not drug dealers or some other criminals, but the police: we knew that they knew what we were doing; and we also knew that some of them were unhappy about it.

By the time I moved back to London on the cusp of the 1990s, the phrase 'stay safe' had already made it on to the club scene. DJs would advise dancers to 'stay safe'; and 'safe' functioned as a term of approval or a form of assent, like 'cool'. The anti-authority sense in which Burris had used it was already absent.

A couple of years later 'stay safe' became one of those phrases that kept appearing in leaflets and advice booklets issued by youth and community projects which saw themselves as streetwise. In the new usage of the phrase, however, the nature of the perceived threat had changed dramatically. No longer referring to the menace of the police, as Burris had done, the term was now being used to suggest that other people on the street could turn out to be a threat; and even to hint that young people could be a threat to themselves unless they behaved responsibly and thereby guaranteed their own safety. From being a word which had connoted an anti-authoritarian stance, 'safe' has become a word that sums up the new form of authority, which works by encouraging us to think of ourselves as essentially vulnerable individuals who must pay heed to the never-ending task of making ourselves 'safe'.

In its emphasis on safety and security, the E scene is probably more immature than any previous incarnation of youth culture. In some ways it seems out of kilter with the reckless rebels of yesteryear. But the banality and infantilism of E culture is not without precedent. It is more than a quarter of a century since Jimi Hendrix remarked that 'music is a safe type of high', and today's music-related culture might well be summed up as the logical outcome of a fifty-year-old tradition which has become more and more preoccupied with safety even as it has grown in popularity and significance.

Forever young

What was once the exclusive preserve of youth − 'youth culture' − is now a popular culture (pop culture) which commands the allegiance of almost everyone under sixty. 'Youth culture ... has become the whole of culture', observed columnist Bryan Appleyard in the *Independent*.[14] It is a lens which both reflects and refracts the experience of its many adherents. The vast majority of people in the Western world now look to the forms of personal expression associated with pop culture as the means to find their self-image and define their experience. In historical terms, this is extraordinary; only during the past fifty years has pop culture become elevated to the point where it has surpassed politics, economics and traditional forms of religion as the primary means of self-definition and the premier thread of public discourse.

What this means is that pop culture, more than politics or religion, is the domain which most people now enter in order to find the iconography which describes their own lives back to them. We come to know ourselves by the images and metaphors of pop culture − a culture which is currently bound up in images of safety and metaphors for risk avoidance. An examination of the iconography of pop culture, therefore, gives us a picture of individuals in society who now see themselves primarily in terms of the quest for safety and the avoidance of risk.

As well as surpassing traditional politics as a focal point in society, pop culture has often been anti-political; indeed, pop culture's anti-political element is what made it appear radical, once upon a time. At its inception in the aftermath of the Second World War it went against the grain of the big ideas, left and right, which had informed political debate and social reform for two centuries. Hence in its original incarnation it was known as 'the counterculture'. But with hindsight we can see that this was a misnomer: the counterculture was not a challenge to the rest of society so much as a preview of where it was already going.

In the 1950s and 1960s the counterculture was developed by the front-runners of a generation whose lack of faith in existing society was exceeded only by disbelief in their own ability to change it. In retreat from the problems of their age, they created the counterculture as a relatively low-risk play area where high-stakes questions about the future of humanity could be avoided. They also originated the combination of childishness and cynicism which has since spread throughout society, and is now writ large in today's pop culture.

Arrested development

The classic dilemma of the modern adolescent is whether to become part of society or to attempt to transcend it. Pop culture describes this moment of indecision, cultivates it as a way of life, and invests the resultant juvenilia with a significance which is hard to justify. What began in the counterculture as a refusal to accept the norms associated with adulthood is now a sad reflection of the successive generations who could not find it in themselves to grow up and instead have lived their entire lives permanently poised on the cusp of the adolescent dilemma.

In the 1950s and 1960s, pop culture was often described as the test-bed for the future development of society. Forty years on, it can be seen as an experiment in arrested development. Unfortunately, the lessons of this experiment remain unlearnt; and what should have been discarded as an occasionally brave but always misguided attempt to transcend the limits of society has now become the mainstream model in which limits and constraints upon human endeavour can be re-presented with even greater force and authority.

Youth came into its own when, despite the economic prosperity of the period, post-Second-World-War society proved unable to develop a credible model of adulthood. Writing in the 1960s about the 'country of the young' which had emerged since 1945, the American critic John W. Aldridge observed that 'anyone in his right mind might hesitate to embrace the joys of adulthood in a time like the present'.[15] Pete Townshend, songwriter and guitarist in The Who, was more succinct; the soundbite in the lyrics to his 'My Generation' is a line which many an ageing pop star has subsequently lived to regret: 'Hope I die before I get old.'

Aldridge noted that the failure of his generation to provide a new model of adulthood had the effect of fetishizing youth, inflating it from a phase to be outgrown into a lifelong excuse for immaturity and childishness. He also recognized that the limited character of youth culture was not the sole responsibility of young people; rather that youth culture and the general preoccupation with it were the joint expression of America's failure to renew itself as a grown-up society. Castigating the intelligentsia for its infatuation with pop culture, Aldridge identified the 'cult of youth' as the avant-garde of a society which had lost the ability to go forward.

These observations seem to have been borne out by subsequent events. Western intellectuals are now obsessed with pop culture. Policy-makers share many of the assumptions which originated within it. Where there used to be a 'generation gap', the preoccupation with 'youth-oriented' cultural forms now spans the entire population. In the 1990s, to say that you have grown out of pop music and its attendant sensibility is to invite accusations of senility. To paraphrase the song by rock artist Bryan Adams, we are eighteen till we die.

Impasse

Widespread infatuation with pop culture is underpinned by the common experience of impasse, i.e. the equally widespread recognition that we are living in a society which cannot understand the problems of its own making, still less overcome them. Standing before the elephantine chaos of today's world, we all have a tendency to feel like children; and pop culture is the focus of everyone's attention because it embodies the pervasive sense of childlike vulnerability which we experience in the face of social problems which seem to be as imponderable as they are gigantic.

Arrested Development

This is the overarching context within which we have come to look upon the world through the prism of the child. It is hardly a ringing endorsement of our adulthood, for the measure of us as adults is surely the extent to which we refuse to accept the sense of powerlessness which external circumstances might impose upon us. But in today's context we seem more than ready to give in to the sense of our own impotence, and even to celebrate it through our perverse identification with those who are necessarily the weakest members of the human race, namely children.

The end of ideology and the cult of the loser

During a Channel 4 documentary on Ecstasy and the dance culture (*Rave New World*, 1995), a spokesman for multimedia artists The Future Sound of London (FSOL) declared that it would be better if consumers felt impotent rather than sexually aroused by FSOL's sounds and images. This statement exemplifies the celebration of powerlessness particularly explicit in today's E culture, to the point where numerous commentators have recommended it as a sexual suppressant which serves to protect women from the unwanted attentions of rampant males. Ecstasy, it seems, is a contemporary substitute for bromide.

The rejection of sexual potency is unusual, although not unprecedented in pop culture (the amphetamine-driven asexuality of punk was a short-lived precursor); however, the renunciation of social power is a long-standing motif in pop culture which can be traced all the way back to the first incarnation of the counterculture in the early 1950s. But whereas the counterculture claimed that the renunciation of power over society would be liberating and somehow empowering for the individual, FSOL and others have now drawn out the logic of abdication from the question of social relations and extended it into the terrain of personal relations.

When asked to explain what the Beats were all about, founder-member Jack Kerouac said that they were 'beat' as in 'beatific' and 'beat' as in 'beaten'. Acceptance of impotent defeat was an intrinsic part of the state of grace to which Kerouac aspired.

While Kerouac was on the road, his fellow American Daniel Bell was moving towards *The End of Ideology*. Bell's thesis was that the great battle of ideas had ended (a notion which had already been mooted by the existentialist Albert Camus and the sociologist Raymond Aron):

ideology on a grand scale had made itself redundant, and pragmatism would henceforth be the key to politics.

On the face of it the two young writers were poles apart. Bell was to become part of the new academia; Kerouac, after breaking his leg playing college football at Columbia, had hobbled away from his chance to become part of the government-sponsored élite. However, what they had in common is of more significance than the different social strata in which they happened to be living at the time.

Both Bell and Kerouac were heralds of the post-ideological era. Bell championed a pragmatic form of social democracy within a reduced terrain of political contestation, while Kerouac stressed the anti-politics of personal experience and self-expression. But in their different ways they were both describing the disaggregation of society and social theory. Furthermore, they described a world without ideological combativity, in which humanity would no longer struggle against its circumstances en bloc; rather (beaten, beatific but above all pragmatic) we would agree to live without combativity and within a more limited range of experience and expectations.

Bell was guardedly optimistic about the prospect of a world without ideology and its attendant aspirations, while Kerouac and his fellow Beats were happy to re-present this loss by initiating the cult of the loser and popularizing the notion that the mad or lost people of the world had a monopoly on authentic experience and true understanding. They advocated what amounted to an abdication from rational calculation and a retreat from the contest for power, which embraced madness as a metaphor for a way of life beyond the traditional politics of collectivized self-interest.

It was against this post-ideological, anti-political background that William Carlos Williams, in his introduction to the City Lights edition, described Allen Ginsberg's influential poem *Howl* (1956) as a 'howl of defeat'.[16] Ginsberg, who was born into a family of communist sympathizers, began his poem with a post-political dedication to Kerouac, 'the new Buddha of American prose'. The second dedication was to 'William Seward Burroughs, author of *Naked Lunch*, an endless novel which will drive everybody mad'. The poem is subtitled 'for Carl Solomon' – a reference to the close friend whom Ginsberg met while they were both resident in the same New York psychiatric hospital. It was Solomon who introduced Ginsberg to the work of Antonin Artaud, the French theatre director and certified lunatic, who died in 1948 but was just then (in the late 1940s) coming into vogue.

This was one of the first episodes in a saga of relationships linking the emerging counterculture to the idea of madness as an elevated and even enviable state of mind. Frustrated by the failure of their parents' big ideas (Ginsberg's left-wing father could never understand what had happened to his son's 'former zeal for a liberal progressive democratic society'), the 'best minds' of Ginsberg's generation attempted, as Burroughs (following Nietzsche) put it, to 'destroy all rational thought'. If the Enlightenment had come to a dead end, they opted to abandon history and invent a timeless new paganism in which rationality was the only heresy. Henceforth madness was regarded by the counterculture not as an affliction but as the mark of superior insight.

The most succinct definition of the new sensibility came from the other side of the Atlantic. 'Good for the imbecile', cried Jean Dubuffet, painter and founder of Art Brût, 'he is our man.' In Britain Dubuffet's paean to imbecility was translated into music-related culture in the form of the 'leapniks' – the precursors of 'slam dancers' who followed the trad jazz bands of the 1950s. Some years later it was re-formatted into the 'idiot dance' originated by singer Roger Chapman of the British 'progressive' group Family. The 'idiot dance' was subsequently imitated by thousands of hippies all over the Western world, and then recycled for the next generation in 1976 when the punks performed similarly deranged and childish movements which they dubbed the 'pogo'.

In the last forty years there have been many other instances in which pop culture has elevated and celebrated the idea of madness. When Pink Floyd vocalist Syd Barrett left the group as a result of mental illness, he entered the holy of holies. After killing off his Ziggy Stardust persona, David Bowie re-invented himself as Aladdin Sane (a lad insane) and paraded his temporary mental instabilty in what is generally regarded as one of the best arts documentaries ever made (*Cracked Actor*, Arena, BBC2, 1974). Actor Jack Nicholson continues to be revered for his part in Milos Forman's film *One Flew Over the Cuckoo's Nest* (1975), in which he played a prankster mental patient struggling to retain his identity in the face of bureaucratic lunacy.

The message of this film, and of the novel by Ken Kesey from which it is taken, is that the bureaucratic madness of mental institutions far exceeds that of their inmates, whose lunacy is not really lunacy at all but a personal and potentially creative vision. This message was repackaged in the 1997 movie *Shine*, which, according to Cambridge don John Casey, 'has invested heavily in the 1960s idea that the mentally ill may really be more sane than the rest of us', particularly in its depiction of pianist David Helfgott as 'a "Holy Fool"'.[17]

The 1960s and 1970s were also the period in which the clown, symbolizing childish innocence and naive irrationality, came to be a favoured icon, featuring in a wide range of films from *Godspell* to Michelangelo Antonioni's *Blow Up*. And when Federico Fellini wrote his autobiography at the end of the 1960s, it was published under the title *I, Clown*.[18]

More recently, the canonization of Kurt Cobain in the wake of his suicide in 1994 shows that the cult of the unhinged loser is still alive and kicking. Moreover, the song that broke the increasingly successful American singer-songwriter Beck into the British market was entitled 'I'm a Loser, Baby (So Why Don't You Kill Me?)'; although Beck's intention was ironic, this aspect of the song tended to get lost over the airwaves. Even the Royals are getting in on the act. In her infamous *Panorama* television interview (November 1995), Princess Diana advertised her experience of bulimia as proof of psychological trauma and victim status. The overwhelmingly favourable response to the interview indicates that the loser's part is the one which almost everyone is now keen to take, especially when it encompasses more than a hint of mental instability.

We know what's good for you
In a radio interview in 1995, soon after announcing that he would not seek re-election to Parliament in the general election of 1997, Conservative MP George Walden remarked that those in positions of authority now treat the public like children with learning difficulties. If Walden was right, and it really is the case that those in authority treat the rest of us like social inadequates who are incapable of making rational decisions on our own behalf, it is important to find out how the great and the good have come to think of the general public in this unusually derogatory fashion. Is it too fanciful to suggest that their mental model of the vulnerable, unstable, childish member of the public is drawn from the canon of pop culture and its 'countercultural' antecedents? It may even be the case that, forty years on, the politicians of today are enacting and enforcing an idea of the inadequate, incapable individual which the Beats and their successors could only dream of.

Arrested Development

Pop culture is certainly the *lingua franca* through which those in the corridors of power seek to engage with those outside. Legend has it that Bill Clinton won the United States presidential election in 1992 because he kept reminding himself that 'it's the economy, stupid'. If that was the catchphrase which got Clinton into the White House, his admission that he had smoked dope 'but didn't inhale' may turn out to be the watchword of his extended tenure there.

New power generation

Clinton is as old as pop culture. As he grew up, so its significance became inflated; hence his eagerness to show awareness of its nuances. During the 1992 election campaign Clinton played the saxophone on nation-wide television, and his younger supporters came to identify themselves as 'the saxophone club'. After the election, the president celebrated his inauguration with a concert that featured a wide range of pop performers, from soul diva Aretha Franklin to a toned-down version of rap. It was broadcast live, with plenty of footage showing the Clinton family tapping their feet and nodding their heads to the music. Clinton's appreciation of pop culture was reciprocated by the music industry, which gave him a Grammy award (spoken-word section) in February 1997.

Clinton's presidency is indicative of a generational shift in the White House. The most powerful people in the most powerful country in the world are now younger than the Beatles; and the culture with which they grew up may well have furnished them with an idea of themselves and the public as permanent adolescents.

With pop culture as its backdrop, the Clinton generation is introducing a new state religion into the United States: counselling. The counselling faith is based on the belief that, left to their own devices, ordinary human beings are so adolescent, immature and unstable that they are always on the point of turning into either another Charles Manson (psychopath and predator) or a Sharon Tate (defenceless victim). This is the nightmare of the counterculture translated into the new mysticism of public policy. It is tantamount to assuming that the average individual is incapable of rational thought and action, and must therefore be a trauma waiting to happen.

A similarly degraded idea of humanity was expressed at the fiftieth Cannes film festival by the actor-turned-director Gary Oldman. Making his directorial debut with *Nil by Mouth* (1997), a film about his alcoholic father's abuse of his mother, Oldman, who has himself undergone treatment for alcohol abuse, declared: 'The sins of the father are visited on the son. We are a lot sicker than we think we are. Most people need therapy.'[19] His combination of religiosity and therapy, patched together in a low opinion of his fellows which is in fact more anti-human than most previous religions, would make Oldman a welcome visitor in either the White House or Number 10 Downing Street.

The religion of counselling conjures up an extremely patronizing image of the permanently 'at risk' individual, prone like a child to uncontrollable and apparently demonic urges and, also like a child, unable to cope with the consequences of such urges in the behaviour of others. The spectre of the immature individual, which is now being projected on to the general population by those in positions of authority, bears an uncanny resemblance to the self-image of childlike vulnerability and madness which, as we have seen, is a staple of pop culture and the counterculture which preceded it.

If the iconography of the counterculture is taken at face value, as an accurate portrayal of everyday behaviour, the only possible conclusion to be drawn from it is that we are all hopelessly alienated, irredeemably childish and permanently hovering on the brink of madness. In which case it really would be the primary duty of government to provide us with counselling and therapy from the cradle to the grave. Thankfully, this is not the case.

We are not half as dumb as our self-image, and the iconography of pop culture needs to be interpreted not literally but metaphorically, as a projection by imaginative means of a broader sense of the inadequacy of society. But the picture is further complicated by the fact that ours is an age in which the distinction between that which is real and that which is metaphorical is increasingly blurred. A growing number of people are now prepared to believe in the bad publicity about themselves and everyone else; and there is a whole new power generation geared up to enact this kind of negative self-image and to factor it into the institutional fabric of society.

Accordingly a new kind of legislation is currently being enacted which corresponds with the picture of widespread inadequacy that originated in the counterculture and has since become a mainstay of pop culture. By enacting such legislation, far from 'selling out' their youthful ideals, the Clintonesque intake into the corridors of power could be said to have stayed true to the impoverished idea of humanity which informed the culture it grew up in. In short, those in authority today have taken pop culture at face value and are now developing government policies which adopt its message of human failure as their starting-point. They are introducing a new legal persona in accordance with the negative cultural personality which originated in the counterculture before entering into the universal currency of pop culture.

With the swearing-in of Bill Clinton as president of the United States, the mindset of the counterculture made it into high office. This does not mean that the old hippie fantasy is coming true and the water supply is about to be spiked with LSD. Rather it means that those in authority treat the rest of us as if we are already tripping. The basic assumption of the new policy-makers is that we are all victims, in constant need of professional advice and regulation to help us through the bad trip called life.

'Clinton-lite' and British victim culture

The cross-pollination between pop culture and state-sponsored victim culture is not confined to the USA. Labour leader Tony Blair, known as 'Clinton-lite' in the White House, has posed for photographs strumming a Fender Stratocaster guitar in much the same way that his American mentor was pictured playing the saxophone. Neil Spencer, former *NME* editor and press officer for old Labour's Red Wedge, noted that Tony Blair has 'a sensibility formed by rock music'.[20] In 1995 Blair told the *News of the World* that rock music 'is the absolute love of my life', but warned that New Labour would lose the 1997 general election if the tapes of his college band Ugly Rumours were ever released. Home Secretary Jack Straw even mimicked Clinton's reference to smoking dope without inhaling. He said the only joints he smoked were 'dopeless'.

In the 1997 general election New Labour sold itself to young people as the party which respects diversity and responsibility – a kind of party political version of the values of E culture. Prior to the election campaign, New Labour was pleased to associate itself with Creation, the record label whose stable of artists includes Oasis, one of the most successful British bands since the Beatles. Noel Gallagher, the songwriter and leader of Oasis, appeared on the front cover of New Labour's in-house magazine and declared that he cried when he heard

Blair's speech to the 1996 party conference. At the end of January 1997, Tony Blair spoke at a music industry meeting hosted in the House of Commons by Creation boss Alan McGee, and McGee's partner Andy Saunders let it be known that Creation has been sitting down with Blair and media strategists Peter Mandelson and Alistair Campbell to advise them about music for New Labour's party political broadcasts. Saunders even mooted the possibility of an Oasis soundtrack for a New Labour party political broadcast. At the time of writing this has not yet occurred, but the relationship between pop culture and the new politics was consummated at a reception for the luminaries of cool Britannia which took place at Number 10 Downing Street in August 1997, and which Noel Gallagher described simply as 'top'.

In the 1960s the Labour prime minister Harold Wilson got close to the Beatles only when he nominated them for the MBE. In the 1990s New Labour has cultivated a much closer connection with the new royalty of pop. As far as pop critics are concerned, it seems to be having the desired effect. 'I can't recognize geeks like John Major,' said Jon Savage, joint editor of the *Faber Book of Pop*. 'Tony Blair is someone I can recognize. He shows an understanding of rock music.'[21]

By the same token, it is Blair's 'understanding of rock music' that will have familiarized him with the cultural personality of the individual as victim, loser and all-round inadequate. Like Clinton, Blair seeks to address our alleged inadequacy through the terminology of failure provided first by the Beat counterculture, and then by its all-enveloping Big Brother, pop culture.

Harvey, Gallagher and the Ecstasy debate

The crossover between pop culture and the politics of victim culture was demonstrated even more clearly in the furore that followed Noel Gallagher's declaration that 'drugs is like getting up in the morning and having a cup of tea'. Gallagher was speaking in defence of Brian Harvey, the aforementioned lead singer in teenybop band East 17 who was sacked (temporarily) for making pro-Ecstasy comments.

In a radio interview broadcast in the early hours of 16 January 1997 Harvey said he enjoyed taking drugs and boasted about how many he could do without suffering ill effects – a boast made by countless young men since the use of illicit drugs began to take off in Britain some forty years ago. Within hours East 17 records were banned by thirteen radio stations and a DJ smashed the band's single on air; television chiefs spiked an interview with Harvey due to be broadcast on the children's Saturday morning programme *Scratchy and Co*; and East 17 was dropped from the launch show of the midweek Lottery.

Harvey was forced to issue a retraction; advised to go for counselling by the other band members who also sacked him; labelled 'irresponsible' and told he would have the deaths of future drugs victims on his conscience; threatened with prosecution for inciting others to offend against the Misuse of Drugs Act; accused of seducing a schoolgirl; and arrested for behaving like a 'football hooligan' in the vicinity of Stringfellow's nightclub.

While Harvey was depicted as the most sacrilegous antichrist since Johnny Rotten, the bereaved relatives of those who have died after taking drugs were accorded the status of saints. Journalists and programme presenters adopted a pious tone of voice when introducing the ubiquitous Paul and Janet Betts, the parents of eighteen-year-old Leah Betts, whose death has become the focal point in any discussion of illicit drug use. Their comments are regarded as sacrosanct.

Gallagher was one of the few music people with enough balls to defend Harvey in public, and for a few hours it looked as if he might be kicked just as hard. But then he issued a statement which referred to the 'harmful side of drug taking' and called for 'an honest and open debate about drug abuse in this country'. His call was taken up in every quarter.

On its front cover the *Daily Mirror* declared 'Why Noel's *right* on drugs' (31 January), and its leader-writer gave Gallagher a pat on the back: 'His words will not persuade a single youngster to turn to drugs', but they may have started an instructive debate, in which case 'he will have achieved much more than the politicians'.

In the space of a few hours the discussion about drugs switched from being a witch-hunt (Tory MP Tim Rathbone, chair of the all-party Drugs Misuse Group, had been calling for Gallagher to be prosecuted) to an open debate in which anyone could express their opinion. Or so it seemed. In fact there was no such transformation. Regardless of what Gallagher had in mind, the debate was an open-and-shut case in which the only possible outcome was the further elevation of the victim as icon.

Even if every television chat show for a whole year had been devoted to the topic of Ecstasy, it would still have been a non-debate. This is because every programme and every newspaper article was built around the sacred testimony of Paul and Janet Betts or some other bereaved parents. Ecstasy 'guru' Nicholas Saunders quickly came to regard such programmes as a set-up to be avoided. On his website (http://www.ecstasy.org) Saunders explained how during the hounding of Brian Harvey he was

> *invited to go on tv twice with the Betts, which I refused since I have found it impossible to have serious debate with a strong emotional element. In fact that is now the seventh time I have refused to go on with the Betts. I also refused the Kilroy show as they said they would have bereaved parents.*

In the non-debate of January and February 1997, the 'strong emotional element' had the status of a Papal Bull. The feelings of bereaved parents as 'secondary victims', took absolute priority, and every other consideration was made to seem insignificant by comparison. The result was not a debate but a theatre of humiliation in which participants were invited to bow the knee before icons of suffering such as the Betts family, or risk being consigned to pariah status like Harvey.

As in previous episodes of E culture and the discussion surrounding it, this was a non-debate. If in earlier episodes the touchstone was 'safety', in this instance the buzzword was 'victim'. In both instances the non-debate proceeded in such a way as to make 'safety' and 'victim' the first and last word on the subject.

It was more than just a set-up by paternalistic television producers, however. The latter would be entitled to claim that, in giving preference to victimhood, they were reflecting the views not only of opponents of Ecstasy but also of many active participants in pop culture, including Brian Harvey, who made a prolific apology to the parents of Leah Betts. Even the usually hard-headed Noel Gallagher was reported to have apologized for any offence he might have caused them. And in clubs all over Britain, ravers welcomed the post-Betts idea of 'safe dancing'.

The irony is that it was their own counterculture which helped popularize the idea of young people as potential victims unable to cope with the vicissitudes of life. Now, in the form of the late Leah Betts and her parents, this image of vulnerability has been taken up by politicians for whom it functions as the pivotal point in calls for more responsibility, restraint and control; and on most of the occasions when they make such calls they can be sure of a fairly favourable response from those involved in what is now the pop version of victim culture.

Thus it was that in the first weeks of 1997 the iconography of victimhood facilitated the passage through Parliament of a Private Member's Bill, introduced by Tory backbencher Barry Legg, which empowers police and local councils to close down any premises (clubs, students' union buildings) where drugs are suspected of being sold and consumed. This legislation, which even the Home Office described as 'draconian', completed its Commons stages on the very day that Brian Harvey was being tailed by journalists brandishing a picture of Leah Betts in a coma, who claimed to have 'shamed' him into making a personal apology to her parents.

DJs and dance-oriented magazines complained about the letter of the Legg law; but they had already acceded to the post-Betts principle of safety first. All of which goes to show that in the 1990s victimhood – the bastard offspring of the Beat counterculture – has acquired a unique moral authority.

Interactivity

While British politicians are paying attention to pop culture and its iconography of victimhood, pop stars are themselves acting out parables of the notion of victim society which now informs political policy. Thus the video for 'Mis-shapes' by Britpop band Pulp (the chart-topping single from the *Guardian*'s 1995 'album of the year' *Different Class*) carried the same message as the anti-bullying films issued that year by the Department for Education (DFE).

In the Pulp video the action took place in the sixth-form disco rather than the school playground, but the moral message was the same as that issued by the Tory government. Lead singer Jarvis Cocker is seen to acquire victim status at the hands of straight white males wearing 'short-sleeved white shirts and moustaches' – the older brothers of the bullies in the DFE material.

The villains of Cocker's piece are insensitive working-class lads unable to recognize that inside everyone, even themselves, there is a victim struggling to get out. Whether or not it was Cocker's intention, in scenes like these his waif-like persona contributes as much to the cult of the victim as the politicians who manipulate personal grief to their own ends. Although he may only be continuing the pop culture tradition in which the victim has often been the protagonist, nevertheless, in circumstances where victimhood has recently become one of the key themes of political policy, merely continuing this tradition necessarily acquires new and perhaps more insidious connotations.

How can we grow up?

In 1995 Jarvis Cocker, then aged thirty-one, said he was proud to be 'imma' (immature).[22] Bjork, also in her thirties, accounts for her youthful appearance by saying that she 'just stayed stupid'.[23] But Cocker is now trying to extricate himself from permanent adolescence and Bryan Appleyard, author and *Independent* columnist, believes it is 'time we all learnt to grow up'.[24] In a penetrating entry on 'infantilisation' in *alt.culture* (a dictionary of pop culture in the 1990s), Eric Konigsberg sounded a similar note of frustration. Noting that 'Americans can no longer think of themselves as grown-ups', he quoted *Movieline* magazine approvingly:

> Grace Kelly *was 22 when she made* High Noon, *the same age as* Winona Ryder *in* Reality Bites. *Lauren Bacall was 19 in* To Have and to Have Not, *the same age as Juliette Lewis in* What's Eating Gilbert Grape? . . . *remember the days when women were women and girls were under 21?*[25]

In a society which may be said to have entered its second childhood, how can anyone grow up? The traditional models of adulthood, stiff-backed and bowler-hatted, are as outdated as the Orange ascendancy in Northern Ireland. Contemporary identities are equally incapable of showing us the way to adulthood. Indeed many of today's models seem to revel in their immaturity, e.g. the tantrums of the petulant homosexual (Queer), the know-nothing cynicism of the teenage gangsta (Rap), the nerdishness of the hacker (cyberculture), the lads and their rude words (Oasis and *Loaded*), and the temperamental tomboy (Riot Grrrl).

If immaturity is stitched into today's collective identities, perhaps the intelligent response is to define oneself by disengagement. But this too seems inherently immature. The celebration of alienation is now a well-worn path, trodden by droves of young people in the fifty years since Albert Camus first published *L'Etranger* (*The Outsider*), followed a decade later by Colin Wilson's essay of the same title. Most of us cannot live for ever on the adolescent alienation effect of not copping off with the right person, even if the kings and queens of bedsitter images (Morrissey, Polly Jean Harvey *et al.*) have made a career out of it.

In short there are no ready-made images of adulthood which we can look to today. The dearth of adult models is the corollary of a culture based on childlike submission, in which the vast majority of viable images are essentially passive and immature.

Arrested Development

Low expectations

At the end of the 1940s, Allen Ginsberg took drugs and claimed to have discovered that the highest plane of human existence was not to do but simply to be. In the 1990s Ecstasy 'guru' Nicholas Saunders feels the same way. Recalling his first time on E, he says 'I'd forgotten what life was all about, how to enjoy, the pleasures of breathing and just being alive. There didn't have to be anything to enjoy – life was so good.'[26]

If a new-born baby could talk, this is what we might expect him or her to say. 'Just being alive' is fine for tiny minds which are not yet able to stretch themselves. But those in their late teens and beyond are degraded by the eagerness with which they throw off any sense of themselves as purposive individuals who aspire to achieve more than 'just being alive'. How sad to think that the realization of such low expectations has now become the high point in the experience of many young people – precisely the people whose reach must exceed their grasp if society is ever to move forward again.

Then again pop culture *is* a sad business. As soon as it started to function as the primary focus for young people, it also served as the original expression of the idea that there is no alternative to the present social system, and that we will always remain alienated from the most important aspects of our own activity. From the moment it became the centrepiece of existence, rather than merely a way of relaxing on a Saturday night, pop culture has both ameliorated and confirmed the bleak assumption that our purposive social activity – work – will always be as dehumanizing as it is today. Therefore, pop culture tells us, the only avenue for the realization of our humanity is our 'free time' in the evening and at weekends.

'The weekend starts here' was the slogo which appeared on black and white television screens at the start of every edition of *Ready, Steady, Go*, the celebrated 1960s pop television show. The subtext was that life began at 6.30 p.m. on Friday, and, as The Clash were to point out a decade or so later, it lasted all of '48 hours' until the time came to get your work clothes ready on a Sunday night. In the 1990s the same sense of fatalism was repeated and indeed amplified in the title of Chris Evans's show for Channel 4: *TFI Friday* (Thank Fuck It's Friday).

So pop culture begins by submitting to the idea that the active part of the week, the five days from Monday to Friday and the underlying social patterns, are simply immutable. By giving up on the possibility of making history and acting for change, from its earliest days pop culture necessarily entailed a broadly passive stance on life – a stance which has set the scene for the submissive victim culture of today.

Moreover this is an outlook which cannot even realize its diminished aspirations. Despite the enormous amount of energy invested in it, our 'free time' turns out to be unfree. Our 'autonomous' social lives mirror the sub-human character of the existing world of collective, social activity (work). Thus, if we are degraded in the workplace and in public life, in E culture we degrade ourselves by performing a caricature of human activity (dancing for eight hours non-stop), a parody of thought (chilling out) and a travesty of collectivity (take a drug which suspends self-interest and enjoy the spurious sense of community which temporarily ensues). The E experience lobotomizes what is uniquely human, namely the capacity for purposive activity based on the combination of intuition and rational appraisal. In this respect our work and our leisure are mirror-images of a society currently dedicated to self-abasement.

Retreatism

In response to the failure of existing big ideas, pop culture arose as a means of avoiding the risk of further failure. In place of bankrupt intellectual traditions, it substituted feeling and emotion as expressed in art and music. Successive generations have subsequently defined themselves in the increasingly banal repetition of this pattern. The philosopher Herbert Marcuse called it the 'great refusal' of big ideas. But as well as discarding existing theories, we threw out the possibility of developing a new system of ideas; and we have all been diminished as a result.

Describing the postwar work of the abstract expressionist painter Jackson Pollock, art critic Peter Fuller noted that 'the only subject available to him was precisely his inability to find a worldview'.[27] This has been the main theme of pop culture ever since, and we are close to letting it make fools of us all.

Notes

1. *Kilroy*, BBC1, 16 November 1995.
2. Joan Smith, 'Saturday night', *Observer*, 1 September 1996.

3. Thomas Pynchon, cited in Bruce Eisner, *Ecstasy: The MDMA Story* (Berkeley: Ronin, 1989).

4. Eisner, *op. cit.,* p. 1.

5. Douglas Rushkoff, *Cyberia: Life in the Trenches of Cyberspace* (London: Flamingo, 1994), p. 110.

6. Paolo Hewitt, *Heaven's Promise* (London: Heavenly Books, n. d.), p. 77.

7. Matthew Collin, *Altered State: The Story of Ecstasy Culture and Acid House* (London: Serpent's Tail, 1997).

8. Jay Stevens, *Storming Heaven: LSD and the American Dream* (London: Paladin, 1989), p. 488.

9. Steve Platt, 'Moral panic', *New Statesman*, 24 November 1995.

10. *The Face*, January 1997, p. 47.

11. Marek Kohn, quoted by Linda Grant, 'The pursuit of happiness', *Guardian Weekend,* 18 November 1995, p. 14.

12. Charlotte Raven, *Guardian*, 18 February 1997.

13. Sheryl Garratt, *New Statesman*, 20 December 1996.

14. Bryan Appleyard, 'Time we all learnt to grow up', *Independent*, 31 May 1995.

15. John W. Aldridge, *In the Country of the Young* (New York: Harper's Magazine Press, 1969), p. 114.

16. William Carlos Williams, introduction to Allen Ginsberg's *Howl for Carl Solomon* (San Francisco: City Lights, 1956), p. 7.

17. John Casey, 'A film that exploits its audience', *Daily Telegraph*, 11 February 1997.

18. Federico Fellini, *I, Clown* (Bologna, 1970).

19. Gary Oldman, quoted in 'Oldman censors his X-rated life for debut script', *The Times*, 9 May 1997.

20. Neil Spencer, quoted by Clare Longrigg, 'Oi, Tony, give us back our generation gap', *Guardian*, 18 May 1995.

21. Jon Savage, quoted in *ibid.*

22. Jarvis Cocker, interviewed by Andrew Smith in 'Pulp TV', *The Face,* July 1995, p. 50.

23. Bjork, in conversation with Clive Anderson on *Clive Anderson Talks Back*, Channel 4, 1 December 1995.

24. Appleyard, *op. cit.*

25. Eric Konigsberg, 'Infantilisation', *alt.culture* (London: Fourth Estate, 1995).

26. Nicholas Saunders, interviewed by Alex Bellos in 'The Buddha of euphoria', *Guardian*, 6 April 1995.

27. Peter Fuller, cited in Stephen Bayley, *Sex, Drink and Fast Cars: The Creation and Consumption of Images* (London: Faber & Faber, 1969), p. 59.

CHAPTER 1

Alienation

The new alienated defined themselves by cultivating a sense of estrangement. Initially this alienated sensibility functioned as a stunted critique of society which was acted out in the form of an exaggerated separation from institutions and from other people. But in the 1990s, at a time when there is no longer an expectation of being able to bring about wholesale change in society, criticism does not spontaneously gel into a critique, however primitive. In these circumstances, all that remains of the alienated sensibility is the assumption that other people are best avoided – the very same sensibility which informs victim culture.

'No one can begin to think, feel or act now except from the starting point of his own alienation.'[1] In *The Politics of Experience* the radical psychiatrist Dr R. D. Laing declared that alienation had become the starting-point of human existence. Laing's claim may seem extravagant. Indeed, in relation to certain moments in history such as war and revolution, when collective engagement has come forcefully to the fore, his proposition would be woefully inaccurate. However, it is the case that the cultural personality of our times originated in the counter-culture of fifty years ago, in which a minority of mainly young people defined themselves by their alienation from the majority and their estrangement from the institutions and belief systems of the main-stream. In the half-century until now pop culture has grown up around this alienated sensibility; and nowadays the motif of alienation is built into almost every aspect of our cultural life.

During the Second World War the eminent sociologist Dr Karl Mannheim had warned of dire consequences if society failed to fully integrate the next generation and neglected to overcome its propensity for alienation:

> *If those who will have to live within the new order, those who have to disseminate its idea – in fact, Youth – are not moved by it, the coming social reconstruction will mean nothing but a set of new regulations decided above the heads of the people.*[2]

Mannheim's warnings were heeded, but to little avail. When 'social reconstruction' took place, the most significant section of 'Youth' was moved not to participate but to take as little part in it as possible. Moreover, these youngsters made non-participation their badge of identity. The American social critic Kenneth Keniston observed that a significant section of the new generation was celebrating its own alienation in a way that had never been done before:

> *Alienation, once seen as the consequence of a cruel but changeable economic order, has become for many the central fact of human existence, characterising man's 'thrown-ness' into a world in which he has no inherent place. Formerly imposed upon men by the world around them, estrangement is increasingly chosen by them as their dominant reaction to the world.*[3]

New notion/new style

Karl Marx was one of the first social critics to make a study of alienation. His research, undertaken during the earlier part of his career, would suggest that alienation has been a constant feature of all our lives throughout the two centuries since capitalism first brought everyone together in a new society, only to disaggregate that society in the recurring process of organizing human activity (production) for profit, rather than need or desire.

Yet the Marxist category of alienation is not the same as the notion of alienation which came to be elevated and even celebrated in the period after the Second World War. Whereas Marx was referring to a general condition inherent in the organization of production for profit, the new alienated were responding to a specific historical context by embracing their own sense of estrangement and displaying it as the distinguishing mark of their separation from society and the other people living in it. The peculiar development of this alienated sensibility was stimulated by the lived experience of the Second World War and its effect on the decades that followed. According to Norman Mailer, one of its foremost chroniclers, this experience was 'a mirror to the human condition which blinded all those who looked into it'.[4] If Mailer was right, the celebration of alienation might best be understood as the impaired vision of those whose perceptions had been scorched by the appearance of man's inhumanity to man.

'There was a percentage of men returning from the wars in both Europe and the Pacific', music journalist Mick Farren subsequently noted, 'who couldn't find it in themselves to go along with the welcome home pacification programme.'[5] In the United States some of these veterans formed motorcycle gangs, precursors of the Hell's Angels (so named because they thought the world was hell). Many more lived in the kind of estranged existence described in the novel *In a Lonely Place* (1948) by Dorothy Hughes (without turning into a murderer like her protagonist). Others adopted the zoot suit as a sign of their refusal to be reincorporated into a menial social role. The social psychologist J. C. Flugel interpreted the wearing of the zoot suit as 'a subcultural gesture that refused to concede to the manners of subservience'.[6]

While the zooties were dressing up, the Beatniks in San Francisco were starting to dress down. 'They developed an anti-fashion', concluded the fashion historian René Konig. 'Its sole basis was opposition. Whereas the San Francisco businessman was smartly dressed, the beatnik simply was *not*.'[7] Meanwhile in Paris, according to Konig, the black jumpers worn by the existentialist chanteuse Juliette Greco 'radiated black humour and the negative philosophy of Jean-Paul Sartre'.[8]

In Europe as well as America young people were modelling their estrangement from mainstream society and turning themselves into mannequins of alienation. *L'Etranger* (1944), Albert Camus' novel of a young man's disconnection from society and its expectations of him, was an essential accessory in a new look which advertised the wearer's distrust of long-established tenets such as family, progress and history.

The ambition to stay outside society had already received some representation in art, music and literature, not least in the social realist fiction of Nelson Algren. Thus the poet and critic Kenneth Rexroth summarized Algren's thesis as 'it is better to be out than in. It is better to be on the lam than on the cover of *Time* magazine.'[9] But it was in the aftermath of the Second World War that this hitherto highly unusual (dis)orientation to society acquired greater resonance – and a new style all of its own.

Arrested Development

The birth of the cool

Postwar jazz musicians were the first to develop a whole new aesthetic dedicated to the expression of the alienated sensibility. Beginning with the album *The Birth of the Cool* (1948), jazzmen premièred a new sound which worked in synchronization with an orientation to the world comprised of indifference (sometimes real, sometimes feigned) and the impression of being inviolable. When a somewhat hostile commentator noted that 'coolness' described 'not only a way of playing' but also 'the glacial stage mannerisms, the lack of body movement, the unresponsiveness to audience reaction',[10] his obvious discomfort was prompted by the uncomfortable psycho-social developments underlying the cool sound, namely the emergence of the alienated sensibility predicated on the perceived desirability of separating oneself from society. This sensibility described a generation of people who were not at ease either with themselves or with the society in which they lived, and who therefore felt ill at ease with their fellow humans also.

The 'cool' aesthetic was both a display of alienation from the society at large and an advertisement of the hipster's estrangement from other people.

Jazzmen of the time often used drugs to achieve their splendid isolation. They were soon followed by writers. In *Cain's Book*, a story of addiction, the Scottish novelist Alexander Trocchi has his protagonist Joe Necchi declare that 'the identity of the junkie was consciously chosen ... The resulting experience is by definition that of an alien in a society of conformers, a personal cosmology of inner space.'[11] For Trocchi heroin was a means of transportation into a realm of alienated inviolability. Using heroin was a sign that he rejected 'the entire system'; and under its influence he felt that he was outside the world and no longer governed by its laws.

Sociologists began to take an interest in the new alienated. 'The participants in the drug subcultures have become alienated from conventional roles such as those required in the family or occupational world', noted Cloward and Ohlin. 'They have withdrawn into a restricted world in which the ultimate values consist in the "kick".'[12]

Some of these sociologists started to feel alienated from their own academic discipline. They felt they had more in common with 'deviant' subjects under investigation than with the patriarchs of their own field such as Talcott Parsons. Howard Becker, in his study of jazz musicians and their use of drugs, refused to make quick moral judgements and instead helped to develop the 'appreciative' style of sociology in which deviance was no longer regarded as a social disease to be treated or condemned.

In his famous formulation, 'deviant behaviour is that which is so labelled',[13] Becker encapsulated the estrangement of his contemporaries from the traditional notions of sociology as both an objective science and a direct instrument of social engineering. His disaffiliation was far from unique. Looking back at the period from the vantage point of the early 1980s, Becker recognized that 'there was a kind of convergence, a lot of people were thinking things like that . . . what I did was to say it more clearly than anybody else'.[14]

A similar sensibility had emerged in Britain with the publication of *The Outsider* (1956). Its author, Colin Wilson, made a stunning literary debut with his account of selected individuals in history who, he claimed, had initiated a new orientation to the world by standing outside conventional society. According to Wilson, the world of the outsider starts with 'a rejection of the everyday world, a feeling that it is somehow boring and unsatisfying'.[15] This was a feeling which Wilson and many of his contemporaries advocated as the start of a new chapter in human history.

The desire to stand outside was even newer than Wilson supposed. It had been expressed before, but its proponents had up to now remained marginal. Moreover, some of the outsiders whom Wilson wrote about were not as permanently estranged as he made them out to be. Wilson began *The Outsider* with a quotation from *Under Fire* by Henri Barbusse, a novel which encapsulated the sense of shock and disillusion prompted by the experience of the First World War. But at the end of the book Barbusse reintegrated himself into what he saw as the essentially progressive dynamic of society. 'A soldier ventures to add this sentence', Barbusse wrote, 'though he begins it with a lowered voice: "If the present war has advanced progress by one step, its miseries and slaughter will count for little".'[16]

Wilson's outsiders from times past were in fact back-projections of a new sensibility of permanent estrangement; and when Wilson, with his mop of hair and heavy spectacle frames, was lionized by Fleet Street as 'the coffee-bar philosopher', this new sensibility reached a mass audience for the first time in Britain.

Arrested Development

Alien nation goes pop

The alienated sensibility soon came to be seen as a mark of integrity. Novelist and journalist Andrew Sinclair later recalled that in his first book he tried to show that 'the worst temptation was inclusion in society';[17] to be alienated was to resist temptation and remain true to oneself.

The new sensibility was also spreading fast. Mary Morse, in her sociological study *The Unattached*, showed that by the beginning of the 1960s young people beyond the narrow band of students and intellectuals were already identifying with it.[18] Morse described a cohort of young people who were soon to be participants in the blossoming of British pop culture. When the British 'Beat boom' got going a few months after her book was published, it became the new vehicle for the expression of the alienated sensibility among the young.

The Beatles were the most influential Beat group, and they themselves had been directly influenced by German 'exis' (existentialists) during their formative years in Hamburg. Furthermore, in 1961 the Beatles visited Paris, where they soaked up the existential ambience of the Left Bank. Paul McCartney, who has since acquired a reputation as the blandest of the band, spoke enthusiastically about American Beat writers such as Allen Ginsberg and Jack Kerouac. Whereas the latter expressed their disengagement from society in rhythmic verse and prose, the Beatles demonstrated their Beat characteristics through rhythm-and-blues covers and, latterly, their own compositions.

A few years later, when The Who smashed their guitars and The Move trashed television sets, both bands were expressing their alienation from the electronic age in which they lived. Likewise blues guitarist Eric Clapton, according to his biographer, 'wanted to perpetuate the myth of "one man versus the world"'.[19] For The Rolling Stones, the alienated Mick Jagger declared, 'I won't accept what other people say is right.'[20] Keith Richards was more basic. 'We'll piss anywhere, man', he is reported to have said, after the band was had up for urinating in public. Alan Price, then of The Animals, invited the rest of society to respect his alienation: 'All I ask is that they leave me alone.'[21] The Jagger–Richards composition 'Get Off My Cloud' expressed a similar sentiment. Although most of the pop songs recorded in the mid-1960s were up-tempo, this does not mean that the underlying sentiments were up-beat. The alienation of the singer/protagonist from the world was as much a staple of pop music as the twelve-bar blues.

Snapshot: I wanna be a Mod

Aged fifteen at The Umbrella Arts Club in Coventry. This was 1971, before the age of municipal arts centres, and The Umbrella was housed in an early Victorian terrace with a tiny cinema in the shed at the back. I was there to watch *Blow Up*, the film set in Swinging London and directed by Michelangelo Antonioni. The scene which made the biggest impression was peripheral to the plot. It took place in the Marquee Club and nothing much happened except that one of The Yardbirds (I think it must have been Jeff Beck) smashed up his guitar. The look of frustration and contempt on his face; the disdain for other people in his eyes; the disrespect for mainstream society and its repressed way of life. I could hardly wait to learn how to play the alienated sensibility and try it out for myself.

Even in its moments of tribalism, pop has never been far removed from the alienated sensibility. The American singer Scott McKenzie, whose song 'If You're Going To San Francisco, Be Sure To Wear Some Flowers In Your Hair' was the signature tune of the hippie summer of love (1967), demonstrated his sense of alienation from society when he declared that 'I live outside it'.[22] That same year, in *The Outsiders* (later filmed by Francis Ford Coppola), the seventeen-year-old novelist S. E. Hinton described the coming of the alienated sensibility to a teenage suburban environment in Middle America. Meanwhile the British critic Angela Carter wrote of the spread of 'outlaw dress' in the metropolis and the way in which it represented 'real dissociation from society'[23] – a dissociation which was no longer confined to an insignificant minority. 'What was once the protest of tiny pockets of intellectuals and artists', noted sociologist Richard Flacks, 'has become a mass phenomenon.'[24]

And when the hippie style lost its alienated edge, punk reinvented it. 'Punk', wrote cultural critic Dick Hebdige, 'was forever condemned to act out alienation.'[25] Under the impact of New Wave, Hebdige continued, 'faces became abstract portraits: sharply observed and meticulously executed studies in alienation'.[26]

Snapshot: Proto-punk

October 1972, a gig at Warwick University, where my schoolboy band The Southside Greeks was outclassed by everybody else on the bill (well, they were all older with more money and much better amplification). Humiliation transformed itself into contempt. Wearing a borrowed leather jacket, I spent an hour in the bar spitting at the students – even though I myself would soon be one of their kind.

A year later, I found myself walking unwillingly towards the Bristol University Drama Department, which seemed to be full of Noël Coward wannabes and others who were more histrionic offstage than on. On the way there, I stopped on a whim to buy a copy of *The Rebel* by Albert Camus together with a pack of cigarettes, although I had not smoked regularly until then. Book in pocket, fag in mouth, I donned a uniform of alienation which I wore like a second skin.

If punk expressed the estrangement of white youth, Rastafarianism was the vehicle for the expression of alienation on the part of blacks. 'The Rastafarian posture was one of detachment', noted E. Ellis Cashmore, a shrewd chronicler of life among black communities in Britain.[27] 'In the 1980s', he added, 'more black youth are striking up this posture.'

Grunge was to the early 1990s what punk was to the late 1970s and alienation is as pivotal to the former as it was to the latter. Newspaper columnist Bryan Appleyard recognized that 'the very point' of grunge 'is the sense of disconnection'. This 'point', Appleyard observed, was 'grimly but at least honestly endorsed by the suicide of Nirvana's Kurt Cobain' in 1994.[28]

Nearly forty years earlier the fans of James Dean had provided an almost identical explanation of the actor's death in a car crash. Many of them viewed it as the almost inevitable outcome of the 'mad driving' which expressed Dean's unwillingness and inability to conform.

We're all alienated now

Mindful of Appleyard's suggestion that 'youth culture ... has become the whole of culture', it should be noted that alienation is a motif which now appeals not only to the mass of youth but also to the even greater mass of ex-youth who make up the majority of the population. The alienated sensibility is now so middlebrow, so mainstream, that it has been taken up by middle-of-the-road Hollywood stars.

In an article entitled 'A very private pain', which depicted him as the latest standard-bearer of the alienated sensibility (talented, troubled and wanting to 'hibernate'), Oscar nominee Ralph Fiennes (subsequently winner of the award for best actor, 1997) described his film *The English Patient* in the following terms: 'I felt it was about the pain and ecstasy of relationships, looking for your inner mate and realising that ultimately, everyone is on their own.'[29] Fiennes could almost have been quoting from Marlon Brando's rendition of the alienated sensibility as Val in *The Fugitive Kind* (1960): 'We are all sentenced to solitary confinement, sentenced to our own little skins.'

Various critics noted that the success of *The English Patient* lies in its capacity to appeal simultaneously to arthouse and multiplex audiences. In a society of what journalist Henry Porter calls 'Lone Rangers' the alienated sensibility is the new universal. In the fifty-odd years since the end of the Second World War, it has come to be one of the prevailing motifs in our culture. Nowadays it is ubiquitous to the point of being banal.

Political as well as personal

This was not always the case, however. At least until recently, besides symbolizing a personal sense of estrangement, the alienated sensibility was also a sign of some kind of rebellion and radicalism in relation to society as a whole. High among the targets of this putative rebellion was what seemed to be a newly repressive combination of bureaucracy and technology.

Tom Wolfe, one of the co-founders of New Journalism in the early 1960s, noticed that the new alienated were wont to 'participate in discussions denouncing our IBM civilization'.[30] Student radicals demanded of their classmates, 'Are you a student or an IBM card?' They were insistent that, in the new world of work, people were subordinated to machines as never before. 'Unlike the tools of workmanship which remain the servants of the hand', remarked one of their mentors, Hannah Arendt, 'the machines demand that the labourers serve them.'[31]

In the 1950s and 1960s the radical sociologist C. Wright Mills railed against 'the personality market' and 'salesroom culture', and warned that the individual felt dwarfed and helpless before managerial cadres of remote organizations and unaccountable institutions.[32] Social critic David Riesman spoke out against such hierarchies and the 'creation of new wants' in a consumerist society. Riesman, author of *The Lonely Crowd*, also questioned 'the *conservative* [my emphasis] belief in progress',[33] adding that 'the belief that one cannot stop technological progress has itself become a tradition, indeed a form of realistic insanity, or what C. Wright Mills calls "crackpot realism"'.[34]

Arrested Development

In *The Pursuit of Loneliness*, a book which set out to explain the embrace of estrangement, Riesman's contemporary Philip Slater likened the old faith in progress to terminal addiction and a cancerous growth:

> The old culture American needs to reconsider his commitment to technological 'progress'. If he fails to kick the habit he may retain his culture and lose his life. One often hears old culture adherents saying 'what will you put in its place?' ... But what does a surgeon put in the place of a malignant tumor?[35]

In their introduction to *Man Alone*, an anthology about 'alienation in modern society', Eric and Mary Josephson warned that 'rocketing through space he [man] is fast losing touch with his own world'.[36] In the same anthology social psychologist Erich Fromm opined that 'alienation is almost total',[37] and the existential philosopher Karl Jaspers observed that 'man shrinks back in alarm from the void he has made for himself'.[38]

The price of progress, warned Jaspers, 'is a dread of life unparalleled in its intensity'; it looked like increasing 'to such a pitch that the sufferer may feel himself to be nothing more than a lost point in empty space inasmuch as all human relationships appear to have no more than a temporary validity'.[39]

The item of technology which above all others symbolized the belittling of humanity was the atom bomb, which President Harry S Truman had ordered to be dropped on the Japanese cities of Hiroshima and Nagasaki in 1945. The bomb was the prime target of alienated angst, but the new alienated tended to think that all modern technology was implicated in this crime against humanity.

Reminiscing about the 1950s from the vantage point of the 1970s, Jeff Greenfield recalled 'the rejection of reason as a tool of death'.[40] When Charles Van Doren, scion of a leading New York intellectual family, was exposed as a television quiz-show fraud, learning itself came into disrepute. 'The same invention that let us witness the stupidities of our elders', Greenfield remembers, 'now gave us a ringside seat to the corruption of the learning process.'[41] Putting corruption and mass destruction together, the possibility occurred to Greenfield and his contemporaries 'that the University was nothing more than a link in the chain of responsibility for mass murder'.[42]

The end of politics?

Jay Stevens, perhaps the foremost chronicler of the drug culture in the USA, has provided a checklist of the new alienated, and suggests that theirs was a rebellion which transposed political opposition to the realm of personal feelings:

> *They were hotrodders who idolised the dead James Dean; they were young existentialists with dog-eared copies of Camus in the back pockets of their chinos; they were drug addicts and jazz buffs who wanted to live with the careering passion of a Charlie Parker solo . . . they were united by feelings of boredom and anger with the status quo; their rebellion was emotional rather than political.*[43]

The rejection of traditional politics was as central to the new alienation as revulsion against the technocratic society. This double disengagement was the subtext of the famous exchange of words in *The Wild One* (1954) between an anonymous smalltown girl and Marlon Brando's Johnny, the leader of a motorbike gang:

> *'What are you rebelling against, Johnny?'*
> *'Whaddya got?'*

In two words Brando turned his back on technology, society and the politics of left and right. Johnny's British counterpart was Jimmy Porter in John Osborne's play *Look Back in Anger* (1956). In a year when the right-wing British tradition was made to look foolish by the débâcle over Suez, and the Russian invasion of Hungary covered the left in ignominy, the jazz-loving Jimmy Porter declared that 'there are no brave causes left'. Whereas some of his predecessors had made 'a journey into communism, and the return',[44] Porter and his contemporaries (dubbed 'Angry Young Men' by the critics) were the first British radicals to make a point of never getting involved in politics in the first place.

The absence of brave causes was explored by the novelist and 'angry young man' Kingsley Amis. In his essay 'Socialism and the intellectuals' Amis complained 'as savagely as possible about the local Labour Party meeting on Suez'. He had gone to the meeting with the intention of joining the Labour Party afterwards, but 'within a quarter of an hour had silently released myself from my vow'.[45] In a thinly veiled reference to George Orwell and his famous essay 'The road to Wigan pier' Amis pointed out that it was harder to romanticize the working class now that they had 'pithead baths and £20 a week'. Amis said he almost envied those who were politically committed but concluded that 'very few causes offer themselves to the cruising rebel'.

In the United States the trend towards a kind of alienated fatalism was confirmed by the assassination in 1968 of Robert Kennedy, whose death, according to one commentator, 'seemed a confirmation of a lesson they [young people] were coming to accept without question: there is nothing ahead that is any good'.[46] Paul Goodman, a middle-aged sympathizer with youthful dissent, felt that 'the young are honourable', but diminished by the lack of any 'persuasive program for social reconstruction'.[47]

In the 1960s alienation from mainstream politics was exacerbated by another war, this time in Vietnam. In *Medium Cool*, a book about the cinema of the decade, Ethan Morden described the 'widespread alienation from belief in our power and wisdom and fairness'.[48] Morden recalled that 'by the summer of 1969, when *Midnight Cowboy* was released, we didn't see ourselves as the world's saviour but as a Mrs Bates, hacking away at the Far East as if the way to save a country from Communism was to destroy the country'.[49]

The 'general disbelief in American politics' reported by Jann Wenner, founding father of *Rolling Stone* magazine, extended to radical politics also. 'The bankruptcy of both sides was what I was seeing', Wenner later recalled, leading him to conclude that 'rock and roll is it'[50] – and politics, by implication, came nowhere near it.

The uncommitted

'Alienation characteristically takes the new form of rebellion without a cause, of rejection without a program, of refusal of what is without a vision of what should be.'[51] In 1960 Kenneth Keniston published what is still perhaps the most perceptive summation of the new alienated. Noting that 'our age inspires scant enthusiasm', he suggested that 'the gains of our technological age' were offset by 'an inarticulate sense of loss, of unrelatedness and lack of connection', leading to an increase in 'alienation, estrangement, disaffection, disengagement, separation, non-involvement, apathy, indifference and neutralism'[52] on the part of young people 'poised hesitantly on the threshold of an adult world which elicits little deep commitment'.[53]

Keniston found that the most alienated were privileged, middle-class Americans 'who have no obvious reason' to be so. He also observed that those who expressed such a 'generalized refusal of American culture' lived 'lives [which] are overexamined', as shown in their overeagerness to psychologize and 'discuss their childhoods'.[54]

Keniston seems to be suggesting that the new alienated exhibited an inward-looking, exaggerated sense of self which was concomitant with a diminished sense of activity and capability in the social world. But not everyone was so sceptical of the alienated stance.

'The ideal man is the non-attached man,' Aldous Huxley had declared.[55] Daniel Bell insisted that 'Alienation is not nihilism but a positive role, a detachment which guards against being submerged in any cause.'[56] And Herbert Marcuse, for the left-wing Frankfurt School, maintained that the alienated sensibility was a sign of political subversion: 'in proclaiming ... the Great Refusal, they recognize the mark of social repression, even in the most sublime manifestations of traditional culture, even in the most spectacular manifestations of technical progress.'[57] Marcuse believed that this 'new sensibility ... expressed the ascent of the life instincts over aggressiveness and death'[58] as represented in the military–industrial complex and monopoly capitalism.

Kenneth Rexroth was equally melodramatic, but from the opposite point of view: 'It is impossible to go on saying "I am proud to be delinquent" without destroying all civilized values ... I believe that most of an entire generation will go to ruin – the ruin of Céline, Artaud, Rimbaud, voluntarily, even enthusiastically.'[59]

Snapshot: Renouncing alienation

Fast forward to 1996, at a gig in a jazz/new-music club in North London. Top of the bill is a woman who seems to have sampled or somehow reprocessed the sound of alienation expressed by twentieth-century composers and songwriters from Stravinsky to Peter Maxwell Davies to Nick Cave. Perhaps the message comes through loudly because the volume is much lower than it would be at a pop concert, but I am suddenly struck by the thought that all we are listening to is the petty complaint of a middle-class thirtysomething with not a great deal to complain about – except that she does not like other people very much. In her expression of it, the alienated sensibility contains nothing critical or challenging. It is no longer part of a 'counterculture', but is now being maintained as part of what Robert Hughes calls 'the culture of complaint'.

A question forms in my mind: is it possible to develop a new aesthetic which is not based on the now entirely negative motif of alienation?

Arrested Development

Positive and negative

Both the positive (Marcuse) and the negative (Rexroth) assessments of the new alienation seem to contain an element of truth. In seeking to distance oneself from the ills of society, there was surely an aspiration to find a new humanity. Likewise seeking to throw off the straitjacket of rigid ideologies, both left-wing and right-wing, was a way of expressing the desire to arrive at a dynamic, open-ended way of approaching lived experience. These are the positive elements within the alienated sensibility; but they have always been expressed through a prism of negativity.

Ned Polsky, one of the earliest chroniclers of the counterculture, was also among the first to investigate its ambiguous character. Noting that the Beats living in Greenwich Village on the cusp of the 1960s exhibited a new attitude of 'political antipathy' which prompted them to ' "resign" from society in so far as this is possible', Polsky characterized their disaffiliation from the 'Permanent War Economy' as a 'Permanent Strike'.[60] It was, said Polsky, a tragic mistake, 'destructive of the self as well as incapable of provoking social change'.[61] In their attempt to extricate themselves from consumer society, Polsky observed, the Beats arrived at a notion of 'holy poverty' which 'enforces comparative poverty of the mind'. Resignation from society necessitated a life of 'scuffling' (compare the Slackers in the 1980s and 1990s) which 'often consumes more time and brainpower than a square job, but its effect on leisure is more stultifying than any job dissatisfaction would be'.[62]

However, although Polsky thought the Permanent Strike was sadly mistaken, he was careful to describe it as a 'virtuous error', and by no means a sign of lumpenization, as some other critics had interpreted it.[63] Like Paul Goodman, author of the influential account of the counterculture *Growing up Absurd*, Polsky seemed to prefer the Beat life to the conformity and conservatism associated with most young Americans in the 1950s.

Powerlessness

Polsky talked about the Beat life as a form of self-imposed impoverishment. Along similar lines various commentators have pointed out that the alienated sensibility, of which the Beat life was one of the earliest incarnations, is derived from a sense of powerlessness. In an article which appeared in Britain in an anarchist magazine, the

American critic George Benello noted 'the familiar assumption of powerlessness which is characteristic of contemporary alienation'.[64] Keniston connected the 'scorn for politics' with 'a feeling of social powerlessness' and 'withdrawal in the face of the complexity of the modern world'.[65]

In *The Jazz Scene* Francis Newton (a *nom de plume* for the Marxist historian Eric Hobsbawm) described the 'escape' of the jazzman and the hipster 'into a world of bop music which the square cannot understand'.[66] Some years later, in *The Bullshit Revolution*, a polemic against the pretensions of radical alienation, West Coast journalist Liza Williams agreed that the new alienated were in the avoidance business: 'their whole time is spent in avoidance of things, landlords, cops, tax men, bills, warrants, girls who love them, anything which would make them pause for a moment and evaluate their position.'[67]

Left-wing commentator Sidney Finkelstein described the new alienated as 'the modern counterpart of the ancient rebel' who 'withdrew to a cave or monastery'. The only new element in the modern method of withdrawal, Finkelstein claimed, is that 'the withdrawal now takes place in the mind'.[68]

'Medievalism' (rejection of industrial society) and 'monasticism' (formation of insulated communities) were two of the trends identified by the British sociologist Jock Young in his investigation into the 'subterranean values of bohemians' at the beginning of the 1970s. In the outlook of the alienated, Young observed, 'Man is seen to have fallen from grace but there is no vision of redemption in the future.'[69]

The artist and critic Jeff Nuttall recognized that, instead of working towards a vision of the future, the disaffiliation of 'the post-Hiroshima teenagers was always automatic rather than deliberate', and as a result, Nuttall said, they remained 'essentially passive, not decisive, in their way of life'.[70]

Arrested development

Newton pointed out that the hipster of the 1950s 'was against the white and coloured status quo ... but he did not know what he was for'.[71] Like Nuttall, Newton depicted a passive sensibility which would soon develop into the fatalism ('no vision of redemption') described by Young in the early 1970s. But the emergence of a mindset in which the progressive development of the external world is virtually inconceivable was by no means a foregone conclusion.

Arrested Development

Not knowing what you are for, initially, is not the same as *never* knowing what you are for. Throughout history those who have gone on to make revolutions did not always start out with a ready-made world-view. More often than not they discovered and developed their own long-term 'cause' in the process of rebelling against the immediate circumstances in which they found themselves. But not in this instance. The new alienated hardly got beyond first base. They are a case study in stunted aspirations; and their arrested development requires further explanation.

With its peculiar stress on the notion of individual isolation, the alienated sensibility was not best suited to grasp the nettle of social questions. Newton noted the extremely individuated character of the new sensibility. Whereas 'the old [jazz] players' ideal had been social', in the hipster's case the collectivity of earlier generations was replaced by 'merely the total inability to get on any terms with the world'.[72] For such a person, 'by definition caged wherever he is', Newton saw that 'every conceivable society must be a prison'[73] – even, presumably, the society of his own, alienated kind. With hindsight we can add that alienation itself became a prison of the hipster's own making.

As the 1950s gave way to the 1960s a wider range of young people came to identify themselves in terms of their alienation. In locking themselves out of mainstream society and its expectations, they were also locking themselves into the confined space of the alienated sensibility.

The Situationists suggested this much when they criticized students in France for wallowing in their own alienation. According to the radical coterie led by the charismatic Guy Debord, the student population was like a 'submissive child', not transcending its circumstances but acting out a 'burlesque repetition' of an alienated society.[74] Nuttall seems to have agreed. 'Young people are not correcting society', he wrote. 'They are regurgitating it.'[75]

Destructive alienation

If the alienated sensibility is a prison of the self, it is a prison made out of an exaggerated sense of separation not only from society and its perceived ills but also from the fellow men and women with whom one might otherwise be able to act collectively, decisively and progressively. By turning its back and walking away from such a possibility, the new alienation did indeed fit the tag applied by the American commentator

Lewis S. Feuer when he described this mode of existence as 'vandalism of the spirit'.[76]

By emphasizing the distance between ourselves and other individuals, the alienated sensibility identified selfhood with separation. This results in a peculiarly fragile sense of self, so much in need of re-affirmation that 'finding myself' has become the top priority for successive generations. Hence Keniston's observation that 'the alienated express themselves more to achieve self-definition than to persuade others'.[77]

The emphasis on the realization of the separate self is unprecedented. At times it has reached absurd proportions, as in the 1950s when a young fan told the journalist (later crime novelist) Gavin Lyall that forming a James Dean fan club would not be true to the memory of the late lamented loner. 'He [Dean] was an individual', said the youth, 'and to appreciate him you have to be an individual, too. You've got to feel as lonely as he did.'[78]

The separation of the self remained paramount even during those moments when the alienated sensibility took on an apparently collectivist tone. Comparing the protest songs of the 1960s with the political songs of the prewar period, Josh Dunson wrote that 'the most significant difference was the change in the personal pronoun from "we" to "I"'.[79] Dunson also observed that the songs of the hungry 1930s 'came out of the unshakable and immense feeling that the singer had discovered some truth, a plan that was going to make the world one of bread and roses', whereas 'the songwriter today is sparked by disillusionment and anger'.[80]

Mario Savio, leader of the radical student movement in Berkeley, California, admitted that he too was thinking primarily of himself when he went to Mississippi as a civil rights activist in the early 1960s. Savio explained how he went there on a mission to find himself: 'My reasons were selfish. I wasn't really alive ... It was not really a matter of fighting for constitutional rights. I needed some way to pinch myself.'[81]

Various commentators also observed that the gripe some protesters seemed to have against the bomb was not so much what it had done to the Japanese people in the cities of Hiroshima and Nagasaki but that it, and the 'totalitarian Amerika' which built it, did not pay sufficient attention to their individual concerns.

Arrested Development

Suspicious minds

Savio chose self-realization by means of charitable work. But the alienated sensibility has not often been so generous towards others. It usually seeks the same end, self-realization, by less generous means. In their unfortunate attempt to realize themselves, however, the new alienated had a habit of minimizing or even destroying their remaining connections with others. They also displayed a tendency to exaggerate the threat posed to them by other people from whom they felt themselves to be so recently disconnected.

In his review of the novel *Lucky Jim* (1954) by Kingsley Amis, the distinguished literary critic Walter Allen described Jim as typical of a new kind of hero, 'bred by existence in the twentieth century to suspect everyone and everything'.[82] The new type identified by Allen not only saw himself as separate from society and from other people, but in the act of separating himself from others he also reconfigured other people into objects of suspicion and fear.

Graham McCann, in his study of the characters played by Montgomery Clift, Marlon Brando and James Dean, and of the actors themselves, seemed to suggest a connection between the search for the new self and the emergence of a new kind of fearful hostility towards other people. The characters associated with the 'rebel males' of 1950s Hollywood, McCann maintained, are 'suspicious of involvement, for they see the world as filled with threats to the self. Only unlimited personal power (or else an outlaw existence) can prevent their losing control over their lives.'[83]

One way of interpreting McCann's thesis is to say that the desire to live 'an outlaw existence', besides being a sign of disdain for mainstream society, is also indicative of unwillingness or inability to interact with other people. As well as being against the status quo, it seems the alienated sensibility is ultimately anti-people.

Fear and loathing

The film *Taxi Driver* (1976), which screenwriter Paul Schrader described as 'an attempt to take the European existential hero ... and put him in an American social context',[84] is perhaps the clearest example of the combination of fear and loathing which has always been inherent in the alienated sensibility. While expressing the subject's sense of alienation from a corrupt social system, this is a movie which also makes everyone else into something intrinsically alien to the subject.

Taxi Driver may have expressed the alienated sensibility in an unusually brutal fashion, but Travis Bickle's fear of others is only an exaggerated rendition of a constant theme which reappears throughout pop culture. From the films of Nicholas Ray (*Rebel Without a Cause*) to the music of Joy Division to Nirvana, the theme of alienation is unavoidable.

'I took up music', said songwriter Richard Thompson, 'so I wouldn't have to talk to people.' Thompson was joking, but the sad fact is that successive generations of young people have formed their cultural personalities in clubs and other venues where the music is so loud and the ambience is so deliberately forbidding that the only possible outcome is to confirm what is, ironically, a *shared* sense of our separation and alienation from each other.

At the birth of the cool, contempt for society and contempt for the society of other people were joined at the hip. The underlying problem with the alienated sensibility is that it does not discriminate between the society in which people currently live and the people who are currently living in it. Within its confines individuals' disgust at existing society and their anxious disdain for other individuals have a tendency to become one and the same. As Gary Kramer observed of cool jazzmen in the 1950s, their 'open disinterest and all but neurotic anxiety to show contempt for their audience were their ways of attacking the "world"'.[85]

In the half-century since the birth of the cool the element of attacking the world has lost out to that aspect of the alienated sensibility which constitutes a rejection, and ultimately an assault, on our common humanity.

The stillbirth of the cool

In today's context the alienated sensibility no longer contains an anti-establishment edge. All that remains is its anti-people aspect, an orientation towards others which, far from being anti-establishment, is on the very same wavelength as the anxious and indecisive new establishment now entering the corridors of power.

If the birth of the cool coincided with the emergence of the alienated sensibility, what we are witnessing today is more like the stillbirth of the cool, and the end of the dual character of the alienated sensibility. In today's context, separating oneself from others is no longer the barely articulated flipside of a stunted social criticism. Already the alienated sensibility is functioning in the mainstream as a straightforward expression of hostility and apprehension towards other people.

This is not to say that there has been a radical departure in the plot lines of popular films or the tenor of song lyrics or the tortured stage personae of actors and musicians. The song remains the same, pretty much; what has changed is the meaning which performers bring to their material and the interpretation which audiences take from it.

Unlike fifty years ago, there are no ideologies for today's alienated to identify themselves against. Our 'cool' predecessors knew who they were by virtue of the fact that they disbelieved in those singular entities known as Marxist–Leninism and the American/British Way of Life. But nowadays there are no absolute belief systems left to disbelieve in. From priests to politicians, everyone is as pragmatic and pluralist as only rebels without causes used to be.

Perhaps the alienated were only ever play-acting at rebellion. But today, even as a fiction, the rebel without a cause experiences increasing difficulty in finding a characterization of himself or herself which is both contemporary and convincing. This does not mean that everyone has turned overnight into an enthusiastic conformist; rather that those who wish to use the alienated sensibility as the means to express their personal rebellion against society now find that it cannot fulfil that aspect of its traditional role. Would-be rebels are left floundering in search of their character, or else they fall back on earlier characterizations of alienated rebels in the vain hope that they can be reapplied in today's context.

The lost cause of the rebel

The malaise of the alienated rebel became apparent when, in Amy Raphael's report on the Lollapalooza 1993 tour for *The Face* magazine, singer Kat Bjelland (Babes In Toyland) warned, 'if the rebellious status quo [sic] is so low that I'm the worst person, then something must be wrong'.

Bjelland is one of many would-be rebels who have lost their bearings. Not long before his death, Kurt Cobain was claiming that 'I still hate the world but not with as much venom as I used to.' After George Bush was pushed out of the White House by the saxophone-playing Bill Clinton, the hell-raising Hollywood star Nicholas Cage confessed that 'I don't have anything to rebel against.' Suede's Brett Anderson dallied with the idea of bisexuality; only 'in theory', he hastened to add, but nobody really cared whether he had practised gay sex or not. At around the same time Madonna's shock value turned to schlock; and in 1996 Roy Carr, author of *The Hip*, a book which serves as the who's who of cool, bemoaned the lack of worthy new entries for the new edition he was compiling.

While today's wannabes are coming unstuck, the public imagination is fixated on the alienated rebels of previous decades, with particular emphasis on the prototypes for the alienated sensibility – the Beatniks.

For some years now publishers have been spurting out reissues of Beat novels faster than William Burroughs could say 'jissom'. Before moving on to the auto-erotic *Crash*, Canadian director David Cronenberg filmed Burroughs's infamous cut-up novel, *The Naked Lunch* (1959). Burroughs himself agreed to appear in a Nirvana video. In 1996 Keanu Reeves was cast in a film about the relationship between Neal Cassady and Jack Kerouac. A recent advertising campaign for Pepe jeans evoked the Beat generation, using archive footage of Allen Ginsberg, Kerouac and Cassady alongside a compressed narrative with Jason Priestly in the Kerouac/Cassady role. The adverts were directed in black and white by Bruce Weber, who had previously made *Let's Get Lost*, a biopic of the bebop trumpeter Chet Baker, whose life story was a parable in alienation from The American Way.

The fashion parade of retro-rebels shows no sign of coming to an end. It seems that nowadays alienated rebels can realize themselves only as a pastiche of their previous incarnations – a far cry from the birth of the cool when Brando and Dean were famous because no one had ever looked like them before.

Why should the figure of the alienated rebel be at once so attractive and so problematic today? In *The Condition of Postmodernity* cultural critic David Harvey suggested that our fragmented lives have put paid to the alienated sensibility, which might explain why the alienated rebel has proved so elusive recently: 'We can no longer conceive of the individual as alienated in the classical Marxist sense, because to be alienated presupposes a coherent rather than a fragmented sense of self from which to be alienated.'[86] This is unconvincing. As is evident from the pop culture of the past fifty years, the alienated self does not have to adhere to a single belief system, but may provide its own coherence as long as there is a substantial, unified body of ideas to identify itself against. It is this external element – and its cohering pressure – which is lacking today.

Arrested Development

Whereas the alienated sensibility began as a badge of identity marking out the bearer as part of a rebel minority opposed to the majority and their allegiance to 'totalitarian' ideology, nowadays the alienated are everywhere and therefore nowhere in particular. Everyone is an outsider, and expressing the alienated sensibility means only that you are as dislocated as the next person. This is not the demise of alienation but its apogee.

Alienation and the new establishment

Along with the ideologies of left and right, the expectation of being able to bring about social change has disappeared also. This too is having a profound effect on the alienated sensibility.

From its earliest expression the alienated sensibility rejected political programmes (social-democratic, reformist and revolutionary) for bringing about social change. This was an antipathy to politics and society which, in the more ideological, less depoliticized age when it arose, could not help but function as a kind of socio-political criticism. It was an anti-ideology which nevertheless acted as a kind of alternative ideology. But in today's context, at a time when it is generally accepted that there is no alternative to society as it currently exists, the alienated sensibility implies no such criticism; nor does it provide any kind of alternative, however inadequate.

Indeed, how could it function even as a truncated critique of the social system when there is apparently no social system to be criticized? Only, as it appears, a continuous, seamless existence in which other people are always causing problems. In this context the alienated sensibility conveys only one message, namely, that other people are scary and to be avoided as often as possible. Moreover every time today's retro-rebels relive earlier versions of the alienated sensibility, they strip them of their ambivalence and their vestigial critical content, and reconstitute them as gestures of this singularly anti-people disposition.

Now that the alienated sensibility is part of everyone's life, it is itself extant only in part – that part which represents hostility and fear of others. In this respect it is on the same wavelength as the new generation now entering the corridors of political power.

Despite its origins in the counterculture, the sensibility of cool disconnection chimes in with the concerns of an establishment which is painfully aware of its own disconnection from the majority of the population. This convergence means that the alienated sensibility is the focal point of contemporary culture, high and low.

R. D. Laing's remark about the centrality of alienation is even more relevant now than when he made it more than thirty years ago. In the popular mindset, as in the ethos of the élite, the current one-sided version of the alienated sensibility is the dominant outlook. Unfortunately, by providing a model of apprehension and hostility towards our fellow human beings, the alienated sensibility now exerts a degrading effect on all those who subscribe to it as the primary means of defining their cultural personality.

Notes

1. R. D. Laing, *The Politics of Experience* (New York: Ballantine, 1968), p. 12.

2. Kenneth Keniston, 'Alienation and the decline of Utopia', *American Scholar*, spring 1960.

3. Karl Mannheim, *Diagnosis of Our Time* (London: Kegan Paul, 1943), p. 47.

4. Norman Mailer, 'The white negro', *Dissent*, summer 1957.

5. Mick Farren, *The Black Leather Jacket* (London: Plexus, 1985), p. 38.

6. J. C. Flugel, *The Psychology of Clothes* (London: Hogarth Press, 1971), p. 110.

7. René Konig, *The Restless Image* (London: George Allen & Unwin, 1973), p. 207.

8. *Ibid.*, p. 198.

9. Kenneth Rexroth, in Gene Feldman and Max Gartenberg (eds), *Protest* (London: Quartet Books, 1973), p. 293.

10. Gary Kramer, 'Skyhook: narcotics and jazz', in Dom Cerulli (ed.), *The Jazz Word* (London: Jazz Book Club, 1960), p. 131.

11. Cited in James Campbell, *Paris Interzone* (London: Secker and Warburg, 1994), p. 263.

12. R. Cloward and L. Ohlin, *Delinquency and Opportunity* (New York: Free Press, 1960), p. 20.

13. Howard Becker, *Outsiders* (New York: Free Press, 1963).

14. Howard Becker, interviewed by Bob Mullan in Chicago 1983; Bob Mullan, *Sociologists on Sociology* (Totowa, NJ: Barnes and Noble, 1987), p. 135.

15. Colin Wilson, *The Outsider* (1956) (London: Picador, 1978), p. 299.

16. Henri Barbusse, *Under Fire* (London: Dent, 1926), p. 342.

17. Andrew Sinclair, *In Love and Anger* (London: Sinclair Stevenson, 1994), p. 36.

18. Mary Morse, *The Unattached* (Harmondsworth: Penguin Books, 1965).

19. Christopher Sandford, *Clapton – Edge of Darkness* (London: Victor Gollancz, 1994), p. 99.

20. Mick Jagger, quoted in *The Permissive Society: The* Guardian *Inquiry* (London: Panther Modern Society, 1969), p. 15.

21. Alan Price, in *ibid.*, p. 15.

22. Scott McKenzie, in *ibid.*, p. 28.

23. Angela Carter, 'Notes for a theory of style', *New Society*, 1967.

24. Richard Flacks, 'Social and cultural meanings of student revolt', *Social Problems*, vol. 15, no. 2 (winter 1970), p. 346.

25. Dick Hebdige, *Subculture: The Meaning of Style* (London: Methuen, 1979), p. 65.

26. *Ibid.*, p. 107.

27. E. Ellis Cashmore, *No Future* (London: Heinemann, 1984), p. 51.

28. Bryan Appleyard, 'Time we all learnt to grow up', *Independent*, 31 May 1995.

29. Ralph Fiennes, quoted in Jan Moir, 'A very private pain', *Daily Telegraph*, 19 October 1996.

30. Tom Wolfe, *The Kandy-Kolored Tangerine-Flake Streamline Baby* (1965) (London: Granada, 1968), p. 233.

31. Hannah Arendt, in Eric and Mary Josephson (eds), *Man Alone: Alienation in Modern Society* (New York: Dell Publishing, 1962), p. 20.

32. C. Wright Mills, in *ibid.*, p. 23.

33. David Riesman, 'Leisure and work in post-industrial society', in Eric Larrabee (ed.), *Mass Leisure* (Glencoe, IL: Free Press, 1958).

34. *Ibid.*, p. 366.

35. Philip Slater, *The Pursuit of Loneliness* (Boston: Beacon, 1970), p. 132.

36. Eric and Mary Josephson, *op. cit.*, p. 9.

37. Eric Fromm, in Eric and Mary Josephson, *op. cit.*, p. 11.

38. Karl Jaspers, in Eric and Mary Josephson, *op. cit.*, p. 15.

39. Jaspers, *ibid.*

40. Jeff Greenfield, *No Peace, No Place: Excavations along the Generational Fault* (New York: Doubleday, 1973), p. 29.

41. *Ibid.*, pp. 142–3.

42. *Ibid.*, p. 156.

43. Jay Stevens, *Storming Heaven: LSD and the American Dream* (London: Paladin, 1989), p. 148.

44. Richard Crossman (ed.), *The God That Failed* (1949) (New York: Gateway, 1987).

45. Kingsley Amis, 'Socialism and the intellectuals', in Feldman and Gartenberg, *op. cit.*, p. 279.

46. Greenfield, *op. cit.*, p. 161.

47. Paul Goodman, *New York Times* magazine, 25 February 1968.

48. Ethan Morden, *Medium Cool – The Movies of the Sixties* (New York: Knopf, 1990), p. 255.

49. *Ibid.*

50. Jann Wenner, cited in Abe Peck, *Uncovering the Sixties: The Life and Times of the Underground Press* (New York: Pantheon, 1985), p. 108.

51. Kenneth Keniston, *The Uncommitted* (New York: Harcourt Brace, 1960), p. 6.

52. *Ibid.*, p. 3.

53. *Ibid.*, p. 4.

54. *Ibid.*, p. 9.

55. Aldous Huxley, *Ends and Means* (London: Chatto & Windus, 1936), p. 3.

56. Daniel Bell, *The End of Ideology* (New York: Collier Books, 1961), pp. 16–17.

57. Herbert Marcuse, *An Essay on Liberation* (Harmondsworth: Pelican, 1972), p. 11.

58. *Ibid.*, p. 31.

59. Kenneth Rexroth, in Feldman and Gartenberg, *op. cit.*, p. 298.

60. Ned Polsky, 'The Village Beat scene' in *Hustlers, Beats and Others* (Harmondsworth: Penguin, 1971), p. 158.

61. *Ibid.*, p. 158.

62. *Ibid.*, p. 158.

63. *Ibid.*, p. 159.

64. George Benello, 'Wasteland culture', *Anarchy 88*, vol. 8, no. 6 (June 1968), p. 173.

65. Keniston, *op. cit.*, p. 416.

66. Francis Newton, *The Jazz Scene* (Harmondsworth: Penguin, 1961), p. 211.

67. Liza Williams, in *LA Free Press*, cited in Peck, *op. cit.*, p. 151.

68. Sidney Finkelstein, *Existentialism and Alienation in American Literature* (New York: International Publishers, 1965), p. 293.

69. Jock Young, 'Student drug use and middle class delinquency', in *Contemporary Social Problems in Britain* (Farnborough: Saxon House, 1973), p. 21.

70. Jeff Nuttall, *Bomb Culture* (London: Paladin, 1970), p. 11.

71. Newton, *op. cit.*, p. 210.

72. Newton, *op. cit.*, p. 213.

73. *Ibid.*

74. Ken Krabb (ed.), *Situationist Anthology* (Berkeley, CA: Bureau of Public Secrets, 1989), pp. 320–1.

75. Nuttall, *op. cit.*, p. 9.

76. Lewis S. Feuer, *The Conflict of Generations* (London: Heinemann, 1969), p. 488.

77. Keniston, *op. cit.*, p. 416.

78. Gavin Lyall, in *Picture Post*, 22 October 1956.

79. Josh Dunson, *Freedom in the Air* (New York: International Publishers, 1965), p. 47.

80. *Ibid.*, p. 47.

81. Mario Savio's speech at Westminster Hall, Berkeley, California, 20 November 1964, cited in Feuer, *op. cit.*, p. 504.

82. Walter Allen, in Feldman and Gartenberg, *op. cit.*, p. 7.

83. Graham McCann, *Rebel Males* (London: Hamish Hamilton, 1992), p. 25.

84. Paul Schrader, in *Film Comment*, March/April 1976.

85. Kramer, *op. cit.*, p. 131.

86. David Harvey, *The Condition of Postmodernity* (Oxford: Blackwell, 1990), pp. 53–4.

CHAPTER 2

Now

In the attempt to escape from the failures of the past, pop culture seeks to climb inside the present moment, thereby removing the possibility of success in the future.

John Lennon once said that 'the whole Beatles message was Be Here Now'.[1] In 1997 the message was echoed in the use of the same phrase, *Be Here Now*, as the title of the third album by Oasis, one of Britain's biggest bands since the Beatles.

In *Revolution in the Head* Ian MacDonald puts the Beatles' records in context. In his illuminating introduction MacDonald observes that the Beatles 'felt their way through life, acting or expressing first, thinking, if at all, only later',[2] and he explains how this mode of existence came together with the LSD-driven West Coast vision of 'reality' as 'a chaos of dancing energies without meaning or purpose. There being no way to evaluate such a phenomenon, all one could do was "dig it".'[3]

MacDonald also suggests that in their orientation to the world – at their press conferences, for example, as well as in their music – the Beatles exhibited what he calls 'simultaneity': simultaneous transmission of ideas and messages which may be conflicting, coherent or both. This, says MacDonald, amounted to a revolution in pop, which 'shifted from a stable medium of social confirmation to a proliferating culture of musical postcards and diary jottings: a cryptic forum for the exchange of individual impressions of accelerating, multifocal change'.[4]

Moreover, in its general application throughout society, simultaneity was an important factor in what MacDonald calls 'the true revolution of the Sixties ... an inner one of feeling and assumption: a revolution in the head'.[5]

Arrested Development

The Beatles, as MacDonald sees them, represent both the radicalism and the incipient conservatism of the 1960s, all wrapped up in the message that everyone must be everything *now*. This is a message which rejects the step-by-step logic of rationality as well as the linear progression of history. As novelist J. G. Ballard said on Radio Three at the end of the 1960s, 'one needs a non-linear technique because our lives are not conducted in linear terms ... we don't live our lives in linear terms the way the Victorians did'.[6]

In life as in art, simultaneity and its close relative 'instantaneity' are modes of expression which privilege the immediacy of the senses over the distancing effect of rational appraisal, while at the same time insisting that perception is all. They also raise the self-expression of the individual to a new status, but only in the interests of dissolving the individual ego and dismissing its potential for purposive activity. Indeed the corollary of the triptych everyone/everything/now is that no one shall amount to anything, ever.

Senses over intellect

'Perhaps I can't explain this to you, but if I had a piano here I could play it.'[7] At a seminar of Anglo-American and continental thinkers during the 1950s the French philosopher Gabriel Marcel expressed dissatisfaction with language and with the limits of philosophical concepts. More famously, Jean-Paul Sartre is reported to have said that he, Sartre, only wrote about existentialism whereas the bebop saxophonist Charlie Parker *was* existentialism. In expressing a preference for the artistic and sensual rather than the rational and intellectual, Marcel and Sartre demonstrated the onset of a new disdain for social theory.

Similar sentiments had already been expressed, albeit unwillingly, by H. G. Wells. At the end of a long career in the service of ideas about rationality and progress inherited from the nineteenth century, Wells expressed his doubts about the human intellect and its application. In *Mind at the End of its Tether* he wrote: 'Hitherto, events had been held together by a certain logical consistency ... Now it is as if that cord had vanished, and everything was driving anyhow to anywhere at a steadily increasing velocity ... The pattern of things to come faded away.'[8]

Wells was articulating the creeping recognition that rationality had somehow been found wanting. Meanwhile the German philosopher Martin Heidegger was initiating the transposition of ideas into the realm of aesthetics, substituting art and culture for intellectual contestation. Thus Heidegger defined Man as 'Being's Poem'[9] – a definition which might itself be defined as an attempt to employ poetry to transcend the exhaustion of theory.

Heidegger's attempt has been endlessly repeated throughout the last half-century. Instead of the arts complementing intellect, artistic creativity has come to serve as compensation for intellectual stagnation. Meanwhile among creative artists society's retreat from reason has long been a core subject in its own right.

Drama critic Martin Esslin noted that the Theatre of the Absurd (a label applied to Samuel Beckett, Arthur Adamov, Edward Albee, Eugène Ionesco and other playwrights who came to prominence in the 1950s) had renounced argument in favour of merely presenting the human condition in all its irrational absurdity – a clear move away from the drama of debate espoused in their different ways by George Bernard Shaw and Bertolt Brecht. On this basis Esslin included the Theatre of the Absurd in 'the "anti-literary" movement of our time'.[10]

But literature itself was being recast in the mould of the irrational. According to the literary biographer Christopher Sawyer-Luçanno, the aim of the cut-up technique adopted by Brion Gysin and William Burroughs in the 1950s was 'to go beyond the conscious mental censor that attempted to impose a rational order on verbal expression'.[11] Their anti-rational experiments have been a continual influence on pop culture, with musicians as varied as David Bowie, Nirvana and The Soft Machine acknowledging the work of Burroughs in particular (The 'Softs' took their name from a novel by Burroughs).

With its reliance on sensory impact, music is the art form best suited to take advantage of the discrediting of intellect. Music critic Wilfrid Mellers observed a retreat to the unconscious as far back as Schoenberg and Debussy.[12] He noted similar characteristics in the work of Pierre Boulez ('[he] abnegates reason and consciousness to enter Nirvana'[13]), and Peter Maxwell Davies, for whom 'a retreat from "consciousness" is also a rediscovery of innocence'.[14] European composers, Mellers claimed, were releasing themselves en bloc from 'the pain of consciousness'.[15] Also descending 'below consciousness' were the American avant-garde composer John Cage, together with jazz musicians such as Jimmy Guiffre and Ornette Coleman.[16]

From the early 1950s the painter Jean Dubuffet called on artists to carry out an assault on reason. Dubuffet demanded 'the complete liquidation of all the ways of thinking whose sum constituted what has been called humanism', to be replaced by 'values of savagery: instinct, passion, mood, violence, madness'.[17]

The cantankerous critic Christopher Booker saw a similar trend in the satire boom of the early 1960s. 'The satirists', Booker claimed, 'were the first expression of a darker longing for sensation, chaos and collapse – without even the dream of "dynamism" to provide hope of a remedy.'[18]

The novelist and academic Malcolm Bradbury concluded that 'by the early sixties, this romantic anarchism ... came to seem the new aesthetic'.[19] The seemingly new aesthetic was 'spontaneous and loose in form', with an emphasis on 'instinct, provisionality and mysticism'. During the course of the 1960s these characteristics, previously found almost exclusively in the avant-garde of high culture, were suffused throughout pop culture, where they continue to be held in high regard.

Bradbury was probably mindful of the fact that such elements had always existed in romanticism. But romantics had always remained marginal, and their preoccupations were generally peripheral to society. Even when attention turned to irrationality at the end of the nineteenth century, the Victorians had no intention of celebrating it. 'The social thinkers of the 1890s', wrote H. Stuart Hughes, 'were concerned with the irrational only to exorcize it ... they sought to tame it, to canalize it for constructive human purposes.'[20] But from the 1960s onwards pop culture has celebrated irrationality for its own sake. It has sought to canalize rationality for irrational purposes; and it has done this from centre stage, not from the margins. 'What *is* new', observed the American critic Theodore Roszak, 'is that a radical rejection of science and technological values should appear so close to the center of our society.'[21]

Repressive rationality

Following the Great Depression, fascism, the Second World War, the atom bomb and subsequently the Vietnam War, rationality, and with it the whole of Western consciousness, stood accused of misleading humanity. According to the radical indictment, it had encouraged us to approach nature in a painfully selective manner. On this count the American intellectual-turned-mystic Alan Watts took Western thought to task in *The Book of Zen*:

To notice is to select, to regard some bits of perception, some features of the world, as more noteworthy, more significant than others. To these we attend, and the rest we ignore — for which reason conscious attention is at the same time ignore-ance (i.e. ignorance).[22]

At the Dialectics of Liberation, a cross between an academic conference and a hippie be-in which took place at the Roundhouse in London in 1968, radical anthropologist Gregory Bateson declared that 'conscious purpose' was both antithetical and inferior to the natural cycle:

[Consciousness] is a short-cut device to enable you to get quickly at what you want; not to act with maximum wisdom in order to live . . . purposive consciousness pulls out, from the total mind, sequences which do not have the loop structure which is characteristic of the whole systemic structure.[23]

A few years later, in a prescient essay on 'men's liberation', Jack Nichols highlighted many of the elements which have subsequently been grouped together as 'the crisis of masculinist reason'. Nichols noted 'an over-reliance on words or symbols as vehicles of communication'[24] and bemoaned the tendency to ignore 'occurrences that do not seem to fit into systematised thinking'.[25] He opposed 'systematisation that imposes on human behaviour plans that often do not fit',[26] together with overemphasis on rationality which restricts other sensitivities'[27] and 'reliance on rational debate as a means of settling matters'.[28] Nichols thought that men were particularly prey to 'overbearing intellectual consciousness' which prevented them from 'letting go and forgetting themselves'.[29] His prescription for men's liberation was to replace the Cartesian observation 'cogito ergo sum' with the motto 'I feel, therefore I am'.[30]

Along similar lines Jeff Nuttall recalled seeing the atom bomb as 'the instrument of a mistaken rationalism'.[31] Nuttall was a prominent participant, albeit a critical one, in the development of a culture which sought to avoid the dangerous mistakes that were assumed to be inherent in the application of rationality.

Singer-songwriter Bob Dylan left his 'protest period' behind and recommended his new songs on the basis that there was no rationally identifiable content to them. On stage at the Albert Hall during his first visit to Britain in 1966, Dylan said he was 'sick of people asking "What does it mean?" It means nothing.'[32] Little Richard's preference for instant intuition over preconceived meaning was more succinct, and without the snide tone of Dylan's reprimand to his fans. He simply said, or rather screamed: 'Awopbopaloobopawopbamboom!'

Holy nonsense

It was just this kind of explosive nonsense which so horrified the conservative academic Allan Bloom, who was prompted to describe rock 'n' roll music as '*alogon* ... not only not reasonable, it is hostile to reason'.[33] But, for others, music's antipathy to reason made it holy. Jeff Greenfield associated 'the rejection of reason as a tool of death' with 'the embrace of rock 'n' roll not as pleasure but as salvation'.[34] Lloyd Grossman, the social historian of rock music, also referred to the music's mission to irrationalize: 'After the Beatles, the rock performer began to be seen not just as an entertainer, but as a social visionary, and archetypal citizen of a new society.'[35] Besides Greenfield and Grossman there were many others who thought of sex, drugs and rock 'n' roll as a kind of sacrament offering protection against rationality and all its terrible works.

By the same token rationality came to be regarded as an unhealthy state which required the quasi-medicinal application of illicit drugs. 'Kant's categories of rationality', claimed the radical psychologist Norman O. Brown, 'turn out to be the categories of repression.'[36] Jay Stevens explains how the Beatniks aimed to undergo a psychological process of 'deconditioning' from rationality, brought about by 'carefully exploiting the disorienting state of drugs like heroin, speed, and the recently criminalized marijuana'.[37]

Norman Mailer noted that the hipsters were trying to invert the 'scientific narcissism' of instinct subordinated to rationality so as to 'have consciousness subjugated to instinct'.[38] In his essay on 'The Holy Barbarians', Lawrence Lipton observed their 'insistence on the non-rational as a way of knowing and a therapy to overcome squareness'.[39]

In a book about The Who Richard Barnes described a kind of deconditioning process which Pete Townshend underwent as an art student:

> Pete had been using his trolley-car for several weeks as part of a serious college project where students were given characteristics different to the ones they had. It was part of a process of breaking down their preconceived ideas about art, design, life and themselves.[40]

This sheds light on Townshend's subsequent career as a performer, which may be interpreted as a continuation of his student experience, with the electric guitar and wall-of-sound amplification as an assault weapon tuned to break down the square (old-fashioned) circles of rationality.

Likewise the editors of underground magazines experimented with various typographical formats through which they attempted to break down the conditioning associated with mainstream news institutions and to escape from the expectation of journalistic objectivity. They were lifting their page layouts away from traditional columns of type in the hope that this would serve as a way of deconditioning their readers from the notion of linear progress and the abstract thought associated with it.

To former Harvard psychologist Dr Timothy Leary, sacked for his advocacy of LSD, abstract thought was tantamount to heresy against the divine ecstasy which occurred spontaneously in nature, or so he claimed. In *The Politics of Ecstasy* Leary declared that 'the nervous system operating free of learned abstraction is a completely adequate, completely efficient ecstatic organ ... To deny this is to rank man's learned concepts above half a billion years of endowment. An irreverent act.'[41]

MacDonald's later assessment is more sober: 'LSD is a powerful hallucinogen whose function is temporarily to dismiss the brain's neural concierge, leaving the mind to cope as it can with the sense information which meanwhile enters without prior arrangement.'[42] But, back in the 1960s, Leary wrote with proselytizing zeal in the hope of making converts to the new religion of irrationality:

Visual transformations. Gone the perpetual machinery which clutters up our view of reality. Intuitive transformations. Gone the mental machinery which slices up the world into abstractions and concepts. Gone the emotional machinery that causes us to load life with our own ambitions and petty desires.

Get rid of all these obstacles, Leary proclaimed, and you would 'wake up' and find 'You are God!'[43]

Authentic and immediate

Within the framework of this new religiosity, premeditated behaviour came to be seen as artificial and therefore false. 'Indeterminacy' became 'a principle' which in turn became 'endemic in the Underground', observed Richard Neville, editor of *Oz* – perhaps the most influential magazine of the period.[44] Spontaneity acquired the status of guarantor of authenticity and truth. Jock Young noted that 'spontaneity' and 'expressive authenticity: the direct unfettered expression of mood' were rated highly among the 'specific subterranean values of bohemians'.[45]

These values may have been peculiarly subterranean back in the 1940s when the abstract expressionist Jackson Pollock, in his desire to make art which had not been sieved through intellect, first committed himself not to erase, redo or touch up his 'action' canvases. But by the early 1960s the celebration of notions of spontaneity and authenticity was going overground as well as continuing underground. In the introduction to an anthology of his early work Tom Wolfe recalls that the article which became one of the founding documents of an impulsive and spontaneous New Journalism was published not in an obscure underground title but in *Esquire*, the coffee-table magazine for the younger echelons of corporate America.

Wolfe gives an illuminating account of how the article came to be written. He had been commissioned to write a serious feature about young people and their car culture – a subject which would previously have been given a comic treatment. But when Wolfe came to write the piece, he found he could not write it in the tone and format of traditional seriousness and journalistic objectivity:

> Finally, I told Byron Dobell, the managing editor of Esquire, that I couldn't pull the thing together. OK, he tells me, just type out my notes and send them over and he will get someone else to write it. So about eight o'clock that night I started typing the notes out in the form of a memorandum that began 'Dear Byron'. I started typing away, starting right the first time I saw any custom cars in California. I just started recording it all, and inside of a couple of hours, typing along like a madman, I could tell that something was beginning to happen. By midnight this memorandum to Byron was 20 pages long and I was still typing like a maniac. About 2am or something like that I turned on WABC, a radio station that plays rock and roll music all night long, and got a little more manic. I wrapped up the memorandum about 5.15am, and by this time it was 49 pages long. I took it over to Esquire as soon as they opened up, about 9.30am. About 4pm I got a call from Byron Dobell. He told me they were striking out the 'Dear Byron' at the top of the memorandum and running the rest of it in the magazine. That was the story, The Kandy-Kolored Tangerine-Flake Streamline Baby.[46]

This is how Wolfe broke the mould of considered, objective journalism. His rejection of the old model itself became a model for a new kind of writing which was fast, furious and above all empathetic – though not necessarily sympathetic – to its subjects. Among its most highly regarded practitioners are Hunter S. Thompson (*Hell's Angels, Fear and Loathing in Las Vegas*), Nick Kent and Charles Shaar Murray (king columnists on the *NME* in the early 1970s, the young Tony Parsons and Julie Birchill (the 'young gunslingers' at the *NME* in the mid- to late 1970s) and the punk fanzine editor Mark Perry, whose boast was that 'most of the things in the Glue [*Sniffin' Glue*] were written straight down, no looking at it later'.[47]

Theirs is a form of writing which aims to reproduce the immediacy of music, and music papers have always been its natural home. But its influence is more widespread than that. To some extent press and broadcasting journalism have been recast in the search for immediacy, and the notion of spontaneity as authenticity is now reaching a new intensity on the Internet.

Snapshot: Who needs objectivity?

My 'A' Levels were in Latin, Greek and Ancient History. One of the Greek authors we read was the historian Thucydides, and I remember being told by my teachers that his work was important not least because it was generally regarded as the birth of objectivity. Instead of a personal story of the Peloponnesian War, Thucydides, we were informed, was significant in that he presented an objective account of the Athenians' defeat by Sparta. But what was so significant about that?, I remember thinking. I wanted immediacy and a highly personalized view of experiences. I needed to feel that it was happening to me *now*; objectivity was what I was trying to get away from.

Herodotus, who writes (pre)history as a personal narrative, was more in my line. And it comes as no surprise to me that the personalized pre-objective histories of Herodotus have found favour with a new generation in the 1990s, following the references to his work in the Oscar-winning film *The English Patient*.

From Pollock to The Clash and the post-Pollock paint-spattered jackets and trousers which were their original stage costume in 1976 (before they went on to combat gear); from Charlie Parker, who according to Jeff Nuttall 'ate up his life and his own system in an utter commitment to sensation and the articulation of that sensation',[48] to the 'on one' ravers who have been known to climb into bass bins in an effort to get inside the immediate sensation of the music; from Juliette Greco on the Left Bank of the late 1950s, singing to her lover that by evening they would have become different people, to the feisty young women's magazine of the 1990s, *Minx*, which recommends itself to potential readers through the shared recognition that only the present exists – throughout its various incarnations, counter/youth/pop-culture has always been searching for a way to get inside the moment that is *Now*.

The moment is *now*

Pop critic Jon Savage believes that 'the total intensity of the moment' is 'the hallmark of youth and its culture', adding that the 'concentration on the Now!' in psychedelia 'made the Now! into a god and thus squared that curious circle between the pop experience (the Now! as frenzy) and Eastern religion (the Now! as eternal stillness)'.[49] No coincidence then, that the record label on which Mods went psychedelic (Itchycoo Park by The Small Faces encapsulates the transition) was called Immediate; or that, nearly thirty years later, when rock band U2 absorbed E culture in a dance-based album, lead singer Bono repeated the observation that pop is all about the present moment.

Kenneth Keniston had noted a similar emphasis among the uncommitted students of the late 1950s. In what he dubbed the 'cult of the present', he remarked upon their 'emphasis on sensation, sentience and experience; the reluctance to make future commitments; the sense of temporal confusion; the extreme emphasis on the present'.[50]

The first anthologists of Beat, Gene Feldman and Max Gartenberg, explained how the term *Beat generation* began as a convenient if not necessarily accurate label but subsequently came to encapsulate an actually existing cohort that sought to extricate itself from past and future: 'the term Beat Generation came more and more to fit an actual generation that was responding in certain ways to existence in mid-century ... [through] the rejection of past and future.'[51] Likewise Mailer's hipsters, according to their chronicler, believed 'there are no truths other than the isolated truths of what each observer feels at each instant of his existence'. They were psycho-existentialists, subscribers to a hip ethic of 'immoderation' which was also 'childlike in its adoration of the present'.[52]

'Adoration of the present' served to divide the hip from the square. According to American commentator Marty Jezer, 'hipsters, hip to the bomb, sought the meaning of life and, expecting death, demanded it now'.[53] 'We want the world and we want it NOW!' screamed Jim Morrison, lead singer of The Doors.

The radical commentator Charles Reich was neither as melodramatic as Morrison nor as pessimistic as Jezer, but he was on the same wavelength none the less. Reich recommended a third consciousness associated with 'a new sense of existence in the immediate present, without fixed points'.[54] From a different vantage point, in a critical portrait of the culture surrounding late-1960s student militancy in Britain, the essayist Bryan Wilson complained that '*Now* is the dominant time' in the mindset of hippyish students, who in their determination to reject 'the routines of everyday society' tried to arrive at a state where 'neither past nor future matters'.[55]

Snapshot: On the One

Aged fourteen, playing bass in a garage band. That moment when it gelled for the first time. Seamless, timeless, the flow of four young people hitting it together (On the One), and nothing mattered in the world outside.

I came home and told my mother that's what I wanted to do. Which is what I did, to no great effect, for another fourteen years. Chasing after that first moment of being On the One.

In conversation with biographer Anthony Scaduto, who described his subject as 'looking for sensations without involving his intellect', Bob Dylan is reported to have said that 'kids realize it's really a drag to plan for tomorrow their whole life ... There is no yesterday, tomorrow never seems to come, so what's left is today, or nothing.'[56]

But it was not just 'kids' who worshipped the present. In a penetrating account of student militancy in the late 1960s and early 1970s, American commentator John R. Searle noted that the students of the period had been brought up by their parents and the authorities to revere spontaneity and self-expression:

From the first parental admiration for his grubby childhood finger paintings

> to the tv and movie glamorization of his undergraduate revolts, the young
> white middle class American is taught by the older generation to regard
> form, structure, discipline and rigour with contempt, and to prize feeling,
> immediacy and self.[57]

Although he welcomes them as 'the flaw in the British Education System', pop sociologist Simon Frith seems to be at least partially in agreement with Searle when he notes that in Britain by the mid-1960s art colleges – not just art students but the institutions themselves – were also geared to the adoration of the present. They functioned, Frith says, as 'a space where both middle class and working class youth could deny the implications of past and future, and live out, however briefly, a fantasy of cultural freedom'.[58]

By this time the cult of the present had extended so far throughout society that even the Christian church was beginning to be influenced by it. 'The Christian ethic is a love ethic primarily', reported the American theologian Joseph Fletcher, 'not a hope ethic ... This means it is for the present, here and now. By faith we live in the past, by hope we live in the future, but by love we live in the present.'[59]

By privileging love in the present over conservative tradition (the past) and progressive aspiration (the future), Fletcher was marrying Christianity to what has since become known as the New Age, as well as prefiguring the Beatles' best-selling mantra 'All You Need Is Love'.

Movement and the moment

The adoration of the present came as one half of an anti-ideological package. The other half was the celebration of movement for its own sake. Indeed movement came to be seen as the way into *now*. What Nuttall described as a 'philosophy of the moment'[60] was also a fetish for movement in the absence of philosophy.

Thus for Marlon Brando's Johnny in *The Wild One*, being on a motorbike was nothing to do with getting from A to B. As he said, the point is 'you just go'. Driven by the same impulse, Beat writer John Clellon Holmes was moved to call his first novel *Go*. In his poem 'Sense of Movement' Thom Gunn seemed to suggest that 'not keeping still'[61] was a kind of compensation for absolutes which were not available. For Kerouac in *On the Road* movement began as an escape from confusion before becoming an end in itself: 'We were all delighted, we all realized we were leaving confusion and nonsense behind, and performing our one noble function of the time, *move*.'[62]

'Movement takes the place of progress', wrote a horrified Allan Bloom.[63] Unlike Bloom's 'progress, which has a definition direction', when Kerouac and his contemporaries got their kicks on Route 66 it did not matter to them which direction they were heading in. The kick was in the travelling, because for them there was nowhere to arrive at.

Indeed the fetish for movement soon dispensed with the spatial element altogether. With its driving beat, music served as a kind of virtual movement, an 'energy centre', as the caption said in the first advert for *Rolling Stone* magazine.[64] To its advocates, one of the benefits of unleashing this momentum was its capacity to obviate the need for thought. As Neil Young put it, 'when I'm really writing, really playing, I'm not thinking at all.'[65] The grandfather of grunge went on to say that 'the worst thing you can do is think. That's the lowest.'[66]

For 'lizard king' Jim Morrison, 'activity that has no meaning' was 'the road toward freedom'.[67] Morrison's notion of freedom was a very personal one. For others the spontaneous, directionless movement of music was tantamount to social revolution, in so far as it was hell-bent on a collision course with a social system that seemed to be both static and premeditated.

'Beginning with foot-tapping', said the American critic Robert Christagu, the 'penchant for activity' which rock music instilled in its audience would probably end with 'state-smashing'.[68] Another American critic, W. T. Lhamon, is equally adamant that the 1950s culture of 'deliberate' speed and movement was a sign of incipient subversion:

> From Brando's omni-rebellion to Jasper Johns's ironic flattening and palimpsesting of the flag, from Martin Luther King's bus boycott to Little Richard's sexual rebellion in Tutti Frutti, from Neal Cassady's stimulated daze to Gary Snyder's Zen ways, fifties culture was an oppositional culture.[69]

As described by *Oz* editor Richard Neville, the 1960s underground rejected political ideology ('it's a brain disease'), maintaining instead that the spontaneous dynamic of self-expression would do the work of a social movement: 'the Underground ... believes that once you have blown your mind, the Bastille will blow up itself.'[70]

In 'Paradise now', an article in the London paper *International Times*, Living Theater director Julian Beck declared his intention of unleashing a violent energy, so as 'to zap them with holiness'.[71] 'We are disruption', claimed Yippie leader Abbie Hoffman,[72] in the apparent belief that energy and movement were in themselves corrosive of the established social fabric. Neville, Beck and Hoffman were all making the assumption that a sense of movement, whether physical or psychological, is necessarily an expression of subversion.

The politics of *now*

In his discussion of student radicalism and the counterculture, Stuart Hall distinguished between 'the expressive and activist poles'. According to Hall, the 'expressive includes the stress on the personal, the psychic, the subjective, the cultural, the private, the aesthetic or bohemian elements in the spectrum of political emotions and attitudes'. Whereas 'by contrast' the activist pole 'stresses the political, the social, the collective, the engagement or commitment to organising the public end of the spectrum'. Hall added that 'the expressive often provides the language through which is tapped the subterranean id forces of rebellion; the activist phase provides the social shaping, organising, driving thrust'.[73]

Hall recognized that 'there is no rigid separation between these "moments"'. Although they are contradictory, he pointed out that both extremes were expressed in the same slogan on the walls of Paris in May 1968: 'imagination au pouvoir' (all power to the imagination). But Hall does not seem to have recognized that in their interaction the 'moments' or 'poles' were themselves re-formulated. The 'expressive' took on some political attributes, but, more importantly, the 'activist' pole came to re-orient itself around the organization of self-expression. When the latter became a political end in itself, the forward-looking thrust of progressive politics was subordinated to the cult of the present, now renamed 'the revolutionary present'.[74] As Lewis S. Feuer described it, 'movement itself was a hallucinogen'.[75]

MacDonald observes that 'all protest demands were ritually required' to be met in the 'revolutionary present: the NOW'.[76] But rather than accept that combining 'the NOW' with political rhetoric was necessarily a sign of radical activism, MacDonald sees through to the underlying immaturity and essentially depoliticized character of even the most ideologically rigid – and rabid – political sects of the time.

'The attraction', MacDonald notes, 'of 1966-vintage Maoist revolution in the age of instantaneity was that it eliminated the preparatory phase of Lenin's model, positing a direct leap to the communist millennium ... All that remained was to take to the streets and "tear down the walls".[77] In this way notions of transposing to Britain the Maoist cultural revolution in China merged with the assumption that new cultural forms in celebration of the moment such as street theatre and pop festivals were in and of themselves tantamount to revolution.

It was the Leninist model that student leader Daniel Cohn-Bendit repudiated when he declared, 'bougeons d'abord; nous ferons la théorie du movement après' (let's move first; we'll write the theory of the movement later).[78] If Cohn-Bendit advocated the immediate theatre of street action rather than theory, Marcuse theorized the poeticization of theory for the left (Heidegger had already done it for the right, and was subsequently accepted into the New Left canon, despite his Nazi past); in subordinating politics to aesthetics he himself came to be championed by the New Left of the counterculture.

Marcuse thought it would be good to 'reverse the direction of progress ... to learn the gay science of how to use the social wealth for shaping man's world in accordance with his Life Instincts'.[79] He championed 'a tabooed logic, the logic of gratification' as against 'that of repression'.[80] And the logic of repression, Marcuse said, was bound up with 'the prevailing principle of reason', which could be challenged primarily by art. According to Richard McCormick, Marcuse imbued art with a liberatory significance, describing it as 'nonalienated praxis in the midst of, and in resistance to, reified industrial society'.[81] Thus Marcuse bridged the gap between Hall's two 'poles' by declaring that Art was Activism so long as it was applied *now*, that is, in accordance with 'Life Instincts'.

Abbie Hoffman performed the same sort of dubious marriage when he declared, 'Reality is a subjective experience. It exists in my head. I am the Revolution.'[82] In this formulation 'revolution' is identified with whatever was going on in Abbie Hoffman's head at the time. This is not the restoration of the revolutionary subject in history, but an expression of gross subjectivism in which history shrinks to fit the size of the individual ego, albeit an inflated one.

Thus even when the fetish for the present was imbued with revolutionary rhetoric, it was expressive of trends away from politics rather than a signal of coherent political developments. 'Development', as MacDonald notes, was 'the crucial thing that died with the rise of the instantaneous/simultaneous outlook.'[83] And without a sense of development there can be no sense of political aspiration. There are means, but no ends – expect the suspension of the traditional relationship between ends and means.

What amounts to the poeticization of politics was not, therefore, the renewal of revolutionary politics but rather the beginning of the end of a political cycle which began in the mid-nineteenth century with the Chartists and the entry of the working class on to the stage of history, and was to end in the 1990s with the eclipse of the working class as a political entity in its own right.

With hindsight it is apparent that in the 1960s the left allowed itself to be re-worked in the image of the counterculture. Furthermore, the substitution of culture for politics and the development of cultural personality in place of political agency have contributed to a new kind of politics. The result is that a new generation of politicians (many of them from a countercultural background) is currently inaugurating a new political cycle by applying assumptions and policies arising from the convergence of the counterculture and the left in the 1960s.

The narrowness of *now*
From its onset the cult of the present had its critics. Kenneth Rexroth, while sympathetic to the notion that 'against the ruin of the world there is only one defence – the creative act',[84] was none the less alarmed by what he saw as a lack of development in the work of two of the earliest icons of the postwar period, namely Charlie Parker and the poet Dylan Thomas.

'They were both very fluent', Rexroth conceded. 'But this fluent, enchanting utterance had, compared with important artists of the past, relatively little content. Neither of them got beyond a sort of entranced rapture at his own creativity.'[85]

Similar criticisms were levelled against the Beats and their cult of irrationality by the liberal critic Norman Podhoretz. In an article entitled 'The know nothing Bohemians', Podhoretz summarized Kerouac's anti-philosophy as: kill the intellectuals who can talk coherently; kill the people who can sit still for five minutes at a time; kill those incomprehensible characters who are capable of getting seriously involved with a woman, a job, a cause.[86]

In the 1960s Theodore Roszak saw the same tendency towards self-indulgence in the instantaneity of the commentary provided by media guru Marshall McLuhan. In reference to McLuhan's expressed preference for writing 'probes' rather than verified analyses, Roszak asked, 'but what is a "probe"? Apparently any outrageous statement for which one has no evidence at all or which, indeed, flies in the face of obvious facts.'[87] If theory could be poeticized, Roszak might have added, it no longer has to be true – except in the mind's eye of the poet who created it.

As exemplified in McLuhan the subordination of objectivity to personal and occasionally illuminating prejudice recently came to the attention of military historian John Kegan, who reported that when he was growing up 'reality was the 9 o'clock news and the front page of the newspaper. Anything else was for one's inner life. Now the distinction between external and internal life seems to be blurring in an alarming way.'[88] The blurring process has in fact been in motion since the 1960s, when, as MacDonald observes, the assumption was first made that 'all human problems and divisions were issues not of substance but of perception'.[89]

For Tom McGrath of the underground paper *International Times* (after legal action by *The Times* of London the title was abbreviated to *IT*) the focus on the immediate was 'essentially optimistic'. *IT*, he said, was part of an 'inner-directed movement' which was 'post/anti-political – this is not a movement of protest but one of celebration', founded on a 'new approach' of making 'positive changes wherever you are, right in front of your nose'.[90] The new approach found resonances in Eastern philosophy, which, as described by William Braden in his influential book *The Age of Aquarius*, is in many respects the opposite of otherworldly. At one level, said Braden, 'its only concern is what you see right before you: the immediately experienced, emotionally moving, all-embracing aesthetic continuum common to all things'.[91]

But this is to subsume 'all things' into the momentary perception on the part of a particular individual. In other words, the corollary of the sole emphasis on *now*, as the repudiation of previous human history and its failures, is the denial of the opportunity to make history and re-make society in the future. Understandable, perhaps, in a primitive society with little scope for social transformation. But nothing short of profligate in the context of advanced economies like Britain or the United States.

Novelist Ralph Ellison observed the abdication from history on the part of young black hipsters in the late 1940s. He depicted them as 'men outside of historical time, they were untouched, they didn't believe in Brotherhood'.[92] Describing the swinging London of the 1960s, critic and jazz singer George Melly wrote that 'the country of "Now" denies having any history'.[93]

London's swingers were paraphrasing Henry Ford and declaring, 'history is junk'. But junking history is to limit oneself to the immediate present, with dire consequences even in terms of one's personal creativity, as art critic Peter Fuller observed in his penetrating analysis of Jackson Pollock:

> *Pollock* never *developed a convincing historical vision in his own paintings. What prevented him from doing so was, at least in part, history itself . . . I am certainly not trying to deny the psychological roots of Pollock's malaise; but I am insisting that, like Goya's, it had a historical component. Pollock had recognised the inadequacies of Benton's conservative, regionalist worldview, and also of the traditional socialist vision (epitomized for him by Siqueiros). But he was unable to find any new way of looking at, or imaginatively grasping, his world or himself.*[94]

From this Fuller concluded that failure was the keynote of Pollock's project, 'not just as a man but also as an artist'.[95] His only success was in representing the desperate situation of a man without a world-view. On similar lines Jeff Nuttall seemed to suggest that the counterculture and its cult of the present ('the Moment, the psychopathic Now') was a kind of refuge or prison which humanity entered into 'when the future became improbable'.[96]

Feldman and Gartenberg, in the introduction to their anthology of Beat writing, note that the hipster's abdication from history tends to preclude subjectivity rather than renew it:

> *By choosing to live only in the present, however, he cuts himself off from those values which have propped up his vision of himself as the hero of history. The sense that he is part of an unfolding design (the religionist's belief in increasing good, the positivist's faith in progress) is no longer accessible to him.*[97]

Snapshot: Off the One

Losing it. Can't stop thinking onstage. It doesn't matter what I am thinking, the problem is that I am thinking at all. Thinking about the next chord and about what's missing from all the chords and riffs and breaks and songs we've been playing. Thinking that maybe when you put it all together, it doesn't add up to all that much.

Result: fluffed notes, bad gigs, raised voices in the dressing-room afterwards. Can't stop thinking that this band I'm in doesn't think. Why have I devoted so much thought to an enterprise devoted to thoughtlessness?

I'm losing it. Time to quit playing music, because I keep trying to lose my mind but it keeps coming back to haunt me.

Of course the Beats and the pop culture which succeeded them were living in response to the failure of that 'unfolding design'. 'The pervasive sense of defeat', observed Feldman and Gartenberg, 'derives from a very real world.' In such a context the Beats were 'desiring not to change the world but rather to deaden the pain of having to live in it'.[98] Their 'return to the primary, known emotions'[99] was a palliative for the forerunners of a culture which cannot bear the burden of thought and adulthood. Instead the Beats were 'forced back into the marginal existence of the adolescent', where they lived out their denial of 'the power to shape and transform experience', reliant on 'exuberance ... propped up by artificial stimulants' to 'conceal the real inertness' of the Beat life.[100] Their permanent, passive adolescence, which when Feldman and Gartenberg described it was the pursuit of only a minority, is now the orientation of pop culture as a whole.

Captivated by the moment

Feldman and Gartenberg recognized that the fetish for movement is the flipside of resigning from any personal responsibility to move society forwards. 'To truly respond', they continued, 'to make the necessary projection of self, would destroy the Beat condition',[101] which, 'in being Beat [it] gives up all desire to control nature, events or people'.[102]

Another American critic, Robert MacIver, in his essay entitled 'The great emptiness', opined that the restless movement of the times was all about running away: 'They try to escape but they run from themselves. They try to forget, but their only recourse is an excitation of the senses.'[103]

MacIver had a point. In so far as it freed the individual from the burden of failed capitalism and the Stalinist travesty of communism, the renunciation of history may have given rise to a temporary sense of exuberant relief. Even Allan Bloom recognized that the onset of disbelief could be thrilling, as when he remarked that 'One has to have the experience of really believing, before one can have the thrill of liberation.'[104] With hindsight it seems that the adrenalin rush of the 1960s was a 'liberation' derived almost solely from the thrill of no longer believing. And one had only to scratch the surface to find the corrosive cynicism beneath.

One of the founding documents of the counterculture, *The Rebel* by Albert Camus, contains moments of just such exuberance, especially in those passages where Camus sought to identify the rebel by extricating him from what had come to be seen as the Hegelian trap of history and revolution.[105] But in response to the failure of grand narratives Camus could come up only with a diminished vision of humanity, defined by our capacity for self-limitation which he re-defined as rebellion itself (see Chapter 9).

The moment of exuberance was short-lived, however. As Christopher Booker observed in his book on the 1970s, 'one of the main reasons why the seventies had such an air of hangover, of aftermath, was that a psychological climax had been passed which could never be worked up to with the same frenzied excitement again'.[106]

Moreover, the excitement at cutting oneself free from the historical failures of capitalism and socialism was inextricably linked to the mounting anxiety about one's own rootless existence. Through the voice of Joe Necchi, the protagonist of *Cain's Book*, Alexander Trocchi described the relationship between his new-found disbelief in objectivity and society and the anxiety which accompanied his lack of faith: 'more and more I found it necessary to suspend such facts, to exist simply in abeyance, to give up (if you will), and come naked to apprehension.'[107]

From a critical perspective Feldman and Gartenberg noted that the disconnected Beats were wont to 'accept life as a state of continuing anxiety ... in the flight from banality they approach the essence of horror'.[108] Their comment is an indication of how the Beats introduced a cultural personality which is so horrified by the world as to be almost immobilized by it.

Asked to endorse a published account of psychedelic music, the American music writer Nick Tosches described psychedelia as 'consciousness expanding for people without consciousness'[109] – an excellent summation of the way in which pop culture has served as an aspirational medium for people with diminished aspirations.

Furthermore pop culture and its participants did not simply have their historical consciousness taken from them by history itself. In some important respects they amputated it themselves, in their mission to elevate the momentary and the irrational. The late Christopher Lasch, whose response to the antics of the New Left was to move out of the left-wing framework altogether, recognized that this was an entirely illegitimate response to the problems of humanity in that it denied the sense of ourselves as active agents with the potential to solve those problems. 'I think humanism is inseparable from the idea of rationality', Lasch told William Braden, 'so I can't see a revolt against rationality as humanism ... I think there is a revolt against humanism going on.'[110]

Anti-humanism was not, of course, the avowed intention of the 1960s revolutionists. In substituting the *now* for their place in history, they thought they were reinstating the individual self in contra-distinction to the discredited collectivism of both the left (communism) and the right (fascism). As Camus saw it, from now on the rebel self must never again be subordinated to the demands of a historical schema, whether of left-wing or of right-wing origin.

In the rebellion of the 1960s the self was made sacrosanct; and the sanctification of the self was itself understood as an act of rebellion. These were the sentiments which connected the existentialism of Camus with the graffito scrawled on the walls of Paris during *les évenements* of May 1968: 'une revolution qui demande que l'on sacrifice pour elle est une revolution à la papa' (a revolution that asks us to make sacrifices for it is an old-fashioned revolution). This was a revolution which would not demand sacrifices from its revolutionists, but instead came up with the puerile demand that society should sacrifice itself to their desire for self-expression.

Ego death

The countercultural radicalism of the late 1960s was an expression of selfhood over and above all other considerations. It was to be a revolution of individuality and diversity that would subsume the public into the private, or 'inner space'. But this privatized expression of selfhood had the contradictory effect of diminishing and sometimes even destroying the self. As Bruno Bettleheim put it in an article on the youth question published in 1969, 'they [student radicals] are convinced that they are struggling actively for personal autonomy, but they are in fact destroying it as radically as those others who withdraw into solipsistic isolation.'[111]

In their eagerness to free the ego from the constraints of rationality and history, the counterculturists – whether retreatist or activist – wanted to dispense with purposive behaviour also. For them 'enlightenment' was the suspension of instrumentality and rational calculation. The self they celebrated was a largely passive entity whose role was to absorb, appreciate and regurgitate the stimuli directed at it. But this diminished role is more like the eclipse of selfhood than its realization – a contradiction which Jay Stevens illustrates in his account of the initiation process for newcomers to Timothy Leary's psychedelic household at Millbrook in New England:

> At the back of the room there were half a dozen film and slide projectors, calibrated to operate in tandem, which threw alternating images of the Buddha etc. on the walls, while a voice would jump from speaker to speaker intoning: 'that which is called ego-death is coming to you. Take advantage of this temporary death to obtain the perfect state – Enlightenment.'[112]

Of course it sounds preposterous. It is the sort of thing which one might expect to see in a flashback sequence in the television comedy series *Absolutely Fabulous*. But the underlying assumption that 'ego death' is tantamount to 'Enlightenment' was influential then, and even more so now. In the 1990s it is often expressed in the form of disdain for the 1980s, a decade associated with all things egotistical and, by implication, venal.

The most clear-sighted participants warned against the cult of the present and the fashion for ego-death in the counterculture. Leary's former colleague Sidney Cohen pointed to the 'mindless' character of the 'sensory whingding' of the LSD circus.[113] After taking STP, Ken Kesey, the leader of The Merrie Pranksters, admitted losing the sense of being able to steer himself through life: 'I lost a thing we take for granted ... the tiller.'[114] Likewise Dick Alpert, a veteran of psychedelia and mysticism, said that the drug made him feel he had lost something human. 'I felt that I had lost my humanity', he told Jay Stevens.[115]

This sense of loss may have been felt peculiarly intensely by such individuals, who may have had drug-induced experiences which were peculiarly intense. But the threat to subjectivity was not really coming from STP, the chemical substance. Theodore Roszak recognized that the entire counterculture raised a question mark over the notion of the purposive, rational individual.

The counterculturists, Roszak observed, 'call into question all that our culture values as "reason" and "reality"'. Roszak also suggested that the ethos of the counterculture was 'to attack men at the very core of their security by denying the validity of everything they mean when they utter the most precious word ... "I"'.[116]

In his film *Death of the Mind* Leary celebrated the dissolution of the purposive ego (at least, it was celebratory on the outside; Diana Trilling was one critic who saw the desperation beneath the veneer). Nuttall observed the same dissolution process at work in the writing of the godfather of the counterculture, William Burroughs.

Burroughs had described his own book of cut-up fiction, *The Naked Lunch*, in terms of the *now*. Explaining how it came to have that title, he wrote '[it] means exactly what the words say: NAKED Lunch – a frozen moment when everyone sees what is on the end of every fork'.[117]

According to Nuttall, Burroughs recognized that 'Man has been cheated of oneness', but his response to the aloneness of Man is to dissolve him and all his works into the present moment: 'His [Burroughs's] way back to it was by the dissolution of language, the dissolution of definition, the dissolution of individual identity.'[118]

Burroughs, Nuttall believed, 'was prepared to do the dissolving', and with some trepidation he observed the 'spread of an ego-dissolving delirium' alongside the development of the counterculture.[119] On the positive side Nuttall noted an attempt 'to re-ignite an overwhelming sense of wonderment at the universe'.[120] But if wonderment was to be overwhelming, it was the rational, purposive ego that was due to be overwhelmed.

There were mitigating circumstances which prompted the fashion for ego death: the Stalinist schema of purposive behaviour in history had been seen to be as bankrupt as the notion of free will associated with the 'free market'. Likewise, what use was there in prolonging a Protestant work ethic that was clearly not working? Surely better to live for sensation in the here and *now*, and to demand, as many radicals did, that everyone else should do the same.

This was the context in which left-wingers like Herbert Marcuse of the Frankfurt School came out in favour of the dissolution of the ego. Moreover, in a bizarre revision of Marxism Marcuse went a long way towards correlating ego-dissolution with the project of liberation:

Today's rebels want to see, hear, feel new things in a new way; they link liberation with the dissolution of ordinary and orderly perception. The 'trip' involves the dissolution of the ego shaped by the established society – an artificial and short-lived dissolution anticipates, in a distorted manner, an exigency of the social liberation: the revolution must be at the same time a revolution in perception which will accompany the material and intellectual reconstruction of society, creating a new aesthetic environment.[121]

Marcuse wanted it both ways. He preferred not to abandon the concept of 'material reconstruction' while at the same time welcoming the dissolution of the only possible agent for the reconstruction of society. For in seeking to dissolve the rational, purposive ego in the endlessly recurring celebration of *now*, the counterculture was both a negation of the potential for solving social problems and the first in a series of barbarous attacks on human agency – a series now culminating in the corrosive notion of ourselves as essentially passive victims.

The bleakness of ego–dissolution, perhaps less discernible in the heady days of Paris '68, was brought to the fore a quarter of a century later in an article by Simon Reynolds about a peculiarly fierce form of techno–music known as 'Ardkore:

With 'Ardkore, the proletarian culture of consolation has become a culture of concussion: hence amnesiac/anaesthetic slang terms for a desirable state of affairs like 'sledged', 'mashed up', 'cabbaged', 'monged' . . .

There's a sampled slice of rap at large in 'Ardkore that goes 'can't beat the system/go with the flow'. On one level it's just a boast about how much damage the sound system can inflict, but perhaps there's a submerged political resonance in there too: amidst the socio-economic deterioration of a Britain that's well into its second decade of one party rule, where alternatives seem unimaginable, horizons grow even narrower, and there's no constructive outlet for anger, what else is there but to zone out, to go with the flow, disappear.[122]

Reynolds's piece indicates that the search for *now* can often mean the annihilation of the self. But there was a time at the end of the 1960s when it seemed like liberation. Nuttall was one of the few who kept their heads throughout the delirium of ego–dissolution. He rejected the notion of mystical oneness in the eternal present, realizing that 'there is a purpose to the human alienation from the cosmos'.[123] Perhaps he also recognized that, throughout human history to the present moment, our alienation from nature has been one and the same thing as our humanity. In any case, Nuttall was right to insist that 'it is now necessary to come back from inner space'.[124]

Notes

1. John Lennon quoted in David Sheff and G. Barry Golson, *The Playboy Interviews with John Lennon and Yoko Ono* (New York: Playboy Press, 1981), p. 70.

2. Ian MacDonald, *Revolution in the Head: The Beatles' Records and the Sixties* (London: Random House, 1995), p. 20.

3. *Ibid.*, p. 16.

4. *Ibid.*, p. 22.

5. *Ibid.*, p. 25.

6. J. G. Ballard on Radio Three, 1969.

7. Gabriel Marcel, quoted in Herbert Kohl, *The Age of Complexity* (New York: Mentor, 1965), p. 11.

8. H. G. Wells, *Mind at the End of Its Tether* (London: Heinemann, 1945), p. 4.

9. Martin Heidegger, quoted by Richard Rorty, *Contingency, Irony and Solidarity* (Cambridge: Cambridge University Press, 1989), p. 116. On p. 114, Rorty also quotes Heidegger on thought 'poeticized'.

10. Martin Esslin, *Theatre of the Absurd* (Harmondsworth: Penguin, 1971), pp. 25–6.

11. Christopher Sawyer-Luçanno, *The Continual Pilgrimage* (New York: Grove Press, 1992), pp. 282–3.

12. Wilfrid Mellers, *Caliban Reborn: Renewal in Twentieth Century Music* (London: Gollancz, 1968), p. 62.

13. *Ibid.*, p. 115.

14. *Ibid.*, p. 174.

15. *Ibid.*, p. 129.

16. *Ibid.*, p. 136.

17. Jean Dubuffet, cited in Christopher Lasch, *The Minimal Self* (London: Picador, 1985), p. 145.

18. Christopher Booker, *The Neophiliacs* (London: Fontana, 1970), p. 172.

19. Malcolm Bradbury, *The Modern American Novel* (Oxford: Oxford University Press, 1984), p. 151.

20. H. Stuart Hughes, *Consciousness and Society* (New York: Vintage, 1958), pp. 35–6.

21. Theodore Roszak, *The Making of a Counterculture* (London: Faber & Faber, 1971), p. 51.

22. Alan Watts, *The Book of Zen* (New York: Pantheon, 1966), p. 28.

23. Gregory Bateson, 'Conscious purpose versus nature', in David Cooper (ed.), *The Dialectics of Liberation* (Harmondsworth: Penguin, 1968), pp. 42–3.

24. Jack Nichols, *Men's Liberation: A New Definition of Masculinity* (Harmondsworth: Penguin, 1975), p. 28.

25. *Ibid.*, p. 29.

26. *Ibid.*, p. 34.

27. *Ibid.*, p. 31.

28. *Ibid.*, p. 33.

29. *Ibid.*, p. 34.

30. *Ibid.*, p. 35.

31. Jeff Nuttall, quoted in Roger Hutchinson, *High Sixties* (Edinburgh: Mainstream, 1992), p. 183.

32. Bob Dylan, quoted in *ibid.*, p. 81.

33. Allan Bloom, *The Closing of the American Mind* (London: Penguin, 1989).

34. Jeff Greenfield, *No Peace, No Place* (New York: Doubleday, 1973), p. 29.

35. Lloyd Grossman, *The Sociology of Rock*, quoted in Michael Bane, *White Boy Singin' the Blues* (Harmondsworth: Penguin, 1982), p. 149.

36. Norman O. Brown, *Life Against Death* (London: Sphere Books, 1968), p. 280.

37. Jay Stevens, *Storming Heaven: LSD and the American Dream* (London: Paladin, 1989), p. 152.

38. Norman Mailer, 'The white negro', *Dissent*, summer 1957.

39. Lawrence Lipton, quoted in Jack Newfield, *A Prophetic Minority: The American New Left* (London: Anthony Blond, 1966), p. 45.

40. Richard Barnes, *The Who: Maximum R&B* (London: St Martin's Press, 1982).

41. Timothy Leary, *The Politics of Ecstasy* (London: Paladin, 1970), p. 59.

42. MacDonald, *op. cit.*, p. 13.

43. Timothy Leary, quoted in Stevens, *op. cit.*, p. 193.

44. Richard Neville, *Playpower* (London: Jonathan Cape, 1970), p. 65.

45. Jock Young, 'Student drug use and middle class delinquency', in *Contemporary Social Problems in Britain* (Farnborough: Saxon House, 1973), p. 21.

46. Tom Wolfe, *The Kandy-Kolored Tangerine-Flake Streamline Baby* (London: Granada, 1968), p. 11.

47. Mark Perry, quoted in Jon Savage, *England's Dreaming* (London: Faber & Faber, 1991), p. 202.

48. Nuttall, *op. cit.*, p. 17.

49. Jon Savage, 'The sound of acid', *Guardian*, 31 January 1997.

50. Kenneth Keniston, *The Uncommitted* (New York: Harcourt Brace, 1960), p. 227.

51. Gene Feldman and Max Gartenberg (eds), *Protest* (London: Quartet Books, 1973), p. 3 (first published by Souvenir Press, 1959).

52. Mailer, *op. cit.*

53. Marty Jezer, in *The Dark Ages*, quoted by Abe Peck, *Uncovering the Sixties* (New York: Pantheon, 1985), p. 10.

54. Charles Reich, *The Greening of America* (Harmondsworth: Penguin, 1971), pp. 302–3.

55. Bryan Wilson, *The Youth Culture and the Universities* (London: Faber & Faber, 1970), p. 196.

56. Anthony Scaduto, *Bob Dylan* (London: Abacus, 1972), p. 177.

57. John R. Searle, *The Campus War* (Harmondsworth: Penguin, 1972), pp. 147–8.

58. Simon Frith and Howard Home, *Welcome to Bohemia* (University of Warwick, Department of Sociology, 1984), p. 9.

59. Joseph Fletcher, *Situation Ethics* (Philadelphia: Westminster Press, 1966), p. 142.

60. Nuttall, *op. cit.*, p. 37.

61. Thom Gunn, *Sense of Movement* (London: Faber & Faber, 1965).

62. Jack Kerouac, *On the Road* (1957) (London: Penguin, 1972), p. 133.

63. Bloom, *op. cit.*, p. 221.

64. *Rolling Stone*'s first advert in the *New York Times*, cited in Joe and John J. Kohut (eds), *Rock Talk* (London: Faber & Faber, 1994), p. 28.

65. Neil Young, quoted in *ibid.*, p. 45.

66. *Ibid.*, p. 142.

67. Jim Morrison, quoted in *ibid.*, p. 113.

68. Robert Christagu, in *Esquire*, June 1970, reprinted in *Any Old Way You Choose It* (Harmondsworth: Penguin, 1973).

69. W. T. Lhamon, *Deliberate Speed* (Washington, DC: Smithsonian Institute Press, 1990), p. 28.

70. Neville, *op. cit.*, p. 18.

71. Julian Beck, 'Paradise now', *International Times*, 12 July 1968.

72. Abbie Hoffman, *The Best of Abbie Hoffman* (New York: Four Walls Eight Windows, 1989), p. 50.

73. Stuart Hall, 'The hippies', in J. Nagel (ed.), *Student Power* (London: Merlin, 1969), pp. 198–9.

74. MacDonald, *op. cit.*, p. 18.

75. Lewis S. Feuer, *The Conflict of Generations* (London: Heinemann, 1969), p. 419.

76. MacDonald, *op. cit.*, p. 18.

77. *Ibid.*, p. 23.

78. Daniel Cohn-Bendit, quoted in Peter Buckman, *The Limits of Protest* (London: Panther, 1970), p. 49.

79. Herbert Marcuse, *Eros and Civilization* (London: Abacus, 1972), p. 11.

80. *Ibid.*, p. 134.

81. Richard W. McCormick, *Politics of the Self: Feminism and the Postmodern in West German Literature and Film* (Princeton: Princeton University Press, 1991), p. 32.

82. Abbie Hoffman, *Revolution for the Hell of It* (New York: Dial, 1968), p. 9.

83. MacDonald, *op. cit.*, p. 32.

84. Kenneth Rexroth, in Feldman and Gartenberg, *op. cit.*, p. 287.

85. *Ibid.*

86. Norman Podhoretz, 'The know-nothing Bohemians', *Partisan Review*, spring 1958.

87. Theodore Roszak, 'The Summa Popologica of Marshall McLuhan', in Raymond Rosenthal (ed.), *McLuhan Pro and Con* (Baltimore: Penguin, 1968), p. 268.

88. John Kegan, 'The bad good news', *Daily Telegraph*, 3 March 1997.

89. MacDonald, *op. cit.*, p. 14.

90. Tom McGrath, in *IT*, no. 10, March 1967.

91. William Braden, *Age of Aquarius* (London: Eyre and Spottiswoode, 1971), p. 235.

92. Ralph Ellison, *The Invisible Man* (Harmondsworth: Penguin, 1952).

93. George Melly, *Revolt into Style* (London: Allen Lane The Penguin Press, 1970), p. 8.

94. Peter Fuller, *Beyond the Crisis in Modern Art* (London: Writers' and Readers' Cooperative, 1980), p. 101.

95. *Ibid.*, p. 100.

96. Nuttall, *op. cit.*, p. 100.

97. Feldman and Gartenberg, *op. cit.*, Introduction, p. 2.

98. *Ibid.*, p. 13.

99. *Ibid.*, p. 38.

100. *Ibid.*, p. 9.

101. *Ibid.*, p. 9.

102. *Ibid.*, p. 4.

103. Robert MacIver, in Man Alone, *op. cit.*, p. 146.

104. Bloom, *op. cit.*, p. 43.

105. Albert Camus, *The Rebel* (Harmondsworth: Penguin, 1972).

106. Christopher Booker, *The Seventies* (London: Penguin, 1980), p. 32.

107. Alexander Trocchi, *Cain's Book* (1963) (London: Quartet, 1973), p. 3.

108. Feldman and Gartenberg, *op. cit.*, p. 2.

109. Nick Tosches, back-cover endorsement of Jim DeRogatis, *Kaleidoscope Eyes* (London: Fourth Estate, 1996).

110. Christopher Lasch, quoted in Braden, *op. cit.*, pp. 192–3.

111. Bruno Bettleheim, 'Obsolete youth?', *Encounter*, September 1969.

112. Stevens, *op. cit.*, p. 359.

113. Sidney Cohen, quoted in Stevens, *op. cit.*, p. 390.

114. Ken Kesey, quoted in Stevens, *op. cit.*, p. 462.

115. Dick Alpert, quoted in Stevens, *op. cit.*, p. 462.

116. Theodore Roszak, *The Making of a Counterculture* (London: Faber & Faber, 1971), p. 54.

117. William S. Burroughs, Introduction, *The Naked Lunch* (London: Corgi Books, Transworld Publishers, 1968), p. 7.

118. Nuttall, *op. cit.*, p. 143.

119. Nuttall, *op. cit.*, p. 239.

120. Nuttall, *op. cit.*, p. 239.

121. Herbert Marcuse, *An Essay on Liberation* (Harmondsworth: Allen Lane The Penguin Press, 1969), p. 37.

122. Simon Reynolds, 'Technical ecstasy', *The Wire*, November 1992.

123. Nuttall, *op. cit.*, p. 241.

124. Nuttall, *op. cit.*, p. 242.

CHAPTER 3

The Child

Rejecting the failure of progress and politics, both of which are associated with the discredited adult world, participants in pop culture have repeatedly sought to turn themselves back into children.

Infants can live only in the immediate present, but all the while they are struggling to get out. Likewise childhood and adolescence are processes whereby the wannabe-individual struggles to leave those stages behind and become an adult. In recent times, however, the state of adulthood has seemed far from desirable, since it connotes either acceptance of an unacceptable world or, in its left-wing variant, an apparently futile commitment to the discredited politics of social transformation. In a situation where the legacy of capitalism is untenable and the communist future is unattainable, many have tried to climb back into the eternal present of childhood. They have taken on the world-view of the child, or rather an arrested adult's notion of a child's-eye view, in an attempt to re-enter the heavenly kingdom of exclusively immediate experience which, ironically they could hardly wait to escape from when they themselves were children.

Stars of the nursery

The elevation of childhood was dramatically displayed at the Brit Awards ceremony in February 1996. When Michael Jackson was lowered from above into the middle of a stage tableau which gave the impression that he, Jackson, is the patron saint of children everywhere, Pulp's lead singer Jarvis Cocker felt deeply aggrieved. In protest at Jackson's self-aggrandizement (in the 1990s proximity to the child is the greatest boast an adult can make) Cocker made his way on stage where he bared an inch or two of his bottom before being hustled offstage by security guards and subsequently arrested by police. Thus Jackson's preoccupation with children was met with an equally infantilized gesture of complaint from Cocker.

In pop culture circles this playground behaviour was widely approved. 'Give him [Cocker] a knighthood', roared the weekly British music paper *Melody Maker*, which also reported that backstage the male stars of the television sitcom *Men Behaving Badly* started a 'Free Jarvis Campaign', while comedian Bob Mortimer ('a qualified solicitor') offered to act on Cocker's behalf.[1] Jackson's child-centred stageshow, Cocker's childlike response and a childish parody of campaigns to free political prisoners – at the Brit Awards that night, it certainly looked as if pop culture belonged in the nursery.

The actors in this charade were the latest participants in a tradition which can be traced all the way back to the 1950s. In an account of the new stars of that decade and the emerging sensibility personified by Montgomery Clift, Marlon Brando and James Dean, film critic Graham McCann notes that these actors came to prominence at a time when 'being an adult' was no longer assumed to be 'something worthwhile'.[2] Accordingly, they began to act out childlike characteristics which in turn were enacted as part of a newly infantilized pop culture.

McCann highlights the 'boyish innocence'[3] of Montgomery Clift in *From Here to Eternity*, and describes him as 'poised on the edge of a gender image, like a lost and bewildered child'.[4] Part of James Dean's attraction to later generations is that 'frozen by death, Dean can be the eternal teenager'[5] who will never grow up. Even Brando's macho characters contained something of the child: as Stanley Kowalski in *Streetcar Named Desire*, according to McCann, he 'takes enormous (perhaps rather childlike) pleasure in opening a bottle of beer, finishing a meal or even changing a T-shirt'.[6]

The child as rebel

McCann points out that, unlike the protagonists of previous generations, the rebel male characters of the 1950s did not initiate action as much as respond to situations beyond their control. In this respect they were childlike rather than adult. He also indicates that the development of childlike personal mannerisms constituted rejection of the adult world in general, and he concludes that 'the childlike or childish rebel was a major figure of the 1950s' – an icon, perhaps, for those who were already exasperated by 'the rituals and rules of adult society'.[7]

Soon after Clift, Brando and Dean broke into Hollywood, the Beat writers began their raids on the literary establishment. The child icon is well represented in Beat writing, and various essayists and biographers have demonstrated the recurring child motif in the lives of counter-cultural luminaries such as Jack Kerouac.

In 'The white negro', the essay which summarized the early years of the Beat sensibility, Norman Mailer came close to recommending the hipster for 'giving expression to the infant in himself'.[8] Gerald Nicosia described Kerouac's sexuality as 'almost infantile'.[9] Ann Charters has Kerouac 'returning again and again to the only fantasy that always held him, the vision of being a child cut adrift in a darkening universe'.[10] Although his image was that of the rootless traveller, Charters demonstrates that Kerouac's life story prefigured the pattern of subsequent stay-at-home generations:

> He was almost 26 and still didn't have a life he could call his. He had the room at his mother's ... All of the chaos that he described in his books ... usually didn't last long. A few weeks, a few months, and he was back with his mother writing it all down.[11]

Children's crusade

Across the Atlantic Colin MacInnes was documenting the rise of the childlike teenager in Britain. 'In this decade', he wrote, 'we witness the second Children's Crusade ... against all "square" and adult nay-sayers'.[12] MacInnes spoke of 'two nations' divided along generational lines: 'the teenagers on the one hand and, on the other, all those who have assumed the burdens of adult responsibility'.[13] He himself was impressed by the 'might' of the children's crusade – 'this new classless class'.

Mary Quant, the fashion designer and the first guru of Swinging London, also spoke of pre-adults as the active agent in a revitalized society. 'Middle age has been abolished by the new fashions', she declared. 'We have perpetuated youth.'[14]

One of the protagonists of the 'new classless class', Bob Dylan, was often described by his associates in childlike terms. When Dylan arrived in Greenwich Village, one of the participants in the folk club scene there remembers him as 'so much like a little boy lost that we were all concerned for him'.[15] Singer Joan Baez recalls Dylan having 'a tantrum. I mean, like a five-year-old'.[16] Dylan himself was keen to get back to the condition of childhood and the creativity which he associated with it: 'I don't write *for* people anymore ... I'm going to have to get back to writing like I used to when I was 10.'[17]

The same sort of ethos was expressed by the heroes of the electric blues and beat scene with which Dylan later joined up – much to the annoyance of his folk fans. Guitarist Eric Clapton, for example, was noted for his 'childlike innocence'.[18] John Lennon, whose published novels were written in a *faux naif* style which owes a lot to Spike Milligan, may not have thought of himself as a fully fledged adult. 'How can I bring up my son', he once asked, 'if I haven't brought up myself properly yet?'[19]

Infantilization

The child motif was by no means confined to teenagers and those catering for their tastes. It was also spreading into academia, high culture and high society.

Whereas Sigmund Freud had endeavoured to extricate his patients from the supposed legacy of their childhood, radical psychologist Norman O. Brown, in a diagnosis of 'the disease called Man',[20] wrote in praise of the 'immortal child in us' and in protest against the frustration of the 'immortal child' by 'the tyranny of genital organisation'.[21]

Music historian Wilfrid Mellers thought he saw a convergence between pop and concert-hall music around the theme of the child. Of the music of Carl Orff Mellers wrote that '*Carmina Burana* may have some historical significance as a genuine halfway house between concert music and pop ... with Orff we really are born again into childhood'.[22]

While grown-up art adopted some of the characteristics hitherto associated with children, New York socialites were abandoning the cocktail lounge sophistication associated with the music of Frank Sinatra and Nelson Riddle and taking on sub-adult styles and mannerisms. Observing this transformation, Tom Wolfe noted that 'socialites in New York today seem to have no natural, aristocratic styles of their own ... They dance the Jerk, the Monkey, the Shake, they listen to rock music, the women wear teenage and even sub-teen styles, such as stretch pants and decal eyes.'[23] It was highly appropriate, then, that the woman whom Wolfe described variously as 'New York's Girl of the Year', 'the most incredible socialite in history', and 'a kind of corn-haired essence of the new styles of life' went by the name of Baby Jane Holzer.[24]

Noting that 'youth had previously been presented as a stage on the path to adulthood', the academic and music critic Simon Frith subsequently summarized the '1960s argument' as follows: 'youth was preferable to age and no one need ever grow old'.[25]

Frith recognized that 'pop songs celebrate not the articulate but the inarticulate ... they measure the depth and originality of their emotions by reference to their inability to find words for them'. He also observed that 'teenage culture, the model of "irregular, spontaneous, unpredictable, exhibitionistic behaviour", became the basis for a more general pursuit of pleasure as a way of life'.[26]

Since the characteristics cited by Frith are usually associated with children rather than adults, it seems reasonable to add that in the 1960s the preference for the childlike rather than the adult was ceasing to be the distinctive motif of scattered groups of Romantics and starting to become widespread throughout society as a whole.

Radical children

At the time, however, no one foresaw that the cult of the child would eventually become part of the mainstream. In its earlier incarnations the child motif appeared as an affront to everything that society in general held dear.

Thus Jeff Greenfield believed that from the 1950s onwards the rejection of the adult world connoted a new kind of radicalism. 'To the Americans of World War Two', he observed, 'Dwight Eisenhower was a Certified Hero ... To the War Babies, Eisenhower was a President as Dumb Grown-Up', who became 'a joke, a symbol of every piece of Grown Up Authority stripped of any sense of legitimacy'.[27]

While Theodore Roszak noted with alarm that 'in every family comedy of the last 20 years Dad has been the buffoon',[28] Greenfield recalled that in children's TV programmes 'the villain was always a grown-up in authority'.[29]

Moreover, Greenfield saw something subversive in the pranksterism of the child–clown: 'Clarabelle the Clown ... darting in from offstage to creep along the front edge of the Peanut Gallery, to avenge the spirit of freedom ... Clarabelle [was] the first Yippie'; and, as such, according to Greenfield, Clarabelle was more influential in the counterculture than either Lenin or Marcuse.[30]

Whether or not he took his cue from Clarabelle the Clown, Yippie leader Jerry Rubin was certainly an advocate of the child over the adult. During student protests at Yale he declared, 'We're gonna take acid with our kids! Our kinds are going to tell us what to do! ... We ain't never gonna grow up! We're gonna be adolescents forever.'[31] Rubin also defined the Yippies as 'children of the middle class, children who refuse to grow up';[32] and he summarized the Yippie message as 'don't grow up. Growing up means giving up your dreams ... The leaders of the revolution are seven-year-olds.'[33]

Similarly, Charles Reich, author of *The Greening of America*, associated the childlike with a superior form of consciousness and looked forward to the day when the whole population 'rediscovers a childlike, breathless sense of wonder; this is the quality that Consciousness Three supremely treasures, to which it gives its ultimate sign of reverence, vulnerability and innocence, Oh Wow!'[34]

Playpower

Alongside the elevation of the child came a new emphasis on play. In 1948 the founder of the Institute of Contemporary Arts in London announced that it would serve as a 'play-centre' for adults. Sociologists commented on the development of a 'fun morality' in which play became as important as work. Noting that 'activities formerly sharply isolated from work have become part of business relations', Martha Wolfenstein observed 'a mutual penetration of work and play' in which 'fun, having been suspect if not taboo, has tended to become obligatory'.[35]

The emerging counterculture took up the emphasis on play initiated in American corporate culture and made it into the *sine qua non* of alternative lifestyles. Beat writer Alexander Trocchi pontificated that 'it is difficult to explain to the underprivileged that play is more serious than work'. He added, 'what is becoming is *homo ludens* in a life liberally constructed'. Providing the essential space for *Homo ludens* meant that 'there is no solution within the conventional economic framework'.[36]

In the 1930s a relatively unknown academic by the name of Johan Huizinga had come up with the notion of *Homo Ludens*, or Man the Player. 'It seems to me', said Huizinga, 'that next to *Homo Faber*, and perhaps on the same level as *Homo Sapiens*, *Homo Ludens*, Man the Player, deserves a place in our nomenclature.'[37] *Oz* editor Richard Neville popularized the Huizinga thesis in a book entitled *Playpower* (which came out in the same year that Huizinga's hitherto obscure tract was republished), in which the notion of *Homo ludens* was translated into the realm of London's counterculture. Henceforth, said Neville, play, not work, was to be the defining activity of human society.

It was its emphasis on play, Neville wrote, which spanned 'the political and cultural denominations of youth protest' and 'converts the Underground to a brotherhood of clowns'.[38] Underground enterprises such as *Oz* already constituted a world of play from which no one felt the need to take vacations ('do children holiday from play?')[39] Playfulness would make traditional politics irrelevant because 'the prank is mightier than the politician',[40] and it would also transform sexuality. Besides declaring that 'the Underground is turning sex back into play', Neville also made the bizarre assertion that 'infants get the most out of their sex life'.[41] Sociologist Bernice Martin later summarized Neville's outlook when she wrote that, for him, 'childhood is the goal of all life'.[42]

The ideas behind *Playpower* found many adherents. In *The Sociology of Youth Culture* Mike Brake has described how leisure replaced work as the major activity of self-definition, so that status came to be derived from non-work.[43] The demand for 'play without restraints' was prominent alongside 'all power to the imagination!' in the graffiti written on the walls of Paris during the student-led disturbances of May 1968.[44] Jim Haynes, founder of the Arts Lab in Drury Lane, also defined the counterculture in terms of play: 'After World War Two everybody was tired and the Beat movement in America began examining why are we alive? ... and one of the answers was: to have fun.'[45]

In the 'summer of love' cover story in *Time* magazine, which first brought the hippies to international attention, the latter were characterized by 'an almost childlike fascination in beads, blossoms and bells, blinding strobe lights and ear-shattering music, exotic clothing and erotic slogans'.[46] *Time* summed up the hippies and their attributes as 'flower power' rather than 'playpower' but the two terms were combined in a third label, 'flower children', which demonstrates the correlation between the emergence of the hippies and the further elevation of the child.

After the hippies' initial flowering in the 1967 summer of love, many of them took up residence and found temporary refuge in the crop of communes that mushroomed across Britain and America during the late 1960s and early 1970s. Subsuming adult work into an idea of childlike play was also an essential part of life in these communes. Thus American sociologist Ron E. Roberts noted that

> *the idea of work as a game means that, in a sense, hip communalists have regressed to childhood. Children play at work. In this way, the young communalists have given new meaning to the biblical dictum that 'whosoever shall not receive the Kingdom of God as a little child shall in no wise enter therein'.*[47]

The elevation of the child was so widespread that even traditional left-wingers tried to absorb the counterculture's emphasis on play and youth into a sub-Marxist idea of the young as 'the new proletariat . . . [which] can become the new revolutionary class'.[48] In the name of the working class the left took the idea of liberatory play to heart, so much so that in the 1970s the left-led Anti-Nazi League thought it had found the ultimate put-down of the far-right National Front in the formula 'NF = No Fun'.

In the 1980s the British sociologist John Davis made a cogent summary of the claims of subversion and revolution which were made in the late 1960s on behalf of the hippies and their playpower ethic. 'The hippies . . . were not merely chronologically and socially post-adolescent and pre-adult in their dropping out from "the system"', he argued. They were seen as actively engaged in a refusal to *ever* 'grow up' and indeed in a subversion of the previously linear structuring of the human life-cycle:

> *In their practical denial of the existential centrality of work . . . the hippies were seen as denying a core component of the conventional, contemporary Western definition of adulthood and maturity. In a post-industrial society, the argument ran, adult work in the accepted sense would no longer be necessary, and play, previously the more or less exclusive property of the pre-adult, would become the dominant social activity and good. In such a society therefore no one would ever need to 'grow up' and youthful values would predominate; such an ideal had yet to be realised, but meanwhile the counterculture was actively exploring the full range of post-industrial possibilities.*[49]

Arrested Development

The search for innocence

The moment of childlike activism was short-lived, but the motif of the child continued to grow in significance as a symbol of the refusal to accept the adult failings of mainstream society and its flawed rationality. In the late 1960s and 1970s groups of musicians like The Incredible String Band and Forest cultivated an atmosphere of childlike whimsy. In *Tommy*, the 'rock opera' which tells a story of a 'deaf, dumb and blind kid', The Who associated 'the complete innocent' with 'pure being'.[50] British psychedelia, pop critic Jon Savage has recently noted, was 'above all concentrating on the child'.[51]

At around the same time students of literature began to reread the classics in search of childlike role models. Characters such as Prince Myshkin in Dostoyevsky's *The Idiot* ('"a perfect child" … a modern saint, a man of unusual moral and spiritual qualities'[52]) were adopted and identified with in so far as they represented the unaffected grace of the childlike.

By the mid-1970s one of the chief complaints against the hippies was that their culture had lost its childlike innocence and mutated into 'adult-oriented rock'. In this respect the term 'adult' carried unwelcome connotations of falsehood, instrumentality and 'selling out'. It became necessary to re-invent the child in pop culture, with its connotations of innocence and authenticity. This the punks duly did, at the same time as they re-presented the alienated sensibility.

Thus for The Sex Pistols' lead singer Johnny Rotten it was 'naivety … a kind of innocence' which attracted him to bass player Sid Vicious.[53] Manager Malcolm McLaren recalls the invention of punk bondage gear as arising out of the desire for something 'that reminds you of Tarzan and babies at the same time. Like a nappy or a beaver tail.'[54] Music critic Mary Harron remembers one of the first American punk bands, The Ramones, as 'dumb smart, smart dumb' – a combination which played with notions of childishness and sophistication.[55]

In the late 1970s and early 1980s the child as represented in punk was succeeded by yet another representation of the child as expressed by the 'shambling' bands of the 'indie' scene. The Manchester-based pop academic Steve Redhead explains that the term 'shambling', first coined by Radio One disc jockey John Peel, was a 'concept born out of "shambolic" and "rambling"'.[56]

Redhead avers that 'shambling' bands such as The Smiths, Mighty

Lemon Drops, The Mekons and Stump emphasized 'the 1960s, childlike innocence and a "refusal to grow up"'. Not that they performed a direct imitation of childish mannerisms, as Redhead points out; rather they expressed 'a desire to keep in mind certain of the "privileges" of innocence'. This amounted not to 'an uncontrollable instinct to behave in a puerile fashion' but to 'a refusal of citizenship'.[57] If Redhead is correct, it means that even when the child motif grew up, as it were, and moved away from some of the silliness associated with the 'flower children', it nevertheless retained its essential function as a way of saying: I want no part in the adult world.

The shambling character of the period has been evoked recently in *Faithless*, a novel by John L. Williams, who was himself a musician in the early 1980s indie scene. Williams has described *Faithless* as a novel about people who have lost their politics,[58] while reviewer, editor and specialist bookshop-owner Maxim Jakubowski, writing in *Time Out*, placed its characters as part of 'a lost generation of Brits who never quite achieved adulthood'.[59]

Abdication

From the mid-1980s the child motif was represented by a new star in Hollywood, Keanu Reeves. Asked to explain why he was cast as the Buddha in Bernardo Bertolucci's film *Little Buddha*, Reeves told *Newsweek* that Bertolucci had informed him that 'it was my innocence'.[60] Reeves made his name as a 'gentle, bumbling and fairly inarticulate' Ted in *Bill and Ted's Excellent Adventure*,[61] and throughout his career various commentators have compared him to James Dean. Like Dean, Reeves has been known to display an unease in public situations which borders on the childlike; and it is partly the childlike element in his personal rejection of Hollywood and its routines which has endeared him both to his dedicated fan base and to the public at large.

By the mid-1990s Reeves came to be regarded as *the* actor of his generation, and American colleges devised whole courses on his work. Keith Mayerson, a student enrolled on the Keanu Reeves course at the Art Center College of Design in Pasadena, summed up the significance of Reeves by describing him as the hero for 'the slacker generation'.[62]

But who are the slackers? As represented in Richard Linklater's film of this name, and in Douglas Coupland's influential novel *Generation X*, slackers were twenty-somethings who avoided entry into the adult world of the career ladder, private health plan and pension scheme. Instead they performed in largely unknown rock bands while working the minimum number of hours in temporary, low-paid 'McJobs'; thus leaving the maximum time for the personal empowerment associated with play.

In his second full-length novel, *Microserfs*, Coupland chronicled the lives of highly paid employees of the Microsoft Corporation. Like slackers, the Microserfs also lived an essentially immature existence in which work was redefined as a sophisticated computer game. Moreover, their line of work, unlike 'McJobs', held out the prospect of earning enough money to retire before reaching the age of thirty. This is the apogee of infantilization, because it means never having to enter the adult world which traditionally combines decades of disciplined work with long-term responsibility and self-denial for the sake of the family.

Absurd

In the 1990s the child motif has appeared in increasingly absurd guises. There are restaurants like *The Playroom* in Battersea where punters play with toys and Barbie dolls along with their food and drink; and there are 'adult baby clubs' where members can play at being infants. The founder of one such club, The Little Rascals, even offers 'counselling to other adult babies'.[63]

Personified by performers such as Bis, Bjork, and Belle and Sebastian (a band which takes its name from a French children's television series about a young girl and her pet dog), infantilism is well represented in today's music industry, where grown men now sport the kind of *Just William* haircut, as worn by Blur's doe-eyed Damon Albarn, which previously they could not wait to grow out of.

Meanwhile Courtney Love is rumoured to carry the ashes of Kurt Cobain 'in a teddy bear in her back pack'.[64] Whether or not the rumour is true, it illustrates the way in which keeping in touch with the child in oneself now constitutes proof of good faith and authentic emotion.

Profiled in the *Observer*, veteran jazz trumpeter Humphrey Lyttleton received the ultimate accolade when he was described as 'the world's oldest teenager ... 75 this week and still refusing to grow up'.[65]

On the London club scene, acting beneath your age is regarded as a sign of freshness and trustworthiness. In a novel set in and around the recently established nightclub Shoom during the 1987 summer of love, music journalist and Oasis biographer Paolo Hewitt described the atmosphere among a new generation of clubbers. Hewitt was pleased to note that 'it was as if the people had become children again, unfettered by manners or hangups or not concerned with what anybody thought of them'.[66]

Likewise in *Altered State: The Story of Ecstasy Culture and Acid House* Matthew Collin reported that 'Ecstasy had opened some kind of psychic door ... Many treated Shoom like a kiddies' ice-cream-and-jelly party, giving each other presents like smiley badges or clip-on hearts.'[67] Collin quotes Spencer Guire and Jason Hawkins, two veterans of the club scene in the late 1980s. The latter recalled, 'we used to have teddy bears ... it was like going back to childhood'; while the former summed up the early days of rave culture by saying 'people were just reverting back to a childlike way'.

The ubiquitous child

The child is now a major theme in advertising and marketing. Panic-stricken opponents of Alcopops, who assume that these drinks are directed at children who will become alcoholics, miss the essential point that, these days, childlike imagery is often used to sell products to adults. Thus in March 1996 Levi jeans provided readers of the trendsetting magazine *The Face* with a child's watercolour painting book and brush inserted into every copy of the magazine. A year later the breakfast cereal Frosties was being sold to British television audiences on the basis that it reaches 'the kid in you'. Along similar lines a television advert for the Cheltenham and Gloucester Building Society counterposes the lithe figure of a child diving for pearls in contrast to the lumbering adult imprisoned in a cumbersome diving suit, representing the alleged burden of technology. The child gets the pearl and the audience gets an implied message about the superior status of children.

A recent advert for British Airways depicted the head and shoulders of a company executive, probably in his fifties, attached to a baby's torso and cradled in his mother's arms. The advert announced the introduction of the 'unique new cradle seat' on British Airways flights. Unless the agency which produced the advert got its market research totally wrong, it also announced that today's senior managers are not averse to thinking of themselves as babes in arms – a notion which would surely have prompted apoplexy on the part of their proud, if stolid, predecessors.

The makers of such advertisements will almost certainly be familiar with the survey and forecasting organization Mintel, which in 1996 found that 41 per cent of childless men between the ages of twenty and thirty-four are doing a Jack Kerouac and still living at home with their parents. In its coverage of the survey the *Guardian* concluded that the 'young generation [is] happy to stay at home with Mum'.[68] The *Daily Mail* adopted a high moral tone, warning of a 'Peter Pan generation' that is 'hooked on pleasure'.[69] Reporter Suzanne O'Shea went on to explain why the Peter Pan generation is such an attractive prospect to advertisers: 'by minimising their financial worries and responsibilities, their ample disposable incomes can be spent on such indulgences as eating out, travel and fashionable clothes'.

The pros and cons of living a childlike existence have become a staple topic for columnists in magazines and newspapers. 'Are you grown up yet?' was the headline on the cover of the American publication *Utne Reader* in May–June 1996. Beneath the first headline was a second question: 'Do you know anyone who is?' Inside columnist Barbara Graham reported that 'I decided at an early age that I would never grow up ... Grown-upness seemed to be ... a dead-end state populated by a bunch of boring people whose primary obsessions were life insurance and Getting Ahead.' The gist of the piece was that Graham had stayed true to her child-self.[70]

A few months earlier the *Guardian*'s Dave Green had noted that, whereas the video game consoles of the 1980s were marketed at children, their 1990s equivalents such as the Sony Play Station are targeted at the eighteen to thirty-five age group. More broadly, Green concluded that 'for every good reason not to become an adult, there's an equally compelling one for remaining a child'.[71] Also in the *Guardian* Suzanne Moore wrote that, in their approach to life, 'most of my best friends are in the 11–15 age group'. She described herself as 'at least 13. I can't say that I have fundamentally altered since then.'[72]

In the *Observer* Peter Beaumont chronicled the lifestyle of the 'thirtysomethings who won't grow up ... you see them in Hyde Park: 30 and 40 somethings on rollerblades and skateboards, hanging out at Glastonbury or discussing Oasis versus Blur at dinner parties. They keep *The Face* folded with their copy of *The Times* and watch *Top of the Pops*.'[73] As one of the characters in the television series *ThirtySomething* once said: 'The tragedy of our generation is that we will always be the kids.'

Even politicians are not immune from the cult of Peter Pan. When NBC's Daphne Barak described Tony Blair (then visiting the USA as leader of Her Majesty's Opposition) as 'like a scared child',[74] she was putting a negative interpretation on the look of wide-eyed non-ideological innocence which Blair seemed to have been cultivating as authentic proof of his good intentions towards the British electorate.

Retreating to the child

In an intelligent discussion of the extensive use of childlike fashion models in the 1990s (that is, models in their early teens alongside older models pretending to be younger), style journalist Jim McClellan touched on the far-reaching effects of the relentless 'pursuit of "freshness"'. We are attracted, he said, to 'something less obvious, something that looks innocent of the tired adult routines'.[75]

This pursuit now involves the whole of society, and McClellan was suggesting that it has arisen in response to the shortcomings of contemporary culture: 'in the absence of consensus elsewhere, child-hood (and the need to protect it) seems the one thing we can all agree on. Some imaginary ideal of innocence is held up by both religious right wingers and communitarians as a symbol of all that we have lost.'[76]

In the *NME* reviewer Mark Sutherland seemed to be thinking along the same lines when he described Crispian Mills of the band Kula Shaker as 'the Tom Hanks of rock: a wide-eyed *ingénue* encapsulating a generation's desire to relive simpler times'.[77]

Life was indeed simpler when we could agree on the inevitability of progress. Now that every section of society has lost faith in its ability to make progress a reality, it seems reasonable to suggest that the cult of the child offers core values (innocence, authenticity) which correspond to the defeat of our adult sense of agency. In other words, the growing cult of the child is the corollary of the erosion of subjectivity in the active, history-making sense.

In the 1990s almost everyone subscribes to the kind of submissive ethos which suggests that most of what happens in the world is necessarily immune to our actions. It is an ethos which originated in the counterculture that defined itself against the last gasp of adult aspirations; and the percentage of those subscribing to it has grown steadily over the last half-century along with the transformation into pop culture of what was once a minority counterculture. The child motif is an intrinsic part of this development, and a number of critics have pointed out that the culture could not exist unless its participants somehow thought of themselves as children. Albert Goldman, for example, once described the whole of youth culture as really only a mother substitute.[78]

Dissatisfaction

McClellan and Sutherland have pointed to the faultlines in adult society which are expressed by the recent growth in the cult of the child. But their dissatisfaction with the childishness of pop culture is far from unprecedented.

Jimi Hendrix identified rock 'n' roll with the play ethos and expressed his frustration with both when he said, 'I don't want to be a clown anymore, I don't want to be a rock 'n' roll star.'[79] John Lennon once said he wanted to do more films because 'unlike pop music it [film] allows you to grow up as a person'.[80] But somehow the possibility of making music or even films for adults seems to have receded still further, prompting one rising star of the 1990s, Beck Hansen, to reverse the sentiments expressed in Neville's *Playpower* and complain that 'we have created this culture where we don't grow up, because we're not allowed to. It bothers me a lot, actually. We are all a bunch of children.'[81]

At the very outset of pop culture, some critics recognized that the growing audience for the celebration of immaturity was a novel phenomenon. Kenneth Keniston recalled the days before the cult of the child when 'adolescence was a matter of "learning the ropes" and memorising the map and timetable for the road of success ahead. Gawky, awkward adolescence was a phase to be outgrown as quickly as possible.'[82]

Looking back to the days when 'Buddy Holly descended on our conformist post-war streets', Philip Norman recalls that 'the majority went directly from childhood to adulthood at about 17, metamorphosing overnight from school uniforms to frocks and twin-sets like their mothers, or tweed jackets, grey flannel trousers and manly briar pipes like their fathers.'[83]

Frank Musgrove observed that this 'metamorphosis' used to be entirely voluntary. Until the end of the 1950s, Musgrove suggested, children could not wait to become adults, and the rush to get married indicated the burning desire to acquire adult status. In Britain it was not until the 1960s that those approaching or even passing what was then described as 'the age of majority' began to prolong their pre-adult existence and increasingly to regress to mannerisms associated with childhood. Musgrove, writing in the early 1970s, summed up this change of heart: 'Ten years ago the young were fighting to get in; today they are often fighting to get out.'[84]

In one of the earliest accounts of embryonic pop culture Caroline Bird was sharply critical of the infantilism which she associated with the Beats. 'It is tempting', she wrote in *Harper's* magazine, 'to describe the hipster in psychiatric terms as infantile, but the style of his infantilism is a sign of the times. He does not try to enforce his will on others, Napoleon-fashion, but contents himself with a magical omnipotence never disproved because never tested.'[85]

In this short paragraph Bird uncovered the common root of the 'cool' and 'naive' styles. From the outset both have expressed a retreat from contestation into a world of childlike fantasy.

Bird was not alone in her condemnation of the Beats. Rejecting one of Kerouac's stories as 'immature', the publisher Putnam's advised him to 'grow up and go to work'.[86] Even those who feel themselves to be close to Kerouac have sometimes felt obliged to make some criticism of his infantilism.

In her largely sympathetic biography of Kerouac Ann Charters pointed out that he 'hadn't offered any real alternative to the conformity of twentieth century America'.[87] The vision of freedom which Kerouac offered was, she admitted, 'a return to the solipsistic world of childhood'. Moreover, this fictional world mirrored the real world of Kerouac's relationship with his mother. Recalling their domestic circumstances, Charters judged that 'he was very much the little boy in her house'.[88] She also quoted the *New York Times* review of Kerouac's *Doctor Sax*, which described it as a 'pretentious and unreadable farrago of childhood fantasy play'.[89]

In an essay entitled 'Adolescence and maturity in the American novel' literary critic Leslie Fiedler complained that American writers were failing to grow up. 'Even our best writers', Fiedler reported, 'appear unable to mature; after one or two inexpert attempts, they find a style, subject and tone, usually anchored in their adolescent experience, and this they repeat compulsively, like a songbird his single tune.'[90] Fiedler made an astute connection between depoliticization and the adoption of an immature sensibility when he wrote that 'it is almost as impossible to imagine a Hemingway character having a child ... as it is to conceive one of them going to a ballot box'.[91] But even Fiedler seemed not to have been immune to the cult of the child: the anthology in which this essay appeared was entitled *An End to Innocence*.

Graham McCann, writing about the Beats' contemporary in Hollywood, James Dean, conceded that there was 'something rather deliberate and tiresome about Dean's irrationality, as though he feared the responsibilities and obligations of adult life and chose to hide from them behind the guise of an incompetent'. McCann repeats the old adage that 'there was no time for Dean to grow up', but adds a note of criticism in the comment that 'if there was time, he did not take it'.[92]

In the 1960s the cult of youth came in for plenty of criticism from the old guard of stiff-backed, bowler-hatted gents. You can almost see the middle-aged pin-stripe worn by the *Weekend Telegraph* leader-writer who, noting that 'once upon a time it was considered normal for adolescents to want to be adults, now the world seems full of adults wanting to be adolescents', declared, 'I don't *want* to worship adolescents.' This tone of voice sounds almost as petulant as the infantile object of his criticism.[93]

Other critics were more penetrating. Paul Johnson, the maverick editor of the *New Statesman* who later switched his allegiance to the right, highlighted the political failings which lay behind the growing infatuation with youth on the part of public figures: 'Bewildered by a rapidly changing society, excessively fearful of becoming out of date, our leaders are increasingly turning to young people as ... geiger-counters to guard them against the perils of obsolescence.'[94] Christopher Booker applied the same analysis to a wider circle of opinion-formers and leaders: 'Unbalanced by change, they display, like an uncertain adolescent, all the symptoms of insecurity.' The cult of youth, Booker suggested, was tantamount to 'trying to resolve an insecurity through what we may call the dream or fantasy level of the mind'.[95]

While public figures were looking to youth, youth itself was looking to the child. In an otherwise favourable account of Swinging London George Melly summed up John Lennon's attempts to go beyond pop: 'His motives are admirable but his means are childish.'[96] In other words, Lennon's hankering for a mode of expression which 'allows you to grow up as a person' turned out to be almost as childish as the infantile pop culture from which he sought to extricate himself. This vicious circle has recently been underlined by Ian MacDonald's account of the Beatles at work, or rather at play, in the recording studios. MacDonald describes Lennon's desire to move on from restrictive pop formulae by experimenting with new musical instruments, without ever having to learn to play them.[97] Instead, Lennon wanted immediate results, or instant gratification in the manner of a child.

Although broadly sympathetic to the aspirations which he saw in the counterculture, Theodore Roszak was none the less concerned that when adolescence became 'a status in its own right', it created 'a limbo that is nothing so much as the prolongation of an already permissive infancy'.[98] Noting the element of retreatism ('it is much more a flight *from* than *toward*'[99]) in the counterculture, he warned that 'such an infantilisation of the middle class young has a corrupting effect. It ill prepares them for the real world and its unrelenting if ever more subtle disciplines.'[100] Countercultural radicalism provided no immunity for this corruption, Roszak observed; it amounted to the 'adolescentization of dissent'.[101]

Lewis S. Feuer was totally unimpressed by the radicalism of Lennon's generation, describing it as 'the last cry of the children in despair at leaving the child's world'.[102] The American educationalist Joseph J. Schwab believed that Keniston *et al.* had given too much ground to the new alienated and their extended period of youth. 'What is so great about it?', Schwab wanted to know.[103] As did Edward Shils, who lambasted the 'flatterers' chorus' of 'middle-aged adults' who came out in favour of youth culture.[104]

Schwab also criticized commentators on youth for tailing trends instead of challenging them: '[they] end up in the attempt to make what *is* the standard of what *ought* to be.' He was equally dismissive of the notion that the retreat into the childlike was an essential part of the search for identity:

> The very phrase 'search for identity' is absurd, because identities are not found lurking in some corner you have not looked in yet . . . Identity is made when you have located and developed the competencies – the potential competencies you have got – and have made something of them.[105]

Daniel Bell condemned the way in which pop culture acted out 'the fantasies and sexual demands of childhood during adolescence on a mass scale' which was 'unprecedented'.[106] The conservative critic Allan Bloom jibed at Marcuse and rock music simultaneously when he observed that the notion of liberation articulated by the former 'will result in a society where the greatest satisfactions are sexual, of the sort that bourgeois moralist Freud called polymorphous and infantile. Rock music touches the same chord in the young.'[107]

Fellow Americans Peter Blos and Carl Frankenstein also recognized 'a retreat from maturity' in the counterculture. Frankenstein thought he could see the same immaturity in the political radicalism of the period, which he described as 'the abandonment of reality in favour of principles'.[108] Along similar lines Bloom declared that 'anti-bourgeois ire is the opiate of the Last Man'.[109]

Although an active participant in the counterculture, the British artist and writer Jeff Nuttall was equally caustic about the childish ethos of the counterculture in which 'naivety was equated with honesty, ineptitude was equated with sincerity, and merit was gauged in terms of proximity to the animal and the vegetable'.[110] His polemical remarks bear some resemblance to the German philosopher Hegel's accurate observation in support of the modern: 'Only the animal is truly innocent.'[111]

Submission

Unlike Nuttall the *Times* columnist and conservative commentator Bernard Levin could not get far enough away from the counterculture. But some of the criticisms which Levin advanced in his account of Britain in the 1960s, *The Pendulum Years*, were not so far removed from Nuttall's. Besides noting with disdain that the influential pop artist Roy Lichtenstein was inspired by 'the popular comics that had for so long entertained children',[112] Levin bemoaned the adoption of the dolphin, in all its supposed innocence, as the 'symbolic beast of the decade, displacing the lemming from the consciousness and conversation of the smart, the sophisticated and the cynical'.[113] In the political radicalism of the time he discerned a childlike submissiveness. Levin described the vogue for Chairman Mao as 'a new bosom' on which the children of the 1960s could 'lay all their cares'. To have accepted the cult of Mao, he added, 'the sixties must have been in desperate need of substitute fathers'.[114] Levin also claimed that a childlike retreatism from reality informed the anti-Vietnam-War protests:

> *Vietnam touched a feeling . . . like that which is said to overcome travellers lost in the snow: a desperate desire to lie down and sleep . . . many, millions possibly — found literally unbearable the thought that the world was the*

way it was; in particular, the reality of aggression simply could not be faced.[115]

Instead of facing reality, the counterculturists went in search of a childlike purity; or, as Levin put it, 'what was sought was real purity, physical and emotional, so that ... the word "macrobiotic", applied to food, made its appearance to denote food untouched by anything artificial'.[116] Just as macrobiotic food was untouched, so the child was admired as a symbol of that which is untouched by age and the experience of reality.

Levin cited Robert Bolt's explanation of retreatism as a response to the absence of sustainable models of adult behaviour. In a preface to his play about Thomas More, *A Man for All Seasons*, Bolt wrote that 'we no longer have, as past societies have had, any picture of individual Man (Stoic Philosopher, Christian Religious, Rational Gentleman) by which to recognise ourselves and against which to measure ourselves; we are anything. But if anything, then nothing.'[117]

Literary critic Malcolm Bradbury noted the same absence, but related it more directly to the cult of the child. After observing that Billy Pilgrim, the hero of Kurt Vonnegut's cult novel *Slaughterhouse Five: Or, The Children's Crusade*, is 'a childlike, gentle-natured but emotionally damaged optometrist',[118] Bradbury concluded that 'one way to respond to the aggressive historical landscape of the sixties was to move through experimental fantasy to a recovered imaginative innocence'.[119]

Right-wing Japanese critics such as Keigo Okonogi formulated a similar but more caustic description of what they dubbed 'the age of the moratorium people', i.e. a generation which had granted itself a moratorium on growing up.[120]

In the 1980s the style journalist and design consultant Peter York demolished the cult of the child – in words if not in deeds – in his book *Modern Times*. York believed that pop culture had been living through a period which he called 'Babytime': 'a magic time when thousands of adult, sane, bourgeois men and women aspired to Babyhood. The man with the child in his eyes, Kickers on his feet and dungarees round the rest, walked the land ... [in] a kitsch version of fifties childhood.'[121] Describing this syndrome as the 'dawn of mass paedophilia',[122] York was clearly wise to its perverse character. He also understood its novelty, as when he pointed out that in the early 1960s 'an adult working woman *presenting* to a doctor in ankle socks and hair ribbons and the rest of the dressing-up and quoting children's books, would have been classifiable – a refugee from the Glass Menagerie'.[123] His mistake was to periodize 'Babytime' too closely as a period 'roughly, from 1968 to 1980',[124] when he should have recognized it as a stage within a broader and more deep-seated trend towards infantilism.

Contemporary diagnoses of Peter-Pan-itis
In the 1990s various critics have tried to account for the growth of infantilism. Reviewing Francis Ford Coppola's *Jack*, *Sunday Times* critic Cosmo Landesman wrote in a tone both horrified and sarcastic about a great director who had lowered himself to making 'a film that celebrates ... the need for we [*sic*] corrupt adults to find the inner child within'.[125] In the *Independent* Mark Simpson criticized the 'Lost Boys stuck in Neverland' personified by 'Keanu and Brad, the boy-men who don't look as if they've started shaving yet'. Simpson correlated the boyishness of men who should know better to the crisis of masculinity:

> In a post-feminist, consumerist age in which being a man is an uncertain business of uncertain worth, Peter Pan-itis, a condition where grown men behave as if they had never grown up at all, has become a benign evolutionary adaption, filling the world with men whose bodies have passed through puberty but whose minds clearly have not.[126]

For other commentators, however, Peter-Pan-itis is not confined to men. Art critic Robert Hughes has written scathingly of a general 'pursuit of the Inner Child'. This, says Hughes, 'has taken over just at the moment when Americans ought to be figuring out where their Inner Adult is, and how that disregarded oldster got buried under the rubble of pop psychology and specious short-term gratification'.[127]

In her book *New Passages* Gail Sheehy suggested that the 'private world' of men and women in their twenties to early forties 'is no longer a flat, linear progression, as it was for their parents. They are leading cyclical lives that demand they start over and over again.'[128]

Robert Bly, one of the founders of the men's movement in America, recently complained that 'people don't bother to grow up, and we are all fish swimming in a tank of half-adults'. Bly compares contemporary icons with the photographs of men and women a century ago, which

> show a certain set of the mouths and jaws that says 'we're adults. There's nothing we can do about it'. By contrast, the face of Marilyn Monroe, of

Kevin Costner or of the ordinary person we see on the street says 'I am a child. There's nothing I can do about it.'[129]

Bly seems to think that the absence of 'effective rituals of initiation' is a key factor leading to a situation in which 'observers describe many contemporaries as "children with children of their own"'.[130] He may be right; perhaps there are no effective rites of passage. But that surely says something about the absent adult world which an individual might be passing into, if only it could be found, rather than simply indicating the lack of a ritual with which to mark the occasion.

In a more penetrating essay Eric Konigsberg suggested that young people's styles have gone into reverse:

American youth seem to be getting, well, younger. Urban outfitters sell Play-Doh to twentysomething customers, indie rock album covers are adorned with baby pictures and childish art trouvee. The kinder-whore look, with its patron saint Courtney Love, pairs Mary Janes with frilly, empire-waisted dresses. Ravers clutch furry pets and cute lunch boxes.[131]

Konigsberg regards infantilization 'as an antidote to the uncertainties of the day. Age regression is a protective shield.' He suggests that the 'conscious abdication of adult responsibility' is derived from living in a world of 'diminished expectations'. And he notes that *faux naif* syntax such as 'Should we do the coffee shop thing?' and 'I have to do the work thing' (the vernacular of TV shows like *Friends*) is not unique to the young. Even ex-president George Bush, Konigsberg observes, 'employed terms like "the vision thing"'.

Konigsberg might have gone on to observe that the use of such childish syntax indicates that George Bush and his successor Bill Clinton lack an adult vision which would of necessity command a mature mode of expression. That their language is babyish speaks volumes about the immaturity of their governance.

Mark Simpson noticed that a similar impression may be drawn from the mannerisms of Tony Blair, whom he describes as 'a man who looks and sounds like every granny's favourite grandson – the library monitor in the Christian Union with a university scholarship lined up'.[132] The cult of the child in politics was further illustrated on 2 July 1997 by the first-ever children's day at 10 Downing Street, when the doors of the prime ministerial home were thrown open to a party of children under the watchful gaze of supernanny Cherie Blair.

Arrested Development

The prevention of adult interaction

Perhaps the most frustrating aspect of the cult of the child is the sense in which it is an extravagant response to the nightmare creatures of our own making. The alienated sensibility made terrible strangers out of ourselves and everyone else. The cult of the child seeks to compensate for life-as-horror-story by inventing a competing fantasy of life-as-a-child's-birthday-party. In this respect the cynical orientation to other people associated with the 'cool' is interdependent upon its mirror image, the naive orientation which accompanies the elevation of the child. But both polarities exclude the possibility of a considered interaction (either competing or co-operative) between mature, adult individuals.

Seen in this light, the vogue for Ecstasy and its childlike fellowship turns out to be the latest antidote to fantastical alienation. Under the influence of Ecstasy, says Jay Stevens, 'existential terrors ... become a little less terrifying'.[133] Likewise, Douglas Rushkoff comments that on E 'the issues that arise in the course of a trip seem less threatening and infinitely more manageable'.[134] The tragedy is that the exaggerated 'terrors' which Ecstasy alleviates (the sense of being permanently at risk, the nightmarish notion of other people and even ourselves) are largely a figment of the alienated sensibility and its tendency to overstate risk.

The absence of adult interaction in the interplay of these mirror images is summed up by *Guardian* columnist Charlotte Raven in her telling description of chilling-out:

> *Go to any nightclub at 5am and you will see not an orgy, but a scene reminiscent of a suburban coffee morning. Everything is 'please' and 'thank you' because, on E, people cannot engage and so they do not talk. What they do instead, therefore, is revert to ritualised forms of interaction in which niceness is valued above any other quality ... E stamps on subversive impulses, nurtures an acceptance of the status quo and is creating a culture of nodding dogs who simply affirm without knowing what they were ever agreeing to.*[135]

While the alienated sensibility has resulted in a world-view in which everyone is nasty, E culture creates a fantasy world in which 'niceness is valued above any other quality'. In both instances the interplay between human beings is seen in exaggerated terms, as a child might see it. Likewise the E experience caricatures human activity to the point of absurdity, in which we are reduced to the level of children's cartoons. It usually involves hours of frenetic dancing, a parody of activity, followed by a spell in the chill-out room which is given over to thinking thoughts of the utmost banality. Both halves of this experience are said to engender a sense of togetherness. But the dancing is done solo: each to his or her own solipsism, even if we are all solipsists simultaneously. And the chill-out consists of facile exchanges rather than substantial interaction. The 'community' created here is equally superficial. It depends on the temporary effects of ingesting the same drug, and disappears as soon as the effects wear off.

In the polarity of fantastical alienation and mythical community, the reality of interpersonal relations and the underlying social context in which they occur remain unexplored. Either we fear each other or we claim to love each other. The ground in between – the ground on which we actually exist in our day-to-day lives – is removed from under our feet. Thus the polarity reflects the way in which our society simultaneously aggregates and disaggregates us, but it represents this contradiction in such a fetishized way as to render it invisible. Taken together, the 'cool' and the naive cult of the child act out this contradiction; but their participants are too embroiled in the charade to make any sense of it.

Sociologist Leonard Broom once declared that 'every society must somehow solve the problem of transforming children into adults, for its very survival depends on that solution'.[136] It seems that pop culture has come up with a novel remedy: it socializes children into adults who would like to go back to being children. This is the consequence of what the American critic Norman Podhoretz described as 'the poisonous glorification of the adolescent'.[137]

After half a century of this 'poisonous glorification', Thom Yorke, the Exeter University-educated lead singer in the highly acclaimed band Radiohead, spoke of 'feeling like ... I don't have an adult frame of mind, 'though I do adult things'. Moreover, Yorke went on to declare that 'being in a band turns you into a child, and keeps you locked into that frame of mind'.[138] He was describing the kind of arrested development that corresponds to the stunted society in which we live, where coming to identify with 'the child in all of us' is one of the pathways through which we have come to accept the closed character of that society and our limited role within it.

Notes

1. Front page headline, *The Melody Maker*, 2 March 1996.

2. Graham McCann, *Rebel Males* (London: Hamish Hamilton, 1992), p. 14.

3. *Ibid.*, p. 19.

4. *Ibid.*, p. 62.

5. *Ibid.*, p. 24.

6. *Ibid.*, p. 99.

7. *Ibid.*, p. 62.

8. Norman Mailer, 'The white negro', *Dissent*, summer 1957.

9. Gerald Nicosia, *Memory Babe: A Critical Biography of Jack Kerouac* (London: Penguin, 1986), p. 164.

10. Ann Charters, *Kerouac: A Biography* (London: Picador/Pan, 1978), p. 14.

11. *Ibid.*, p. 83.

12. Colin MacInnes, in *Twentieth Century* magazine, February 1958.

13. Colin MacInnes, *England, Half English* (London: McGibbon and Kee, 1961), p. 56.

14. Mary Quant, quoted in Jonathan Aitken, *The Young Meteors* (London: Secker and Warburg, 1967), p. 13.

15. Camilla Horne, quoted in Anthony Scaduto, *Bob Dylan* (London: Abacus, 1972), p. 60.

16. Joan Baez, quoted in *ibid.*, p. 193.

17. Bob Dylan, quoted in *ibid.*, p. 180.

18. Christopher Sanford, *Clapton – Edge of Darkness* (London: Gollancz, 1994), p. 85.

19. John Lennon, quoted in *The Permissive Society: The Guardian Inquiry* (London: Panther Modern Society, 1969), p. 15.

20. Norman O. Brown, *Life Against Death* (1959) (London: Sphere Books, 1968), p. 16.

21. *Ibid.*, p. 37.

22. Wilfrid Mellers, *Caliban Reborn* (London: Gollancz, 1968), p. 95.

23. Tom Wolfe, *The Kandy-Kolored Tangerine-Flake Streamline Baby* (1965) (London: Mayflower/Granada, 1968), p. 12.

24. *Ibid.*

25. Simon Frith, *Sound Effects* (London: Constable, 1983), pp. 33–4.

26. *Ibid.*, pp. 34–5.

27. Jeff Greenfield, *No Peace, No Place* (New York: Doubleday, 1973), pp. 19–20.

28. Theodore Roszak, *The Making of a Counter Culture: Reflections on the Technocratic Society and Its Youthful Opposition* (London: Faber & Faber, 1971), p. 31.

29. Greenfield, *op. cit.*, p. 120.

30. *Ibid.*, p. 121.

31. Jerry Rubin, quoted in *ibid.*, p. 247.

32. Jerry Rubin, in *Oz*, no. 11, March 1968.

33. Jerry Rubin, *Do It!* (London: Simon and Schuster, 1970), p. 87.

34. Charles Reich, *The Greening of America* (Harmondsworth: Penguin, 1971), p. 221.

35. Martha Wolfenstein, 'The emergence of fun morality', *Journal of Social Issues*, vol. 7, no. 4 (1951), reprinted in Eric Larrabee (ed.), *Mass Leisure* (Glencoe, IL: The Free Press, 1958), pp. 86–93.

36. Alexander Trocchi, a version of the Situationist International manifesto, 1960, item 18 in the Sigma portfolio, issued privately in 1964/5.

37. Johan Huizinga, *Homo Ludens* (London: Paladin, 1970), p. 3.

38. Richard Neville, *Playpower* (London: Jonathan Cape, 1970), p. 278.

39. *Ibid.*, p. 263.

40. *Ibid.*, p. 258.

41. *Ibid.*, p. 274.

42. Bernice Martin, *A Sociology of Contemporary Cultural Change* (Oxford: Blackwell, 1981), p. 129.

43. Mike Brake, *The Sociology of Youth Culture* (London: Routledge and Kegan Paul, 1980), cited in E. Ellis Cashmore, *No Future* (London: Heinemann, 1984), p. 31.

44. Quoted in Stanley Cohen and Jock Young, *The Manufacture of News: Social Problems, Deviance and the Mass Media* (London: Constable, 1973), p. 9.

45. Jim Haynes, quoted in Jonathon Green, *Days in the Life* (London: Minerva, 1989), pp. 14–15.

46. *Time* cover story, 'Summer of love', anthologized in J. D. Brown (ed.), *The Hippies* (New York: 1968), pp. 1–13.

47. Ron E. Roberts, *The New Communes* (Englewood Cliffs, NJ: Prentice Hall, 1971), p. 45. Roberts quotes the Gospel according to Luke, chapter 19, verse 17.

48. John and Margaret Reynolds, 'Youth as a class', *International Socialist Journal*, February 1968.

49. John Davis, *Youth and the Condition of Britain: Images of Adolescent Conflict* (London: Athlone Press, 1990), p. 204.

50. Gary Herman, *The Who* (London: Rockbooks Studio Vista, 1971), p. 75.

51. Jon Savage, 'The sound of acid', *Guardian* Review, 31 January 1997, p. 10.

52. Maurice Friedman, *Problematic Rebel* (London: University of Chicago Press, 1963), p. 229.

53. John (Rotten) Lydon, quoted in Jon Savage, *England's Dreaming* (London: Faber & Faber, 1991), p. 116.

54. Malcolm McLaren, quoted in *ibid.*, p. 210.

55. Mary Harron, quoted in *ibid.*, p. 132.

56. Steve Redhead, *The End-of-the-Century Party* (Manchester: Manchester University Press, 1990), p. 81.

57. *Ibid.*, p. 55.

58. John L. Williams, interviewed in *Living Marxism*, March 1997.

59. Maxim Jakubowski, reviewing *Faithless* by John L. Williams (London: Serpent's Tail, 1997) in *Time Out*, 22–9 January 1997.

60. Keanu Reeves, talking to *Newsweek*, quoted in Chris Nickson, *Keanu Reeves* (New York: St Martin's Press, 1996), p. 133.

61. *Ibid.*, p. 66.

62. Keith Mayerson, quoted in *ibid.*, p. 69.

63. *Time Out*, 11–18 December 1996.

64. Joseph Gallivan, 'Kurt reminders', *Telegraph* magazine, 19 January 1997, p. 22.

65. *Observer*, 19 May 1996.

66. Paolo Hewitt, *Heaven's Promise* (London: Heavenly Books, n. d.), p. 72.

67. Matthew Collin, *Altered State: The Story of Ecstasy Culture and Acid House* (London: Serpent's Tail, 1997).

68. 'Young generation happy to stay at home with Mum', *Guardian*, 5 June 1996.

69. Suzanne O'Shea, 'Hooked on pleasure: a Peter Pan generation says no to family life', *Daily Mail*, 5 June 1996, p. 11.

70. Barbara Graham, in *Utne Reader*, May–June 1996, cover story and pp. 64–5.

71. Dave Green, 'Just kidding', *Guardian Weekend*, 25 November 1996.

72. Suzanne Moore, 'Young at heart', *Guardian*, 15 May 1996.

73. Peter Beaumont, 'Thirtysomethings who won't grow up', *Observer*, 19 May 1996.

74. NBC's Daphne Barak, quoted in *Daily Telegraph*, 4 February 1997, p. 4.

75. Jim McClellan, 'Lolita: the phenomenon', *Esquire*, April 1997, p. 66.

76. *Ibid.*

77. Mark Sutherland, reviewing *Kula Shaker* in *NME*, February 1997.

78. Albert Goldman, cited by Dylan Jones in 'Will of irony: the tribulations of ironic existence', *Arena*, September 1989.

79. Jimi Hendrix, quoted by Sheila Weller in *Rolling Stone*, 15 November 1969.

80. John Lennon, quoted in Ray Coleman, *John Lennon* (London: Futura, 1985), p. 179.

81. Beck Hansen, interviewed in *The Face*, no. 200 (February 1997), pp. 70–4.

82. Kenneth Keniston, *The Uncommitted* (New York: Harcourt Brace, 1960), p. 394.

83. Philip Norman, extract from his *Buddy Holly: The Biography* (London: Macmillan, 1996) which appeared in the *Sunday Times News Review*, 8 September 1996.

84. Frank Musgrove, *Ecstasy and Holiness: Counter Culture and the Open Society* (London: Methuen, 1974), p. 3.

85. Caroline Bird, 'The lost generation', *Harper's Bazaar*, February 1957.

86. Quoted in Nicosia, *op. cit.*, p. 230.

87. Charters, *op. cit.*, p. 265.

88. Charters, *op. cit.*, p. 284.

89. *New York Times* review of 3 May 1959, quoted in Charters, *op. cit.*, p. 265.

90. Leslie Fielder, *An End to Innocence – Essays on Culture and Politics* (Boston: Beacon Press, 1952), p. 193.

91. *Ibid.*, p. 193.

92. McCann, *op. cit.*, p. 155.

93. *The Weekend Telegraph* supplement, 28 May 1965.

94. Paul Johnson, 'The menace of Beatlism', *New Statesman*, 28 February 1964.

95. Christopher Booker, *The Neophiliacs* (London: Fontana, 1970), p. 55.

96. George Melly, *Revolt into Style* (Harmondsworth: Penguin, 1970), p. 228.

97. Ian MacDonald, *Revolution in the Head: The Beatles' Records and the Sixties* (London: Random House, 1995), p. 19.

98. Roszak, *op. cit.*, p. 32.

99. *Ibid.*, p. 34.

100. *Ibid.*, pp. 32–3.

101. *Ibid.*, p. 41.

102. Lewis S. Feuer, quoted in William Braden, *The Age of Aquarius* (London: Eyre & Spottiswoode, 1971), p. 59.

103. Joseph J. Schwab, quoted in *ibid.*, p. 60.

104. Edward Shils, 'Plenitude and scarcity', *Encounter*, May 1969, p. 46.

105. Schwab, quoted in Braden, *op. cit.*, p. 60.

106. Daniel Bell, *The Cultural Contradictions of Capitalism* (London: Heinemann, 1979), p. 144.

107. Allan Bloom, *The Closing of the American Mind* (London: Penguin, 1988), p. 78.

108. Peter Blos and Carl Frankenstein, quoted in Braden, *op. cit.*, p. 61.

109. Bloom, *op. cit.*, p. 78.

110. Jeff Nuttall, *Bomb Culture* (London: Paladin, 1970), pp. 37–8.

111. Hegel, quoted by Richard Mills in *Young Outsiders: A Study of Alternative Communities* (London: Institute of Community Studies/Routledge and Kegan Paul, 1973), p. 172.

112. Bernard Levin, *The Pendulum Years: Britain in the Sixties* (London: Pan, 1970), p. 308.

113. *Ibid.*, p. 412.

114. *Ibid.*, p. 276.

115. *Ibid.*, pp. 256–7.

116. *Ibid.*, p. 184.

117. Robert Bolt, preface to *A Man for All Seasons* (London: Heinemann, 1960), p. xi, quoted by Levin, *op. cit.*, p. 349.

118. Malcolm Bradbury, *The Modern American Novel* (Oxford: Oxford University Press, 1984), p. 168.

119. *Ibid.*, p. 171.

120. Keino Okonogi, 'The age of the moratorium people', *Chuo Koron*, October 1977.

121. Peter York, *Modern Times* (London: Heinemann, 1984), p. 64.

122. *Ibid.*

123. *Ibid.*

124. *Ibid.*

125. Cosmo Landesman, in *Sunday Times*, Culture section, 13 October 1996.

126. Mark Simpson, 'Lost boys in Neverland', *Independent*, 23 May 1996.

127. Robert Hughes, *The Culture of Complaint* (New York: Oxford University Press, 1993), p. 8.

128. Gail Sheehy, *New Passages* (London: HarperCollins, 1996), extracted in *Utne Reader*, May–June 1996.

129. Robert Bly, *The Sibling Society*, extracted in *Utne Reader*, May–June 1996.

130. Robert Bly, 'The society of children', *Independent*, 6 November 1996.

131. Eric Konigsberg, 'Infantilisation' in Steven Daly and Nathaniel Wise (eds), *alt.culture.usa* (London: Fourth Estate, 1995).

132. Simpson, *op. cit.*

133. Jay Stevens, *Storming the Gates: LSD and the American Dream* (London: Paladin, 1989), p. 490.

134. Douglas Rushkoff, *Cyberia – Life in the Trenches of Hyper-space* (London: Flamingo, 1994), p. 111.

135. Charlotte Raven, 'To E or not to E?', *Guardian*, 18 February 1997.

136. Leonard Broom, *Sociology*, 7th edn (New York: Harper & Row, 1981), p. 216.

137. Norman Podhoretz, quoted in Andrew Sinclair, *In Love and Anger* (London: Sinclair Stevenson, 1994), p. 58.

138. Thom Yorke, interviewed by Caroline Sullivan, 'Bride and sighs', *Guardian*, 16 May 1997.

CHAPTER 4

Vulnerable

Alongside the elevation of the child, pop culture sings of the virtues of vulnerability.

In 'an infantilised culture of complaint', says Robert Hughes, 'to be vulnerable is [to be] invincible.'[1] In this topsy-turvy world it is acceptable to respond to stress by making a great show of being unable to cope with it. And, if there is not enough stress from which to improvise such a pantomime, then it will have to be invented.

For Hughes the reverential response to the black artist and drugs victim Basquiat (whose life was subsequently celebrated in an eponymous biopic released in Britain in March 1997) exemplifies the sort of 'solemn exercise in Heroic Victimology'[2] which characterizes pop culture today. By no means convinced that Basquiat's work is anywhere near as profound as it is made out to be, Hughes adds that 'the abiding traits of American victim art are posturing and ineptitude'.[3]

In today's context, says Hughes, 'to be infantile is a regressive way to defy the stress of corporate culture: don't tread on me, I'm vulnerable. The emphasis is on the subjective: how we feel about things.'[4]

This is not a definition of the 'subjective' which either Hegel or Marx would recognize. Their concept of the subjective meant making oneself the subject, i.e. the actor, in the lived experience of history, rather than being subjected to the forces of nature or allowing oneself to become the mere object of someone else's attention and manipulation. But if we allow the Hughes definition to stand temporarily, what seems to be suggested here is that a 'subjective' culture focusing on 'how we feel', with particular emphasis on how vulnerable we feel, will necessarily lead to an atmosphere of closure, passivity and regression. On this topic Hughes quotes Goethe to good effect:

> *Epochs which are regressive . . . are always subjective, whereas the trend in all progressive epochs is objective . . . Every truly excellent endeavour turns from within toward the world, as you see in the great epochs which were truly in progression and aspiration, and which were all objective in nature.*[5]

The Hughes/Goethe definition of 'subjective' is what I would prefer to call 'subjectivism', where the feelings and aspirations of the individual are not grounded in the experience of trying to alter the course of events in the outside world, but rather are allowed to continue untested in the internal world of our private thoughts. Where I agree wholeheartedly with Hughes is that the trend today is directly opposite to Goethe's recommendation: i.e. more and more people are turning from the external world to an inner world, which then comes to be celebrated as the only world we have.

The upshot is a subjectivist mindset which is unwilling and increasingly unable to distinguish between perception and objective reality (in fact the use of drugs is often an attempt to lose all sight of that distinction, albeit temporarily). In this postmodern solipsism the contemporary mood of vulnerability (often unwarranted by external circumstances) acquires the status of a universal law (I perceive it to be, therefore it is), and our increasingly limited experience is coloured accordingly. This is an ethos which is entirely antithetical to the Marxist or even the progressive bourgeois concept of subjectivity as history-making; and it has developed within the framework of a pop culture which itself emerged from the 1950s onwards in response to the dual failure of both left- and right-wing notions of how to make things happen in society. If becoming vulnerable is now considered the most appropriate mode of presentation for the individual in our society, this is because our society has come to see itself as ineffective and therefore vulnerable: a self-image which was originally developed and piloted within the iconography associated with the counterculture.

Damaged but beautiful
Vulnerability has been a key theme of pop culture since its inception. 'An allegory of vulnerability' is how the poet Craig Raine described J. D. Salinger's *Catcher in the Rye*,[6] in an article marking the fortieth

anniversary of this epochal novel and its protagonist Holden Caulfield, who has been described as the world's first teenager.

While Salinger was inventing Caulfield in all his vulnerability, the existentialist philosopher Albert Camus was discussing 'this vulnerable universe'.[7] At the same time a new generation of actors articulated a Hollywood version of existentialism using vulnerability to symbolize their rejection of the purposive roles embodied in previous generations of Hollywood heroes. Instead of ambition and effectiveness, they posed confusion and disintegration.

Thus Graham McCann, writing about Montgomery Clift as the confused Private Prewitt in *From Here to Eternity*, notes that it is 'never entirely clear whether he is in rebellion against society or in flight from it'.[8] McCann cites Clift's observation about the roles he himself played that they 'have a skin missing', which creates an aura of tragic fragility;[9] and he recalls Jane Fonda's commendation of Clift, that he was 'vulnerable . . . like a wound'.[10]

Along similar lines McCann describes James Dean as 'a personality that seemed on the verge of disintegration',[11] and he refers to Andy Warhol's pronouncement that Dean was the soul of our time in so far as he was 'damaged but beautiful'.[12] McCann also notes that Marlon Brando's Johnny (*The Wild One*) is 'physically tough but oddly insecure' and that he 'rarely instigates anything; usually he merely reacts'[13] – all of which is entirely in keeping with a leading role which represents the subjectivist rather than the historically subjective.

McCann goes on to describe Brando in *On the Waterfront* as representing the 'blood-soaked . . . loser of the modern world'.[14] He also notes that in *The Men* (1950) Brando played a paraplegic maimed by the war – one of the first among many instances in which the vulnerability associated with mental or physical disability comes to be seen as a sign of superior wisdom. Even Brando's macho mannerisms are seen by McCann as 'defence mechanisms, hiding the vulnerable self'.[15]

In their various ways ('Clift's silent stare, Brando's mumbling and Dean's giggle') these three actors communicated a new 'inarticulacy'. 'Comfortable neither with words nor without them', as McCann puts it,[16] they were at a loss with language as they were with purposive activity. Summarizing the significance of the new generation of Hollywood males, McCann is fairly sympathetic to 'the obsessions with inwardness and privacy' (the very tendencies to which Goethe was hostile) which they represent.[17] He also describes how their characteristic vulnerability came to be part of the currency of pop culture: 'the vulnerability of the ideal screen male became the experience of all, and on the screen it was not now merely acceptable but desirable'.[18]

In a hagiography entitled *Beautiful Loser* – the title itself a reference to Leonard Cohen's cult novel of the 1960s, *Beautiful Losers* – Barney Hoskyns describes Clift in terms which are similar to McCann's, as the harbinger of 'a velvet revolution of shyness and introversion' who was so vulnerable that 'even as a "rebel" ... he let life happen to him'. Hoskyns celebrates this beautiful loser as 'the original non-macho rebel and misfit of the American cinema', and suggests that Clift's personal life and the role he played are all asking the same question: 'how to remain thin-skinned, vulnerable, and stay alive?'[19]

Encounter culture

While Clift was developing his thin-skinned screen presence, the Beats were cultivating the notion of vulnerability as a sign of superior consciousness. Allen Ginsberg wrote in admiration of the way in which William Burroughs 'gives the impression of suffering terribly and continuously'.[20] Jack Kerouac saw a doleful beauty in the vulnerability of a 'crippled kid': 'a great big beautiful face, much too large, in which enormous brown eyes moistly gleamed'.[21] In a polemic against the rock-solid characters of previous generations and their literature, Kerouac announced a new fragility: 'everybody is going to fall apart, disintegrate, all character structures based on tradition and up-rightness and so-called morality will slowly rot away.'[22]

In *Protest* Feldman and Gartenberg associated vulnerability with the Beats' attempt to strip away staid identities: 'to be oneself is also to be vulnerable'.[23] Gerald Nicosia, in his critical biography of Kerouac, likened the Beats 'verbalising their feelings' in all-night rap sessions to 'a modern encounter session', which seems to suggest that they were vulnerable individuals seeking solace and support in their self-expression.[24]

Writing in the 1950s about the career of jazz-age novelist F. Scott Fitzgerald, the literary critic Leslie Fiedler suggested that Fitzgerald's current high status among the American reading public depended on his reputation as a vulnerable loser. Fiedler observed that 'the essential appeal of Fitzgerald is ... in his failure'; he also noted that the novelist cultivated a sense of vulnerability as part of his self-image: 'Fitzgerald *willed* his role as a failure ... long before his own actual crack up, he dreamed it, prophesied it in his stories and novels.'[25] In the next essay in the anthology *An End to Innocence*, published in 1952, Fiedler discussed the adoption of 'the bum' as an 'American cultural hero', and, in a reference to the trend-setting youthful protagonist of Goethe's eponymous novella, described the elevation of the bum into a 'Dead-end Werther'. With particular reference to the contemporary novel *From Here to Eternity* by James Jones, from which the Montgomery Clift film was taken, Fiedler opined that new American heroes were remarkable for being put-upon and done to. The antithesis of historical subjectivity, they 'could not fight back and win, so they were very strict in their great pride of losing'.[26]

Writing about 1950s Americana and its effect on 1960s Britain, Jeff Nuttall described 'hipster heroes' as '*pain* heroes',[27] indicating that these characters took their place in the iconography of British pop culture by virtue of their ability to represent the discomfiture of the fashionably fragile self at the mercy of an unrelenting world. Nuttall also noted that one of the attractions of the new culture was that it 'protected' the impression of vulnerability, suggesting that this latter was something to be nurtured and cultivated. 'We flew to this culture', Nuttall reported, because 'it provided a formalised mode of behaviour to compensate for our own directional poverty'.[28] Moreover, it would seem that the identification with vulnerability was itself an expression of 'directional poverty', which in turn became a rich source of imagery for a counterculture that identified itself against causes and direction.

In an age which looks to anti-heroes rather than heroes, vulnerability rather than ambition has become the key component in the cultural personality of our times. It should come as no surprise, therefore, that vulnerability has been an essential element in both the public make-up and the private persona of most countercultural anti-heroes.

For example, the comedian Lenny Bruce, the man who took the world apart and exposed its prejudices, was inseparable from the Lenny Bruce who repeatedly fell apart ('Eric is hip to Lenny's moods. He's seen him fall apart before', recounts his biographer Albert Goldman).[29] Indeed it is likely that a Lenny Bruce who did not fall apart himself would not have been allowed to take the world apart so venomously in his stand-up routines. The tenor of the times, as Hughes points out, is such that the victim is granted more leeway and greater legitimacy.

Arrested Development

Likewise fragility was always an important part of Bob Dylan's charisma. He took his stage name from the Welsh poet Dylan Thomas, an unstable alcoholic. Anthony Scaduto's book on Dylan begins with the singer Joan Baez describing him as 'more fragile than other people';[30] and in the late 1960s, when Dylan disappeared from public view as a result of what was rumoured to be a serious motorcycle accident, his kudos within pop culture reached new heights.

While Dylan remained in seclusion, the counterculturalists of the 1960s scoured the literature of earlier generations searching for role models of vulnerability. The new taste for vulnerability brought a number of authors to a much wider readership than they had ever enjoyed before. Franz Kafka was one such writer. In a letter to a friend, Kafka had defined the creative person in terms of frailty and vulnerability, which was very much in tune with the thoughts of those reading him for the first time in the 1960s:

> The poet is always much smaller and weaker than the social average.
> Therefore he feels the burden of earthly existence much more intensely and
> strongly than other men. For him personally his song is only a scream . . .
> only suffering . . . He is not a giant, but only a more or less brightly
> plumaged bird in the cage of his existence.[31]

These sentiments were highly appealing to the kind of mentality which wanted to 'worship' Leonard Cohen for 'his suffering';[32] and Kafka, largely ignored during his own lifetime, duly became one of the fashionable novelists of the late twentieth century.

Among the hippies of the late 1960s and early 1970s vulnerability was cultivated as a sign of creativity, to the point where Rolling Stones guitarist Keith Richards felt able to look back at the mayhem and murder which occurred during the Stones' free concert at Altamont on the West Coast of America and declare 'people were just asking for it . . . They had victims' faces.'[33]

Therapeutic radicalism

The vogue for vulnerability was not confined to the non-activists among the counterculture. Various commentators also observed the motif of vulnerability among the radical activism of the 1960s. Thus Nat Hentoff, primarily known for his commentary on jazz, described some participants in the anti-Vietnam-War movement as individuals whose fragile sense of self prompted them to use peace protests as a form of therapy. 'Their act's essential effect', suggested Hentoff, describing one particular protest, 'was to make them feel relevant ... I am all for self-therapy, but if that's what it is, let's call it that.'[34] Lewis Yablonsky agreed that ' "the revolution" ... is simply a shield of immunity that allows people to act out violent and bizarre behaviour.'[35]

Literary critic Martin Esslin suggested that the attraction of Che Guevara, one of the most popular icons of 1960s radicalism, lay chiefly in his aura of vulnerability:

> Would Che Guevara, an unsuccessful revolutionary and an unoriginal thinker, have ever acquired the influence he wielded among the young generation of 1968, had not his image, the beautiful martyred face of his murdered body, captured the imagination and embodiment of a whole complex of doctrine, passion and lifestyle?[36]

Likewise, in his introduction to the *New Left* reader, Carl Oglesby suggested that vulnerability was an essential part of the mental make-up of the New Left, some of whom found their moment of personal verification in the experience of being beaten up by the police:

> The policeman's riot club functions like a magic wand under whose hard caress the banal soul grows vivid and the nameless recover their authenticity – a bestower, this wand, of the lost charisma of the modern self: I bleed therefore I am.[37]

Oglesby's epigram on 1960s radicalism – 'I bleed therefore I am' – suggests that its real function was not so much to do, in the active, history-making sense, but rather to be done to, in the hope that authority bearing down on the vulnerable would indict itself and act as the force of its own destruction, while at the same time endowing its targets with the sense of authenticity which they had previously lacked. Once again the gradual eclipse of subjectivity as history-making can be seen as the corollary of the emergence of vulnerability as an acceptable, even desirable, mode of existence.

For all the rhetoric of social transformation in the radical counter-culture, the embrace of vulnerability should be seen rather as the renunciation of the transformative potential of humanity since it connotes an idea of selfhood which is primarily receptive and essentially passive.

In the 1970s the notion of vulnerability was represented in the form of Tommy, the boy whose deafness, dumbness and blindness raised him to a higher consciousness (as well as pinball wizardry). As depicted in the 'rock opera' written by Pete Townshend and performed by his band The Who, Tommy is heroic by virtue of what would previously been regarded as frailty. Along these lines, rock biographer Gary Herman described him as 'an ideal' who is ideal because he is frail and inadequate: '[Tommy] has withdrawn into himself and is incapable of interacting with the world or with other people, except through the most elementary and direct senses'.[38] Meanwhile the late Janis Joplin was wise to the fact that she was being sold to the public as a vulnerable individual. 'Maybe my audiences can enjoy my music more if they think I'm destroying myself', she quipped.[39]

By the end of the 1970s vulnerability was re-presented in punk, which 'celebrated its patheticness',[40] according to Nuttall. In the early 1980s Bernice Martin reviewed what she called 'the expressive revolution' of the previous two decades, and summarized the correlation between prominence in pop culture and the expression of vulnerability:

> Dylan makes extended play on his own Christ-role in some of his 1960s lyrics; Tommy is crucified . . . at the end of Pete Townshend's rock opera; [Ray] Gosling was drawn to the same image in 1962 when he described the pop star as 'paid to be crucified twice nightly'. The murder of John Lennon makes the point with tragic eloquence.[41]

The point is that John Lennon remains the 'cool' Beatle to this day, unlike George Harrison, Ringo Starr and in particularly sharp contrast to the infuriatingly jaunty Sir Paul McCartney, primarily because his assassination endowed his persona with victim status and an unassailable aura of vulnerability.

Snapshot: Electric crucifixion

Aged twelve, I lived half my life in a make-believe world of Mod, arguing with friends about which of us was the first to become 'far out' and refusing to submit to the short back and sides haircut which our teachers tried to foist upon us. But the other focus of my pre-teen existence was the local church, where I served at the altar while my newly ordained Dad officiated at various services.

Problem: how to resolve these half-lives? Answer: through the idea of suffering and images of crucifixion, which seemed somehow as applicable to Jimi Hendrix and Che Guevara as to Jesus Christ. One year I even read a biography of Guevara as part of my Lenten devotions.

I think my parents had the same sort of idea. I remember that, in keeping with the house style of the newly consecrated Coventry Cathedral, my Mum made my father's vestments out of a rough cloth called hessian, which to them (and me) was both modish and representative of the suffering of Christ, the Son of Man.

Eccentric? I do not think we were too far out on a limb: the notion of Christ as vulnerable like a pop star was also expressed in the religious rock operas of the time, such as *Jesus Christ Superstar* and *Godspell*.

Miserabilism

The cultivation of vulnerability continued through the 1980s, for all the brashness and 'power dressing' associated with the decade. The shaven heads of the skinheads were meant to invite comparison with Nazi storm troopers. But shaven heads and striped pants on the indie scene were more reminiscent of their concentration camp victims. The latter look was popularized by, among others, Sinead O'Connor, who used her Irishness as a badge of vulnerability – authenticated, she alleged, by the Great Hunger of the mid-nineteenth century.

Writing about one of the most successful bands of the period, pop journalist Simon Reynolds described The Smiths and their 'miserabilist' lead-singer Morrissey as merely 'a synopsis of pain', whereas in Reynolds's eyes Kristin Hersh of the lesser-known Throwing Muses went even further, representing 'the presence of pain ... the inconsolable wrestling with the insoluble'.[42]

Reynolds sensed that the experience of life as an 'insoluble' problem prompts an 'inconsolable' response, which in turn is represented through the wearing of an expression of pain, thereby advertising one's experience of being pained by the world and all its vicissitudes. This is how an expression of vulnerability – of being the defenceless object of cruel forces at work in society – comes to function as a desirable identity.

In the 1990s the world of fashion has clasped this identity to its flat chest. In previous decades skinny models like Twiggy toyed with a look of vulnerability. But when Twiggy was the icon of Swinging London, vulnerability was part of an experiment in trying to live outside the traditional power nexus. Three decades later the thinness first associated with Twiggy is intended to give the impression that, say, Jodie Kidd or Kate Moss is vulnerable to the point of being damaged by the knocks she has taken from the outside world. The claim that what President Bill Clinton calls 'heroin chic' (the fashion editor of the *Daily Mail* refers to it as the 'cocaine addict look'[43]) is really physically harmful, either to fashion models or to young readers of fashion magazines, remains unproven. But there is no question that an aesthetic of vulnerability has emerged, in which bruising – or the impression of having been bruised – is regarded as highly desirable.

Even women who are billed as powerful draw some of their moral authority from an aura of victimization. Describing Kurt Cobain's widow Courtney Love (Hole) and Kat Bjelland (Babes in Toyland) for her book on women in rock, *Never Mind the Bollocks*, *The Face* journalist Amy Raphael could not pass over the element of vulnerability in their appearance: 'It's child-woman, a fucked-up Lolita, innocence disturbed. It is a potent, on-the-edge image which toys with vulnerability and power. It hints, disturbingly, at a "rape victim" look, although both women would insist that they are ultimately in control.'[44]

Raphael noted that both women would insist that they are ultimately in control, and she herself seemed to give credence to this idea with the suggestion that the Love/Bjelland image 'toys' with 'power' as well as vulnerability. However, it seems more accurate to suggest that this image plays with the fact that the victim is the person with the most status in today's society. This is not a representation of 'power' but a reflection of the moral authority that is ascribed to the powerless.

Autopathology

The literary counterparts of skinny models and their 'heroin chic' are what *Independent* journalist Ruth Picardie dubbed 'the new illiterati'. With the accent on the 'ill' in 'illiterati', Picardie grouped together a host of writers who have made a name for themselves, or improved on their previous status, by describing, at great length, their illnesses, frailty and vulnerability. Her list of 'autopathography' includes recent books by Ben Watt, Tim Lott, Kay Redfield Jamison, Susanna Kayser, William Styron, Oscar Moore, Harold Brodkey, Caroline Knapp, Laurence Slater, Elizabeth Wurtzel, Robert McCrum, Fiona Haw, Elisa Segrave and Gillian Rose. Literary agents, according to Picardie, now operate on the basis that 'illness has become hip'.

Picardie contextualized 'autopathology' as a symptom of a victim culture which elevates vulnerability – a culture in which *psychiatrists have their own chat shows . . . doctors are sex goods . . . Oprah Winfrey's daily mess fest has made her one of the richest entertainers in America, Dennis Potter is lauded because he has cancer, and in which celebrities do not hide their problems as they did in the fifties, but shout about them on prime time tv: Imogen Stubbs' paralysis-inducing fear; Adam Faith's post-traumatic stress, Ludovic Kennedy's depression.*[45]

Picardie might also have included newscaster Jon Snow's account of the lifelong effects of his mother's alleged denial of emotional warmth to him.

The connection between sickness and creativity is now being applied retrospectively. In spring 1997 programme-makers Blackwatch Productions publicized a new series for Channel 4. Entitled *Post-Mortem*, it sought to establish a causal connection between the ill-health of particular artists and their creative genius. The press release issued by Blackwatch described *Post-Mortem* as follows:

a creative arts series which examines the mortal remains of five great artists to determine how their physical ailments might have had a bearing on their genius. In effect the series makes art television of the autopsy. The programmes explore the connection between art and affliction and the tortuous path toward creativity.[46]

The five featured artists were Beethoven, Montgomery Clift, Francis Bacon, Virginia Woolf and Nijinsky (also featured in Colin Wilson's *The Outsider*). The gist of the programmes was that their unique creativity depended on mental and physical vulnerability. The overall effect of this kind of programme is to extend the contemporary fashion for vulnerability into history, so that past achievements are recast as accessories in today's victim culture.

The parade of vulnerability is now so all-embracing that journalist and television personality Michael Parkinson was recently moved to comment that he feels like the only person not to have been marked by some kind of abusive experience during childhood. It has now reached the point where not to be vulnerable is regarded as a sign of untrustworthiness: if one is not abused, one is taken to be an abuser.

Snapshot: Hunched

As I was walking out of the dinner hall one day, an upright schoolmaster called me over. 'Why are your shoulders hunched like that, boy?' 'I don't know what you mean, Sir.' 'You do very well, and if you carry on like that you'll end up a hunchback.' I walked away well pleased with myself. The hunched posture I had adopted – in imitation of James Dean – was meant to represent my refusal to be 'straight' like most of my sixth-form contemporaries, who were dutifully lining up to read law at Cambridge. And to think that, if I carried on with this posture, it might get into my bones and become part of my physical as well as mental make-up. There could be no better proof of my preference for a vulnerable self rather than the seemingly stolid personalities of my peers.

In films the childlike vulnerability which arises from mental or physical disability has come to be associated with insight and authenticity in an otherwise dumb, adult world of pretence and duplicity. Films which elevate disability in this way include *Above Suspicion*, *My Left Foot*, *Rainman*, *Mute Witness* and *Passion Fish*.

When Christopher Reeve, the actor who played Superman, broke his neck in a riding accident, he acquired new status as a paraplegic. Reeve's own accounts of what happened to him after his accident are eminently sensible. None the less he has been allotted a perverse role in public life in which the wheelchair-bound ex-Superman is called upon to act out the fatalistic assumption that the expectation of power will necessarily lead to destruction. In recognition of his personal suffering, he is also allotted a kind of wisdom that is assumed to accompany physical impotence. The cult of Christopher Reeve, which is not to be confused with the eminently sensible things which Reeve himself has said about his own condition, is a parable of the expectation of human failure and disaster, in which the role imposed upon Reeve is somewhere between that of Sophocles' Oedipus at Colonus and Pete Townshend's Tommy.

The vulnerable politician
The status that comes only with vulnerability and victimhood propelled Reeve into the centre of President Bill Clinton's successful re-election campaign in 1996; he was the star attraction of the Democrats' national convention that year. More recently, there have been calls for the re-imaging of one of Clinton's predecessors as president, namely Franklin Delano Roosevelt. FDR was never photographed in the wheelchair to which polio had consigned him. This is now interpreted as a sign of

censorship and prejudice against the disabled. Such is the respect attached to the wheelchair in the 1990s that pictures of Clinton in this vehicle of victim status were splashed all over the newspapers following an operation on the President's knee in 1996.

Likewise, a halo of vulnerability was one of the signposts along Tony Blair's route to Number 10 Downing Street and the British premiership. In contrast to the rugger-blokeishness of former Labour leader Neil Kinnock, the avuncular tone of Labour premiers Harold Wilson and James Callaghan or the air of nit-picking precision conveyed by the leader of the 1945 Labour government, Clement Attlee, Blair portrayed himself as a sensitive individual who is discomfited by the grubby contestation of party politics.

On the radio programme *Desert Island Discs* Blair confessed to Sue Lawley that he disliked the tough exchanges which occurred at Prime Minister's Question Time (this was in 1996, when he had only to ask the questions, not answer them), so much so that the first of his selection of records was an anthem to vulnerability called *Cancel Today*. It was the sort of song which could well have been chosen by the 'beautiful loser' Montgomery Clift, and it was entirely in keeping with the media's nickname for Blair when he first became Labour leader – Bambi.

More ominously, Blair did indeed 'cancel today'. He rearranged the parliamentary schedule so that Prime Minister's Question Time now occurs only once a week. Moreover, the session has been redesigned to reduce the atmosphere of combativity, derided as 'Yah-Boo politics' in current parlance. Thus the aesthetic of vulnerability has already made its debut on the parliamentary stage.

A few months after he appeared on *Desert Island Discs*, Blair's keynote speech at the New Labour Party's pre-election conference was notable as a theatrical presentation of himself as a man whose emotional vulnerability is also an indelible mark of his integrity. The performance prompted a sceptical response from Adam Nicholson in the *Sunday Telegraph*, who resented Blair's fragmented grammar and broken sentences. These, thought Nicholson, were contrived to give the impression of a man moved by his own emotion to the point of inarticulacy. Comparing Blair to the religious evangelist Billy Graham, Nicholson located him in 'that twilight zone of the almost overcome'.[47]

But not all responses were so hostile. The front cover of the magazine for Labour Party members, *New Labour New Britain*, featured pop star Noel Gallagher saying 'Tony Blair's speech brought tears to my eyes'.[48] For all his laddishness, Gallagher had clearly experienced the speech in the way in which it was intended, as an invitation to come together now in the shared experience of our vulnerability.

A few months later, in the run-up to the general election, the Tories sought to turn the tables on Blair's aura of vulnerability when they issued a controversial advert showing Blair as a childlike puppet dangling on German Chancellor Kohl's knee, with the caption 'You don't send a boy to do a man's job'. But in today's climate vulnerability is regarded as a plus not a minus, and it was the Tories who came off the worse in the ensuing furore.

In today's pop culture, as designed and developed by counter-culturists from the 1950s onwards, performers and audiences are invited to enter into a mutual appreciation of their vulnerability. And in a political culture which distrusts ambition, vulnerability is a quality – formerly regarded as a weakness – which commands respect and adulation. It even functions as the focal point for a fragile sense of togetherness.

Yet there is nothing substantial or even truly co-operative about this togetherness. Arising from the absence of history-making subjectivity, it amounts to a huddling together in the shadow of the failure of left- and right-wing ideologies. In this respect political culture now functions not as a vehicle for activating change but more as a shelter from the consequences of ideological failure. It operates, therefore, in much the same way as the counterculture which preceded it.

Notes

1. Robert Hughes, *The Culture of Complaint* (New York: Oxford University Press, 1993), pp. 9–10.

2. *Ibid.*, p. 196.

3. *Ibid.*, p. 186.

4. *Ibid.*, p. 10.

5. Goethe speaking to Eckermann, quoted in *ibid.*, p. 10.

6. Craig Raine, commenting on *The Catcher in the Rye*, *Sunday Times*, 7 August 1994.

7. Albert Camus, *The Myth of Sisyphus* (New York: Alfred Knopf, 1955), p. 66.

8. Graham McCann, *Rebel Males* (London: Hamish Hamilton, 1992), p. 19.

9. *Ibid.*, p. 24.

10. *Ibid.*, p. 47.

11. *Ibid.*, p. 24.

12. *Ibid.*, p. 125.

13. *Ibid.*, p. 15.

14. *Ibid.*, p. 109.

15. *Ibid.*, p. 47.

16. *Ibid.*, p. 17.

17. *Ibid.*, p. 49.

18. *Ibid.*, p. 30.

19. Barney Hoskyns, *Montgomery Clift: Beautiful Loser* (London: Bloomsbury, 1991), pp. 6–8.

20. Jay Stevens, *Storming Heaven: LSD and the American Dream* (London: Paladin, 1989), p. 162.

21. Jack Kerouac, *On the Road* (1957) (London: Penguin, 1972), p. 273.

22. Jack Kerouac, in *The Town and the City* (London: Eyre & Spottiswoode, 1950), quoted by Jeff Nuttall, in *Bomb Culture* (London: Paladin, 1970), p. 112.

23. Gene Feldman and Max Gartenberg (eds), *Protest* (London: Quartet Books, 1973), p. 234.

24. Gerald Nicosia, *Memory Babe: A Critical Biography of Jack Kerouac* (London: Penguin, 1986), p. 151.

25. Leslie Fiedler, 'Some notes on F. Scott Fitzgerald', in *An End to Innocence – Essays on Culture and Politics* (Boston: Beacon Press, 1952), pp. 175–6.

26. Leslie Fiedler, 'Dead-end Werther: the bum as American cultural hero', in *ibid.*, pp. 187–8.

27. Nuttall, *op. cit.*, p. 31.

28. *Ibid.*, p. 21.

29. Albert Goldman, *Ladies and Gentlemen – Lenny Bruce!* (London: Picador/Pan, 1976), p. 508.

30. Anthony Scaduto, *Bob Dylan* (London: Abacus, 1972), epigraph.

31. Kafka's letter to Janouch, quoted by Maurice Friedman, *Problematic Rebel* (Chicago: University of Chicago Press, 1963), p. 31.

32. Richard Goldstein, *The Poetry of Rock* (New York: Bantam, 1969), p. 128.

33. Keith Richards, quoted by Julie Burchill and Tony Parsons, in *The Boy Looked at Johnny: The Obituary of Rock 'n' Roll* (London: Pluto Press, 1978), p. 23.

34. Nat Hentoff, 'Them and us: are peace protests therapy?', in Walt Anderson (ed.), *The Age of Protest* (California: Goodyear, 1969), p. 255.

35. Lewis Yablonsky, *Robopaths* (Baltimore: Penguin, 1972), p. 140.

36. Carl Oglesby (ed.), *The New Left Reader* (New York: Grove Press, 1969), p. 15.

37. Martin Esslin, *Artaud* (Glasgow: Fontana Modern Masters, 1976), p. 11.

38. Gary Herman, *The Who* (London: Rockbooks/Studio Vista, 1971), p. 74.

39. Janis Joplin, quoted in Amy Raphael, *Never Mind the Bollocks: Women Rewrite Rock* (London: Virago, 1995), p. xiii.

40. Jeff Nuttall, quoted in Roger Hutchinson, *High Sixties* (Edinburgh: Mainstream Publishing, 1992), p. 194.

41. Bernice Martin, *A Sociology of Contemporary Cultural Change* (Oxford: Blackwell, 1981), p. 157.

42. Simon Reynolds, *Blissed Out* (London: Serpent's Tail, 1994), p. 32.

43. Remark made at a talk on fashion at the Institute of Contemporary Arts, London, March 1997.

44. Raphael, *op. cit.*, p. xxii.

45. Ruth Picardie, 'Did I ever tell you how ill I was?', *Independent*, 6 August 1996.

46. Press release issued March 1997 by Blackwatch Productions, Glasgow.

47. Adam Nicholson, commentary on Tony Blair's speech in *Sunday Telegraph*, quoted in *The Week*, 12 October 1996.

48. *New Labour New Britain*, autumn 1996.

CHAPTER 5

Madness

Since the 1950s madness has been regarded as both a reaction to a crazy world and a superior strategy for dealing with it. After nearly half a century of identification with an iconography of madness, it is small wonder if those in authority treat us like imbeciles.

In 1964 two *Sunday Times* journalists published a book on the new culture among the young. Culled mainly from interviews with teenagers, it was seized upon as one of the most authoritative documents of its time. The book was called *Generation X*, and the title was taken from a poem, included in the book, composed by a twenty-year-old woman, who wrote it 'in the peace and tranquillity of the trees and gardens of a psychiatric hospital'. The poem begins 'I am me/I must suffer because I am me'.[1] Noting that the writer was hospitalized as a result of depression and neurosis, Charles Hamblett and Jane Deverson reported that 'the more we read it, the more it seemed to tell us'.[2]

Their repeated reading of this doggerel tells us something about the fashionable status of madness in the 1960s. The mere fact that these lines were written in the gardens of a mental hospital seems to have endowed them, in the mind's eye of Hamblett and Deverson, with insight and aesthetic quality. The fact that they chose to describe a whole generation in relation to the jottings of an unstable (and, in literary terms, unexceptional) mind; and, furthermore, that theirs was the description which found favour with so many other commentators, serves as further indication of the kudos attached to the idea of being mentally disturbed. It was as if youngish journalists, and the young people about whom they were writing, came together around the notion of madness as an exotic and exciting state of mind, preferable and in some ways superior to the mundane, everyday consciousness of commuters and factory workers.

At about the same time the following graffito appeared on the walls in and around Swinging London: 'Tube-work-dinner-work-tube-armchair-tv-sleep-work. How much more can you take?' The notion that it was better to go mad than carry on taking it was widespread.

The kudos associated with madness has remained high ever since. Then and now, few people really want to be mentally ill; but the notion of being bounced by mental instability out of traditional, bankrupt patterns of thought into an alternative consciousness – this is a motif which recurs throughout the development of the minority counter-culture into mainstream pop culture.

'Today's rebels', noted Marcuse in 1969, 'want to see, hear and feel things in a different way: they link liberation with the dissolution of ordinary and orderly perception.'[3] Likewise Jacques Ellul, in a polemic against the technological society, praised madness on the grounds that 'only madness is inaccessible to the machine'.[4]

Feldman and Gartenberg observed that among the Beats an idea of 'insanity' served as 'the ultimate retreat, more insulating than heroin, weed or bop'. They also explained how the idea of madness functioned as an antidote to the failure of rationality: 'In a world where the "upward and onward" assurance of positivism always rings false, madness is the most sure way (next to death) ... of splintering life into a stream of acutely felt sensations that impose no demands.'[5]

Writing about the fashionable idea of madness in Britain nearly twenty years after the Beats came on the scene, Frank Musgrove observed that 'the counterculture embraces madness and disorder. Its committed members describe themselves as "freaks" and those who are not "alternative" as "straights".'[6] In the years since Musgrove wrote this, the ethos previously associated with first a handful of Beats and then a minority of 'freaks' has gone mainstream. In the late 1990s the roles are reversed, and the 'straight' believer in positivism would be regarded as the 'freak'.

'Embryonic storm-trooper'

Back in the 1950s, when Kenneth Keniston first discussed the new alienation among the young, he noted that they often 'overexamined' themselves in psychological terms. He remarked upon 'their readiness to discuss their childhoods, their intense interest in their own psychology', adding that 'they often tend to interpret their own behaviour as "merely" a reaction to an unfortunate past'.[7]

Keniston's observations suggest a cohort of young people already dallying with the idea of psychological disturbance as a not unattractive explanation for their sense of alienation. To be alienated and unhinged was beginning to be thought of as preferable to integration into the corporate career ladder and submission to the parallel doctrine of *mens sana in sano corpore*.

Some critics viewed this development with alarm. Giving evidence to a Senate subcommittee, Vance Packard expressed concern about the combination of 'monotony tinged with hysteria' in rock 'n' roll.[8] Novelist Ralph Ellison felt apprehensive about the aura of insanity associated with beboppers. 'What if history was not a reasonable citizen', he ruminated in his novel *The Invisible Man*, 'but a madman full of paranoid guile, and these boys his agents, his big surprise?'[9]

Reviewing Jack Kerouac's *On the Road*, *Time* magazine lambasted the Beats for their 'degeneracy' and described them as 'a disjointed section of society acting out of its own neurotic necessity'.[10] The *New York Times* described Kerouac's *Doctor Sax* as 'largely psychopathic'.[11] In a left-wing journal, *The Nation*, Herb Gold dismissed Kerouac's work as 'a naive paean to madness'.[12]

A number of medical experts conducted scaremongering studies of the Beats. One such study, of the Beat enclave in San Francisco, was performed by psychiatrist Dr Francis Rigley, who reported that 60 per cent of his subjects 'were so psychotic or crippled by tensions, anxiety and neurosis as to be non-functional in the competitive world'.[13]

In a more famous study, *Rebel Without a Cause*, from which the still more famous film took its title, Dr Robert M. Lindner warned that contemporary culture might be giving rise to a new kind of psychopath: 'a religious disobeyer of prevailing codes and standards ... a rebel without a cause, an agitator without a slogan, a revolutionary without a programme'.[14] Lindner thought that the new psychopath was an 'embryonic storm-trooper'. Writing in the shadow of the Second World War, he suggested that this proto-fascist could be identified by his infantilism:

a prolongation of infantile patterns and habits into the stage of physiological

> *adultism ... the inability to marshal the requisite determination for the achievement of specific goals of a socially acceptable order — these reflect to a startling degree the loose, undetermined, easily-detoured and almost purposeless conduct of the very young child.*[15]

Lindner's psychopath, like some children, might be expected to display short snatches of brilliance: 'Like the play-pattern of the very young, he shows an intensiveness, even a brilliance, at the outset of work ... as with the playing child, boredom follows rapidly.'[16] Faced with the emergence of the new psychopath, the task of the researcher, Lindner said, was to 'examine him thoroughly as we would a virulent bacillus; to dissect him and obtain his measure; perhaps even ... to make a good citizen of him in a new world'.[17]

For Lindner, whose loyalty to the positivist tradition remained firm if not entirely unquestioning, the alienation exhibited by some young people was tantamount to sickness — and a dangerous sickness too. In Britain the jazz critic Francis Newton (aka Marxist historian Eric Hobsbawm) did not accept the Lindner diagnosis at face value; but, as a participant in left-wing politics and debate, he was equally wary of the celebration of inarticulacy in the new hip-dom. Newton seems to have been suggesting that the hipsters brought the unwelcome attention of the psychiatrists down on themselves, when he wrote that 'there is now a good deal of literature about the hipster, most of which reads like a psychoanalyst's case diagnoses, and for a good reason: because the hipsters do not explain themselves, and show the world only their symptoms, which have to be interpreted'.[18]

Neurotica

Lindner warned that the new unhinged would be a problem for society; but his analysis was quickly adapted so as to suggest that society itself was a patient in need of therapy — an attitude first articulated by avant-garde American criminologists in the 1930s. Thus, when director Nicholas Ray borrowed the title of Lindner's book for his film starring James Dean, he presented mental instability, personified in Jim Stark, as the natural response of a basically sound young man to an unsound society.

In their small magazine *Neurotica* Jay Landesman and G. Legman had already been playing with the same idea. In the editorial for issue number five, they wrote:

> *It is our purpose to implement the realisation on the part of people that they*

*live in a neurotic culture and it is making neurotics out of them. The
practitioners have their own journals.* Neurotica *is for the patients –
present and future . . . We want to describe a neurotic society from the
inside . . . We believe that the psychiatric perspective can best describe and
most clearly interpret the impact of human society on the human
individual.*[19]

In *Neurotica*, as in Ray's *Rebel Without a Cause*, there remains a
dualism: mental instability is caused by an unstable society; it is
preferable to conformity, but it also causes problems which society
must remedy in order to heal itself. But in his essay 'The white negro'
Norman Mailer moved away from this ambivalence, towards embracing the idea of psychosis on behalf of the hipster, whom he described
as 'the American existentialist'. With typical bombast Mailer suggested
that only the psychopath knew how to live in contemporary society:
'The decision is to encourage the psychopath in oneself . . . and exist in
that present, that enormous present which is without past or future,
memory or planned intention.'[20]

For Mailer the enormity of the Second World War had broken the
continuum of past, present and future. Through the barbaric experience
of infantry battles and aerial bombings, traditional certainties about
controlling our environment ('by mastering time, mastering the links of
social cause and effect . . . the confidence that time could be subjected to
our will') had been discredited by the 'intolerable anxiety that death
being causeless, life was causeless as well'.[21] Hence for Mailer 'time
deprived of cause and effect had come to a stop'. So too had traditional
assumptions of moral worth. 'If society was murderous,' asked Mailer,
'then who could ignore the most hideous questions about his own
nature?'[22]

According to Mailer, existential psychopathy provided a kind of
answer to such a question. While noting that 'there is a depth of
desperation to the condition', he nevertheless regarded existential
psychopathy as a necessary mode of existence whose time had come: 'a
philosophic psychopath . . . may indeed be the perverted and dangerous
front-runner of a new kind of personality which could become the
central expression of human nature before the twentieth century is
over.'[23]

As a description of the flight from rationality and the motivation for
this trend, 'The white negro' is an illustrative, if ultimately uncritical,

essay. It is uncritical, and unfortunate, in that Mailer tried to make out that blacks are born existential psychopaths who spontaneously provide the model for a new white psychopathy. Jay Stevens noted that Mailer, in seeming to exhort his readers to cultivate the psychopath, was 'standing the condemnatory label on its head'. Stevens also realized that this reversal did not amount to a critical understanding of either social problems or the people in whom they were mirrored. 'A better defence', Stevens pointed out, 'would have attacked the legitimacy of the label psychopath, which had a distressingly glib currency in the fifties.'[24]

Throughout the 1950s and 1960s the term 'psychopath' was used as a catch-all explanation and as proof of increasingly fashionable distress. Many enlisted in the ranks of the *faux* psychopath. Speaking of this period, a literary lady told Stevens that on the New York scene 'it was all in fashion to go crazy'.[25] Writing in 1968, Erik Erikson, the eminent commentator on the psychology of youth, noticed that a certain cohort of young people had been histrionically acting out the diagnoses which psychiatrists had previously applied to them:

> *The history of the last 20 years seems to indicate that there are clinical terms which are taken over . . . by those who have been overdiagnosed, and, in this case, by a section of a whole age group which echo our very terms and flamboyantly display a conflict which we once regarded as silent, inner and unconscious.*[26]

From the 1950s onwards, in other words, growing numbers of individuals started to play at being mad. First they identified themselves with the label 'psychopath'. Then in the 1970s they labelled themselves 'paranoid', and verified this self-labelling with reference to the Black Sabbath song with the same title.

Rigley and Lindner were wrong in interpreting the alienated sensibility as a form of real madness; and equally wrong in taking the new rhetoric of madness at face value. Nevertheless the Beats, for example, did correlate madness with creativity; and since then scores of subcultures have followed suit. In the light of the continuing fad for mad, it seems legitimate to extend the point made by Newton, and to suggest that, if participants in pop culture have been unduly subjected to a psychotherapeutic approach on the part of those in positions of authority, this may have something to do with the way in which pop culture has celebrated inarticulacy and presented an image of its own participants as being only one step away from mental illness. We have played the fool, and now we are living with the consequences of our play-acting.

The fad for mad

In the beginning, however, it seemed as if identifying with insanity would free us from the straitjacket of the inane society. Hence Dean Moriarty was the hero of Kerouac's *On the Road* in so far as he 'was becoming the Idiot, the Imbecile, the Saint of the lot'.[27] Also in *On the Road* Kerouac declared, 'the only people for me are the mad ones'.[28] He felt sufficiently strongly about this to repeat the phrase in an article he wrote for *Encounter* on the origins of the Beat generation.[29]

'For years', noted biographer Gerald Nicosia, 'Jack Kerouac had more or less treasured the notion of his own madness'[30] – perhaps from the days when he was given what he called 'an indifferent character discharge'[31] from the navy. Nicosia also recognized that in Kerouac 'exhilaration was the flipside of his mental exhaustion'.[32] In *Desolation Angels* Kerouac described himself as looking 'like an escaped mental patient'.[33] Elsewhere he described himself as a 'sick clown'.[34] His close friend Allen Ginsberg referred to Kerouac affectionately as a 'Zen lunatic',[35] and as 'a type of simpleton'.[36] Ginsberg once wrote to Kerouac and explained that he (Ginsberg) had gone mad from too much suffering. Now he wanted to live in a world where 'the heroes were holy idiots'.[37] The notion of idiocy as something inspirational and to be aspired to was in the process of being established among the Beats.

While still a student of English literature Ginsberg spent a few weeks in a mental hospital, where he befriended another young patient by the name of Carl Solomon. It was to Solomon that Ginsberg dedicated the poem *Howl*, widely regarded as the document which heralded the Beat generation and the counterculture which developed from it. Ginsberg set the tone for fifty years of countercultural history in a poem which bemoans the destruction of the 'best minds' by madness, but which also groups together 'the madman, bum and angel' in holy communion against suburban conformity.[38] Henceforth madness could be regarded as both a burden and a mission – the countercultural equivalent of Christian vocation.

Ginsberg's mother spent many years in various asylums, where she underwent repeated doses of electric shock treatment; but proximity to real mental illness does not seem to have prevented Ginsberg's dalliance with the idea of madness as alternative consciousness. When he and Solomon were assigned to adjoining beds, the latter introduced the former to the writings of Antonin Artaud, the French actor, dramatist and originator of the 'theatre of cruelty' who had died in obscurity in the 1940s. Artaud was a revelation to them both.

Solomon took Artaud's essay on the nineteenth-century Dutch painter Vincent van Gogh and used it as a kind of intellectual ejector seat that lifted him out of what he regarded as the stifling world of rational conformity. In 'Report from the asylum', his contribution to Feldman and Gartenberg's *Protest* anthology, Solomon quoted Artaud's favourable definition of a lunatic: 'a man who has preferred to become what is socially understood as mad rather than forfeit a certain superior idea of human honour'.[39] After many years as a mental patient himself, Artaud had gone on to describe psychiatry in equally unfavourable terms and to define it as an apologetic for barbarism: 'A vicious society has invented psychiatry to defend itself from the investigations of certain superior lucid minds whose intuitive powers were disturbing to it.'[40]

This was music to the ears of a new generation of anti-rationalists, for whom Artaud became the embodiment of a madness which was perceived to be as enlightening as it was nonconformist. With Solomon and Ginsberg among its founding members, a cult of Artaud was established, which later grew to enormous proportions.

By the mid-1970s Artaud was one of the 'modern masters' featured in the Fontana series of booklets, although the author assigned to him, Martin Esslin, acknowledged that his 'modern' was not a 'master' in the traditional sense: 'not a thinker ... nor was he a doer ... his actual work in that sphere [theatre] is generally acknowledged to have been a failure.'[41]

Nevertheless, wrote Esslin, the impact of Artaud 'manifests itself in a number of different spheres; in the theatre certainly, but also in poetry, literary criticism, psychology, political ideology, philosophy, the drug-cult and the search for alternative lifestyles'.[42] Esslin also noted that philosophers such as Gilles Deleuze and Félix Guattari regarded Artaud as 'a kind of saintly model'. Much of what passes for philosophy or political science in France, said Esslin, is 'Artaudian rhetoric, words used for their emotional charge'.[43]

In a counterposition borrowed from Nietzsche, Esslin suggested that 'Artaud's rejection of the Apollonian principle in favour of the unrestrained ecstasies of Dionysos has rallied a whole generation'.[44]

Esslin maintained that Artaud was 'a figure whose influence must be recognised among the forces that shape the thinking and feeling of our time'.[45] Noting that Artaud is one of those figures 'whose impact . . . arises from what they are and what they have *suffered*',[46] Esslin summed him up as 'one of the archetypal heroes – or sacrificial victims – of our age'.[47]

It is a peculiarity of our age that its archetypes are sacrificial victims rather than conquering heroes; and in this respect Artaud is indeed the template. With madness as his *bona fides*, Artaud, as Esslin put it, has 'become the embodiment of a lonely individual persecuted and victimised for his individuality and lifestyle by the upholders of convention and propriety'.[48] In this capacity, noted Esslin, Artaud's letter to the chancellors of Europe's universities was 'one of the first leaflets issued by the students of the Sorbonne in 1968'.[49] The students and counterculturists were attracted to the madness of Artaud the 'drug-addicted mystic and visionary believer in the Cabbala, the Tao and Eastern religions' as an antidote to 'the spirit of rationalism, analytic and discursive thought, formal logic and linguistic pedantry which has desiccated the fullness of man's emotional life'.[50]

While the real-life Artaud approached his deathbed (before the cult of Artaud was born), the painter Jean Dubuffet took up where he left off. In 1948, in a statement entitled *Crude Art Preferred to Cultural Art* Dubuffet declared that 'madness gives man wings and helps his power of vision'.[51] The art critics Charles Harrison and Paul Wood have since surmised that for Dubuffet, 'the human and the civilised were at opposite poles – a conclusion which must have seemed to be supported by the experience of war'.[52] In this respect Dubuffet was the European counterpart of Norman Mailer, whose romance with the psychotic went along with his rejection of the combined rational and technological forces which seemed to have conspired to produce the Second World War.

Similar currents were at work in Britain. In her debut novel *Under the Net* (1954) Iris Murdoch introduced a new kind of anti-hero in the form of Jake Donaghue, who was thirtysomething, 'talented but lazy', living in bohemian London 'by literary hack-work' and as little original writing 'as possible'. Donaghue is characterized by self-effacement and an approach to others which is both warm and ironic. But his defining characteristic ('what is more important for the purposes of this tale') is his 'shattered nerves'.[53] Here is a protagonist who is not battling with others as his literary predecessors had done throughout the history of the novel; rather than striving to overcome his own weaknesses he has learnt to enjoy life within them, to the extent that his 'shattered nerves' are the submerged co-ordinates of his very existence.

In *The Outsider*, the most fashionable book of non-fiction in mid-1950s Britain, Colin Wilson discussed a number of historical role models for a new spirituality, some of whom, as Wilson subsequently stated, were 'lop-sided ... capable of becoming insane'.[54] For Wilson, madness – or something close to it – was a sign of an individual breaking out of narrow conventions.

Following Wilson's lead, others began scouring the classics for examples of enlightened lunacy. Some began to identify with the character of Prince Myshkin, the protagonist of Dostoyevsky's *The Idiot*. Myshkin was described by the American critic Maurice Friedman as a perfect child and a modern saint, whose mystical qualities were inseparable from his epilepsy.[55] (When Ginsberg met Carl Solomon in an asylum the former introduced himself as Myshkin and the latter dubbed himself Kirilov, the most demonic of Dostoyevsky's *The Possessed*.) By the mid-1960s the notion of madness as a creative frame of mind was so widespread that the literary critic Al Alvarez declared that 'the modern artist ... cultivates not his own garden but his psychosis'.[56] Alvarez may well have had in mind the opening line of Saul Bellow's influential novel *Herzog*: 'If I am out of my mind, it's all right with me, thought Moses Herzog.'[57]

'Schizoid subterfuges'

In the world of humour also, the notion of madness acquired a new significance. The American magazine *Mad* portrayed postwar American society as an exercise in absurdity. Editor Al Feldstein conceptualized this depiction as 'a kind of service for young people ... in at least alerting them to what was going on around them in the areas of advertising, politics, manufacturing, packaging etc.'.[58] It seems to have had the desired effect on the young Robert Crumb, who was to become the premier cartoonist of the counterculture. 'If you were growing up lonely and isolated in a small town,' Crumb recalled, '*Mad* was a revolution. Nothing I read anywhere else suggested there was any absurdity in the culture. *Mad* was like a shock, breaking you out.'[59]

Mad magazine decoded the madness of society. It was also interpreted as an invitation to subvert official madness by acting it out and taking it to even more ridiculous extremes. This is the self-consciously warped logic of the prankster mentality, in which a creative madness is regarded as the antidote to the stifling, respectable madness of 'normality'.

In Britain the premier representatives of this outlook were The Goons. Spike Milligan, himself diagnosed as a manic depressive, explained the healing quality of such supra-madness in a commentary to the published version of the *Goon Show* scripts: 'Its starting point is one man shouting gibberish in the face of authority and proving by fabricated insanity that nothing could be as mad as what passes for ordinary living.'[60] This approach was imitated and refined by the likes of Marty Feldman, Monty Python and Vivian Stanshall. It also informed countless products of pop culture such as the Beatles' film *Help!* and The Monkees' eponymous television series.

The Goons struck a chord with many young people across society, including the youthful heir to the throne, Prince Charles. According to Nuttall, The Goons were at once protest and surrealist art, and also populist, in that 'the Goon Show was every National Serviceman's defence mechanism'.[61] Among future participants in the counter-culture, the influence of The Goons was particularly strong. Biographer Christopher Sanford recounts that '[Eric] Clapton would awake from an apparent coma to engage in the kind of comic monologue characteristic of the Goons'.[62] Nuttall recalled that 'Goon Show caricature voices spread into everybody's conversation and provided us all with schizoid subterfuges, vocal disguises'.[63] Note the association of 'schizoid' with 'subterfuges', as if normality was something to be dodged by using the mannerisms of Milligan's 'fabricated insanity'.

Snapshot: Marxism, tendency Harpo

Christmas in Coventry after my first term away at university. On Christmas Eve I went back to the same pub we always went to as sixth-formers. In a room full of former classmates I caught sight of one who had clearly become a Marxist; not in the manner of Karl Marx, or even a member of the tendency Groucho. An exhibitioner in *Literae humaniores* at Oxford, this young man had rejected the humanist tradition in favour of the look and the mannerisms of Harpo Marx, the maddest of the Marx Brothers. He had the hair and the costume down to a T. Fortunately the adoption of the prankster mentality had not struck him dumb like Harpo – not yet, anyway.

Arrested Development

The prankster aspiration to find a different kind of sanity by means of contrived lunacy was further represented in the Netherlands by the Provos of Amsterdam; and most famously by Ken Kesey's troupe of LSD missionaries, The Merrie Pranksters. In the mid-1960s, before LSD was ruled illegal, they roamed California in a psychedelic bus, spreading acid as if it were a holy sacrament of enlightened madness. This latter was the aspect of the 'trip' which Marcuse recommended, as 'the dissolution of the ego shaped by the established society' – a dissolution which anticipated, albeit in a 'distorted' fashion, what Marcuse chose to call 'an exigency of the social liberation'.[64]

As an author Kesey had already advocated that the lunatics should take over the asylum. In his 1962 novel, *One Flew over the Cuckoo's Nest*, which was made into a widely acclaimed film directed by Milos Forman and starring Jack Nicholson, Kesey used a mental hospital and its white-coated staff as a metaphor for a technological order which was both obsessive and repressive. Ranged against the authorities are a prankster-patient, McMurphy, and his secret ally (and narrator of the novel) Chief Bromden, a native American who the staff believe is deaf and dumb. In Kesey's scenario it is McMurphy and his inspired madness which have a therapeutic effect on the patients, as when Chief Bromden describes McMurphy 'drawling, winking, joking his best to wheedle a skinny laugh out of some acute who'd been scared to grin since he was 12'.[65] McMurphy's prankster-therapy operates on behalf of the incarcerated patients against the sinister madness of the nursing staff and, by implication, contrary to the status quo outside the hospital.

One Flew over the Cuckoo's Nest is a prime example of what Carl Oglesby defined as 'the modern sensibility' in which it is assumed that 'neurosis is man's ordinary condition and can even be husbanded to a certain eerie grace'.[66] The personification of such 'eerie grace' is the narrator of Kesey's story, Chief Bromden.

Taking over the asylum

Kesey's wishes came partly true, when in the form of 'anti-psychiatry' the lunatics did indeed take over some of the asylums. The novelist Angela Carter, reminiscing about the 1960s in Sara Maitland's anthology *Very Heaven*, recalled that the prime mover behind 'anti-psychiatry' was one of the figureheads of the period:

R. D. Laing's The Divided Self *was one of the most influential books of*

*the sixties – it made madness, alienation, hating your parents – it made it
all glamorous. God knows what he did for people who were really mad . . .
but he certainly set the pace for that crazy hinge of the decade.*[67]

Dr R. D. Laing was a Scottish psychiatrist who became disillusioned
with his own discipline, in much the same way that Matza, Becker *et al.*
had reacted against the discredited positivism of mainstream sociology,
particularly the way in which, as they saw it, the process of labelling the
misfit had the effect of 'bottling' him or her within a self-fulfilling
prophecy. In *The Divided Self* Laing warned against the pressures to
conform and live 'life, without feeling alive'; and he went on to suggest
that what had been labelled madness was an essential, if as yet
uncharted, element in our common humanity: 'Generally, it is evident
that what we shall discuss here clinically is but a small sample of
something in which human nature is deeply implicated and to which
we can contribute only a very partial understanding.'[68]

Laing maintained that 'true sanity' necessitated the 'dissolution of the
normal ego, that false self completely adjusted to our alienated social
reality'. This would allow for 'the emergence of the "inner" archetypal
mediators of divine power' and bring about a new frame of mind with
'the ego now being the servant of the divine, no longer its betrayer'.[69]

When Laing gave a paper to the Sixth International Congress of
Psycho-Therapy, his starting-point was that 'we, the sane ones, are out
of our minds'.[70] According to Laing, the certified insane could teach us
much of what we needed to know about ego-dissolution. 'Schizo-
phrenics', he told journalist Geoffrey Moorhouse, 'have more to teach
psychiatrists about the inner world than psychiatrists their patients.'[71]
Along similar lines Nuttall remembered Laing for the suggestion that
'schizophrenia was a tortured means to a fuller experience'.[72]

In *The Deviant Imagination*, an intelligent discussion of the intellectual
currents of the period, sociologist Geoffrey Pearson described 'anti-
psychiatry' as 'a sort of fellow-traveller of the counter-cultural
rebellion'[73] and summarized its 'position' thus: 'that the requirements
of normality, conformity and reasonableness . . . are a suffocation which
stifles, blocks and distorts the expression of a fully human consciousness.'[74] Pearson noted that contemporary descriptions of the 'acid trip'
and 'the schizophrenic voyage' indicated that the two experiences were
commensurate, although he himself remained sceptical about this
suggestion. He also observed that among radical activists such as the

Situationist-inspired publishers of *King Mob* magazine there was a Laingian assumption that schizophrenia had a 'key role' to play in 'the subversion of the *reasonable* society'.[75] But Pearson recognized that the relabelling of 'personal distress' as 'an inarticulate political consciousness … the murmurings of personal and crypto-political dissent' was entirely illegitimate.[76] He also saw the contradiction in the interpretation of madness as 'at one and the same time both a product of a crazy alienating family *and* a legitimate, authentic mode of experiencing the world, which can heal'.[77]

In America the distinguished scholar Lionel Trilling also cast a critical eye over the liberatory claims of 'anti-psychiatry'. Trilling began his essay 'The authentic unconscious' by addressing the introduction to the English edition of Michel Foucault's *Madness and Civilization*, which was penned by a long-standing associate of Laing, Dr David Cooper. 'Madness', Cooper had written, 'is a form of vision that destroys itself by its choice of oblivion in the face of existing forms of social tactics and strategy. Madness, for instance, is a matter of voicing the realization that I am (or you are) Christ.'[78]

In madness Laing and Cooper saw a sane man struggling to get out of an insane society, and, as Artaud had suggested thirty years previously, choosing honourable oblivion rather than settling for 'our alienated social reality'. Trilling admitted to harbouring an initial sympathy for some of these ideas. 'Who', he asked, 'will not be disposed to find some seed of cogency in a view that proposes an antinomian reversal of all accepted values, of all received realities?' But he also regarded 'anti-psychiatry' as a kind of wishful thinking which could have the effect only of betraying those in real need of psychiatric treatment: 'But who that has spoken, or tried to speak, with a psychotic friend will consent to betray the masked pain of his bewilderment and solitude by making it the paradigm of liberation?'[79]

Besides being harmful to the mentally ill, 'anti-psychiatry' was of dubious benefit to those of the counterculture who empathized with it. Feldman and Gartenberg had already pointed out that, by reducing experience to a stream of 'acutely felt sensations', the fad for mad offered an ontology which was totally undemanding. Likewise Trilling noted that Cooper's notion of 'an upward psychopathic mobility to the point of divinity, each one of us a Christ' was a means of canonizing the solipsistic individual without requiring him or her to earn elevation by acting in the external world, i.e.

*with none of the inconveniences of undertaking to intercede, of being a
sacrifice, of reasoning with rabbis, of making sermons, of having disciples, of
going to weddings and to funerals, of beginning something and at a certain
point remarking that it is finished.*[80]

Not only did the Laing–Cooper outlook take the onus from the
individual; in its rejection of rationality it actually prevented him or her
from shouldering the burden of trying to make history. In other words
the Laing–Cooper outlook was not so much 'anti-psychiatry' as a form
of anti-subjectivity, which insisted that the individual should do
nothing but keep faith with 'the truth' of his or her own madness.

Disbelief as a form of authority

Besides rejecting the tenets of 'anti-psychiatry', Trilling sought to
explain why it had become a reference point among the intelligentsia.
Noting that 'many among us find it gratifying to entertain the thought
that alienation is to be overcome only by the completeness of
alienation',[81] Trilling observed that the attraction of 'anti-psychiatry'
lay in the absolutism of its alienation from society:

> *The enthusiasm for Laing is a response not to the originality of his
> conception but to its extremity – his inculpation of society comes so near to
> being absolute that it is experienced as an exhilarating liberation, if not,
> alas, from the bondage of social necessity, then at least from the duress of its
> moral authority.*[82]

Trilling added that 'no expression of disaffection from the social
existence was ever so desperate'.[83] His observations prefigured Esslin's
explanation of the status of Artaud: 'the chief appeal ... was the
vehemence of his denunciations, whatever the target.'[84]

Trilling hit upon an intriguing contradiction. If 'anti-psychiatry' was
as essentially passive as he understood it to be, how come it was
interpreted – and not only by its practitioners – as a kind of liberation?
The answer to this question lies, as Trilling himself began to indicate,
both in the intensity of its rejection of discredited positivism and in its
simultaneous dismissal of history-making activity. Thus, while playing a
part in the corrosion of an old order oriented around traditional
ideologies, the underlying assumptions of 'anti-psychiatry' have also
played a role in the construction of a new, anti-ideological order which
is already turning out to be even more restrictive than its predecessor.

Arrested Development

In the 1960s anyone who allied himself or herself with anti-psychiatry would have been participating in the 'great refusal' of traditional ideologies, and in so doing would have absolved himself or herself of the burden of their failure. Pearson understood that, under the terms of the new outlook, the 'deviant victim' was raised to the status of the 'deviant hero';[85] in which case we could all become heroes simply by abdicating from the discredited norms of society.

At the time it must have felt like having a dead weight lifted from one's mind: if progress had stopped and society did not work out the way we had planned it, there was no longer any need to feel even indirectly responsible. The failures had all been caused by a rational, instrumental approach to the world from which one had resigned and for which one was in no way responsible.

Entwined with the relief that comes with the onset of disbelief, the end of responsibility accounts for much of the euphoric rush of the period. But in time the first principle of anti-ideology – to wit, that there is nothing to believe in except the negation of ideology – has come to be the new orthodoxy. It leaves us trapped not in the prism of failed positivism but in the open prison of our own negativity, which cannot but translate into a disbelief in our own capabilities and an inability to see ourselves as the makers of history.

In this respect 'anti-psychiatry', and all the other anti-ideologies, replaced discredited ideas with the discrediting of ideas. In the 1990s anti-ideology has now gone mainstream, to the point where 'ideological' is the ultimate pejorative term in a political debate which is appropriately bereft of ideas. Such is the resulting diminution of politics that, as the *Daily Telegraph*'s editor Charles Moore pointed out during the 1997 general election campaign, New Labour does not 'have a dream' like Martin Luther King, but only 'a dream home' and a narrower mindset to match.[86]

In this profoundly anti-ideological context, to 'have a dream' is regarded as deeply suspect. Big ideas are ruled out of order wherever possible. Thus, in the mouths of the new power generation, anti-ideology is now a means of curtailing discussion and exercising a new form of authority – a new model authority in which the discrediting of earlier incarnations of order plays an integral part.

The familiar imbecile
But the essentially negative thrust of 'anti-psychiatry' could not have

leapt directly from the pages of Laing to the statute books. Once again, the mediating links are to be found in the flow of countercultural currents into mainstream pop culture, which soon began to absorb, reproduce and popularize notions of madness as a creative frame of mind and, in so doing, familiarized its consumers with an imbecilic image of themselves. This anti-subjective self-image is now drawn upon by a new generation of politicians who assume instability – or 'vulnerability', in current parlance – on the part of the general public, and who take our alleged frailty into account when legislating 'for our own good'.

As indicated by Angela Carter, the key figures of the swinging sixties liked to play around with the idea of their own mental instability. 'If I didn't write,' declared Bob Dylan, 'I think I'd go insane.'[87] In 1965 Dylan announced, 'I'm afraid of losing my sanity sometimes.'[88] Joan Baez said she thought 'Bobby comes closer to being psychotic than neurotic'.[89] At times Dylan 'was busy being Dada, everything's crazy, sort of comical, cynical, or however you want to put it'.[90]

In the late 1960s Cream, the first of the 'supergroups', played on the image of themselves as 'three musicians who, far from plying their trade for pleasure, did so in order not to jump out of the nearest window'.[91]

When a colleague by the name of Charles Slack proposed to Timothy Leary, half-jokingly, that they form a Psychopath Club, Leary, according to Jay Stevens, 'gave him an amused look and said "you know, I really am a psychopath"'.[92]

Emmett Grogan, an associate of Abbie Hoffman, informed a group of radical students that their problem was that they did not have 'the balls to go mad'.[93] Daniel Foss and Ralph Larkin described the counterculture and its pop festivals as 'what amounts to mass therapy',[94] which indicates an attempt by self-labelled 'freaks' to 'cure' themselves by a higher madness. Counterculturists complained that 'straight' society made them feel 'paranoid', which in turn could only be remedied by a sacramental combination of music and drugs to 'blow your mind'.

'Be wise, be a fool' was a prominent slogan in the German counterculture, where the fool, as Sabine Von Dirke has explained, was interpreted 'as an articulation of spontaneity, energy and fun'.[95] Von Dirke cites Michael Kramer's declaration that 'Fools are dropouts, outsiders, and anti-heroes'.[96] And vice versa: a large number of counterculturists were happy to identify with an image of themselves as 'fools', to the point where 'entire festivals of fools were organized', with the 'Festival of Fools in Amsterdam' being 'the most successful and copied one'.[97]

Fashion designers gave themselves names like 'The Fool', and the tragedy of the crazed King Lear (filmed under the direction of Peter Brook) became Shakespeare's most fashionable play. A prestigious theatre company translated a minor work by Laing, *Knots*, into a stage play. Ken Loach directed *Family Life*, a film based on Laing's notion of the family as the locus of repression and the wellspring of madness.

The eccentric British composer Peter Maxwell Davies wrote *Songs for a Mad King*, while the avant-garde American composer John Cage described mental hospitals as the 'localization of a resource we've yet to exploit'.[98] On the long-running BBC radio show hosted by John Peel, pride of place went to eccentrics such as Ivor Cutler and Kilburn and The High Roads and to full-blown crazies like Wild Man Fisher and the incomparable Captain Beefheart.

The vogue for insanity was such that when an old-fashioned headmistress with the wonderfully appropriate name of Elizabeth Manners castigated the hippie for being 'a bedlam creature in a costume of satin rags' her reproach would have been taken as a compliment by most of those to whom it was directed.[99]

The love affair with madness carried on throughout the 1970s. Apart from David Bowie's presentation of himself as Aladdin Sane (a lad insane), Andy Warhol advertised his neurotic lifestyle in an autobiography *From A to B and Back Again*. Warhol also said that crazy people tended to be more creative because they could not do things in a routine fashion. In *The Music Lovers*, the flamboyant film director Ken Russell depicted the Russian composer Tchaikovsky as a man driven mad by his repressed homosexuality. Woody Allen reached the top rank of Hollywood stardom by portraying himself as a debilitatingly nervous young man whose acute indecision took him to the brink of insanity.

A band by the name of Sparks consisted of twin brothers: Russell Mael (the nice one) and Ron Mael (the mad one), complete with Hitler moustache. And just when the 1970s rock stars' flirtation with madness began to come up against the limits of credibility, the whole affair was played out all over again with the punks in the lead role. Proto-punk-band Dr Feelgood was fronted by a lead singer (Lee Brilleaux) and a guitarist (Wilko Johnson) who both gave the impression of being psychotic.

Then, in 1976, The Sex Pistols came to the fore with a frontman who presented himself as mentally and physically crippled. In his autobiography *No Irish, No Blacks, No Dogs* John Lydon (Rotten) explained that the idea for bondage gear came about after he did a photo-shoot in a straitjacket. 'I really liked being in that straitjacket', he recalled;[100] and bondage gear, he claimed, was arrived at as a compromise which would allow him to give the impression of being constrained like a lunatic while still being able to move around on stage. More than twenty years later, with the title of his 1997 album, *Psycho's Path*, Lydon was still playing with the same idea of himself as mad, bad and dangerous to know.

In the late 1970s the idea of madness was softened somewhat by the Two-Tone band, who took their name from a song of political satire by the Jamaican Prince Buster, and turned it into a celebration of adolescent nuttiness in preference to the world of sober adulthood. But the fad for mad was brought back into the framework of depression and psychosis in the form of Nick Cave and his portrayal of cool alienation permanently on the point of a frenzied outburst. In *Blissed Out* Simon Reynolds described Cave as 'morbidly inward ... sick but refusing to be healed and integrated', adding that Cave's 'obsessions are wounds he deliberately keeps open'.[101]

Snapshot: On the edge

'So what are you going to do with your life, then?' The disdain in her voice was unmistakable. Here was a mature, professional woman quizzing me, a twentysomething musician who had recently become disillusioned even with music, about when I intended to grow up. This was in the early 1980s, when she was climbing up the career ladder and I was going nowhere. That we shared the same bed was no longer a sufficient counterweight to the rapidly growing divergence between her social status and mine. I felt less like her lover and more like a patient in a surgery.

But all I had to do was play the patient role to the full. I, at least, was going to stay true to the craziness of all those years in bands and bedsits. I replied without a moment's hesitation. 'I want to live on the edge': the edge of experience, outside the mainstream, on the cusp of sanity/insanity. 'What does that mean?' she retorted, and with that the conversation came to an end. If she did not know, or had chosen to forget, there was really no point in going on.

Writing towards the end of the 1980s, Reynolds rehashed the comparison between 'the schizoid experience', with its emphasis on the present ('the insupportable dazzle of the moment') and the acid trip ('timeless, beyond words, transcendental'). He mentioned The Sex Pistols, Black Flag, Loop, The Pixies, The Birthday Party and The Stooges as bands whose 'vision of the rock 'n' roll essence as disinhibition attained via the cretinous and cretinizing effects of repetition, noise and self-abasement' put them closer to the 'schizoid' version of the perpetual present.[102] Reynolds also used words like 'seizure' and 'convulsive' in relation to the 'bliss' associated with this kind of pop music. And he quoted musician and theoretician Genesis P. Orridge as saying that the participants in dance culture have 'put themselves through psycho-therapy, which is what Ecstasy was originally used for'.[103]

All of which seems to suggest that the idea of madness has been a recurring motif throughout the recent development of pop music, to the point where, if indeed the latest cohort of devotees are now seeking 'psychotherapy' from Ecstasy and the scene related to it, they may well be doing so in order to ameliorate the aura of madness which is so virulent in the surrounding culture.

Occasionally the fixation with madness in pop culture is recognized as laughable, as when the millionaire co-founder of The Eurythmics, Dave Stewart, complained that he was suffering from 'paradise syndrome', which he defined as a mental condition that plagues the successful with imaginary ailments.[104] But for the most part, proximity to madness, or an idea of madness, is still regarded as a sign of authenticity and creativity. Thus Nirvana became *the* band of the early 1990s only after Kurt Cobain's suicide. The Manic Street Preachers became *the* British band of 1996–7 after the disappearance of their original lead singer, which was widely understood to have been prompted by mental instability. And the early success of Bristol's trip-hopper Tricky was inextricably linked to the image he projected of being on the brink of derangement.

In the pop culture lexicon neurosis remains an admirable quality, as when Ben Watt, one half of the pop duo Everything But the Girl, who has written a highly acclaimed account of his own recent illness and its mentally disorienting effects, says that part of the reason why he likes jungle music is its 'neurotic' feel.[105]

In the same month that Watt's remarks about ragga were published, a new American pop band called The Eels broke into the British music scene for the first time, fuelled by an acute sense of musical dynamics and the persona of frontman E, who presents himself in the manner of a recovering mental patient.

In the winter of 1996–7 the Hayward Gallery on London's South Bank mounted a widely acclaimed exhibition, *Beyond Reason*, drawn from the Prinzhorn collection of drawings and paintings produced by inmates of the Heidelberg mental hospital. On British television one of the most popular characters in recent years was the borderline schizophrenic Joe Wicks (Paul Nicholl) of *EastEnders*, the only member of the cast with his own fan club. In the theatre one of the most important productions of 1997 was the National Theatre's new staging of Peter Weiss's *The Persecution and Assassination of Marat as Portrayed by the Inmates of the Asylum of Charenton under the Direction of the Marquis de Sade*, the first British production of which, directed for the Royal Shakespeare Company by Peter Brook in 1964, was a high point in the early flowering of the fad for mad.

Shortly before the *Marat/Sade* opened at the National in May 1997, director Jeremy Sams gave an interview to Heather Neill of *The Times* in which he declared, 'there are parallels between acting and lunacy – making something up and calling it "real", inventing an intact alternative reality'. Sams also said that he wanted his audience to come to 'know what it's like to feel that much pain'.[106] After nearly half a century the readiness to identify ourselves with images of trauma and lunacy and the propensity to misconceive madness remain unabated.

Equally hard-wearing is the notion of madness as a form of subversion bordering on the revolutionary. Ginsberg once described himself as a 'philosophical anarchist',[107] and he seems to have thought of 'reasoned *derangement of all the senses*. All shapes of love, suffering, madness'[108] as his equivalent of the anarchist's bomb. Forty years on, Spike Milligan seems to have been referring to a similar notion when, in an interview with Sean O'Hagan for the *Observer*, he declared that 'myself and Sellers always thought of ourselves as comic Bolsheviks'.[109] In the preceding paragraph of the published interview, however, Milligan declared that 'humans are boring', confirming his previously documented preference for the natural world over the destructive aspects of human society, and thus indicating a casual disregard for the existing worth as well as the unrealized potential of humanity. Likewise idiot-wannabe Jack Kerouac once declared that he felt 'guilty for being a member of the human race'.[110]

Arrested Development

Such anti-human sentiments are not out of kilter with the fad for mad; indeed throughout its fifty-year history the latter may be said to have been predicated upon them. It's no joke. The idea of lunacy as lifestyle not only belittles the achievements of human society so far but also wants to dispense with one of the essential tools for achieving more than we have done already – our rationality. In this respect the fad for mad cannot be subversive; starting out as an attitude struck against a discredited way of life it has become part of a new and perverse way of life in which madness is imbued with moral authority, Big Ideas are discredited *per se*, and the anti-ideological doctrine of ultimate failure is proving to be more stifling than Victorian values.

Notes

1. Charles Hamblett and Jane Deverson, *Generation X* (London: Tandem Books, 1964), p. 58.

2. *Ibid.*, p. 59.

3. Herbert Marcuse, *An Essay on Liberation* (Harmondsworth: Allen Lane, 1969), p. 37.

4. Jacques Ellul, *The Technological Society* (London: Jonathan Cape, 1965), p. 404.

5. Gene Feldman and Max Gartenberg (eds), *Protest* (London: Quartet, 1973), p. 134.

6. Frank Musgrove, *Ecstasy and Holiness: Counter Culture and the Open Society* (London: Methuen, 1974), p. 42.

7. Kenneth Keniston, *The Uncommitted* (New York: Harcourt Brace, 1960), p. 9.

8. Vance Packard's evidence to the 1958 Senate Committee on Interstate Commerce, quoted in Joe Kohut and John J. Kohut (eds), *Rock Talk* (London: Faber & Faber, 1994).

9. Ralph Ellison, *The Invisible Man* (Harmondsworth: Penguin, 1952).

10. Review in *Time* magazine, quoted in Ann Charters, *Kerouac: A Biography* (London: Picador/Pan, 1978), p. 264.

11. *New York Times*, 3 May 1959, quoted in *ibid.*, p. 286.

12. Herb Gold in *The Nation*, quoted in Gerald Nicosia, *Memory Babe: A Critical Biography of Jack Kerouac* (London: Penguin, 1986), p. 557.

13. Cited in Jack Newfield, *A Prophetic Minority: The American New Left* (London: Anthony Blond, 1966), p. 45.

14. Robert M. Lindner, *Rebel Without a Cause* (New York: Grove Press, 1944), p. 2.

15. *Ibid.*, pp. 2–3.

16. *Ibid.*, p. 3.

17. *Ibid.*, p. 14.

18. Francis Newton, *The Jazz Scene* (Harmondsworth: Penguin, 1961), p. 209.

19. Cited in Jay Landesman, *Rebel Without Applause* (London: Bloomsbury, 1987), p. 78.

20. Norman Mailer 'The white negro', first published in *Dissent*, summer 1957, subsequently in a retrospective anthology, *Advertisements for Myself* (London: Panther, 1976), p. 271.

21. *Ibid.*, p. 270.

22. *Ibid.*, pp. 270–1.

23. *Ibid.*, p. 275.

24. Jay Stevens, *Storming Heaven: LSD and the American Dream* (London: Paladin, 1989), pp. 172–3.

25. *Ibid.*, p. 176.

26. Erik H. Erikson, *Identity: Youth and Crisis* (1968) (London: Faber & Faber, 1983), p. 19.

27. Jack Kerouac, *On the Road* (1957) (London: Penguin Books, 1972), p. 193.

28. Quoted in Charters, *op. cit.*, p. 265.

29. Jack Kerouac, 'Beatific – on the origins of a generation', *Encounter*, August 1959.

30. Nicosia, *op. cit.*, p. 178.

31. Charters, *op. cit.*, p. 349.

32. Nicosia, *op. cit.*, p. 577.

33. Charters, *op. cit.*, p. 250.

34. Nicosia, *op. cit.*, p. 627.

35. Allen Ginsberg, quoted by Charters, *op. cit.*, p. 201.

36. Ginsberg on Kerouac in a letter to Mark Van Doren, 1 June 1948, quoted by Charters, *op. cit.*, p. 349.

37. Ginsberg, letter to Kerouac, April 1948, quoted in Nicosia, *op. cit.*, p. 210.

38. Allen Ginsberg, *Howl* (San Francisco: City Lights, 1956).

39. Artaud, quoted by Carl Solomon, in 'Report from the asylum', contribution to Feldman and Gartenberg, *op. cit.*, p. 141.

40. *Ibid.*, p. 141.

41. Martin Esslin, *Artaud* (Glasgow: Fontana, 1976), p. 10.

42. *Ibid.*, p. 9.

43. *Ibid.*, pp. 111–12.

44. *Ibid.*, p. 112.

45. *Ibid.*, p. 10.

46. *Ibid.*

47. *Ibid.*, p. 14.

48. *Ibid.*

49. *Ibid.*, p. 107.

50. *Ibid.*, pp. 108–9.

51. Jean Dubuffet, 1948 manifesto *Crude Art Preferred to Cultural Art*, cited in Charles Harrison and Paul Wood (eds), *Art in Theory 1900–1990* (Oxford: Blackwell, 1992).

52. Harrison and Wood, *op. cit.*, p. 552A.

53. Iris Murdoch, *Under the Net* (1954) (Harmondsworth: Penguin, 1960), p. 21.

54. Colin Wilson, introduction, written in 1976, to the 1978 edition of *The Outsider* (1956) (London: Picador), p. 12.

55. Maurice Friedman, *Problematic Rebel* (Chicago: University of Chicago Press, 1963), p. 223.

56. Al Alvarez, quoted in Andrew Sinclair, *In Love and Anger* (London: Sinclair Stevenson, 1994), p. 135.

57. Saul Bellow, *Herzog* (1964) (Harmondsworth: Penguin, 1965), p. 7.

58. *Mad* editor Al Feldstein, quoted in Maria Reidelbach, *Completely Mad: A History of the Comic Book and Magazine* (London: Boxtree, 1992), p. 38.

59. Robert Crumb, quoted in *ibid.*, p. 36.

60. Spike Milligan, introducing *The Goon Show Scripts* (London: The Woburn Press, 1972), quoted in Elizabeth Nelson, *The British Counterculture* (Basingstoke: Macmillan, 1989), p. 43.

61. Jeff Nuttall, *Bomb Culture* (London: Paladin, 1970), p. 116.

62. Christopher Sanford, *Clapton – The Edge of Darkness* (London: Gollancz, 1994), p. 53.

63. Nuttall, *op. cit.*, p. 116.

64. Herbert Marcuse, *An Essay on Liberation* (Harmondsworth: Allen Lane, 1969), p. 37.

65. Ken Kesey, *One Flew over the Cuckoo's Nest* (1962) (London: Picador, 1973), p. 10.

66. Carl Oglesby (ed.), 'Introduction: the idea of the New Left', in *The New Left Reader* (New York: Grove Press, 1969), p. 5.

67. Angela Carter, in Sara Maitland (ed.), *Very Heaven: Looking back at the 1960s* (London: Virago, 1988), p. 215.

68. R. D. Laing, *The Divided Self* (Harmondsworth: Penguin, 1965), pp. 40–1.

69. R. D. Laing, *The Politics of Experience and the Bird of Paradise* (London: Penguin, 1967), p. 119.

70. Quoted in Nuttall, *op. cit.*, p. 110.

71. Laing, interviewed by Geoffrey Moorhouse in *The Permissive Society: The* Guardian *Inquiry* (London: Panther Modern Society, 1969), p. 48.

72. Nuttall, *op. cit.*, p. 109.

73. Geoffrey Pearson, *The Deviant Imagination* (London: Macmillan, 1975), p. 31.

74. *Ibid.*, p. 19.

75. *Ibid.*, p. 101.

76. *Ibid.*

77. *Ibid.*, p. 20.

78. D. Cooper, Introduction to Michel Foucault, *Madness and Civilization* (London: Tavistock, 1967), pp. vii–ix.

79. Lionel Trilling, 'The authentic unconscious', in *Sincerity and Authenticity* (London: Oxford University Press, 1974), pp. 170–1.

80. *Ibid.*, p. 171.

81. *Ibid.*

82. *Ibid.*, p. 161.

83. *Ibid.*, p. 171.

84. Esslin, *op. cit.*, p. 109.

85. Pearson, *op. cit.*, p. 24.

86. Charles Moore on the Radio Four news programme *Today*, 11 April 1997.

87. Anthony Scaduto, *Bob Dylan* (London: Abacus, 1972), p. 137.

88. Robin Deneslow, *When the Music's Over* (London: Faber & Faber, 1989), p. 73.

89. Joan Baez, quoted in Scaduto, *op. cit.*, p. 199.

90. Scaduto, *op. cit.*, p. 201.

91. Sandford, *op. cit.*, p. 108.

92. Stevens, *op. cit.*, p. 192.

93. Emmett Grogan, quoted in Abbie Hoffman, *The Best of Abbie Hoffman* (New York: Four Walls Eight Windows, 1989), p. 23.

94. Daniel Foss and Ralph Larkin, *Theory and Society*, spring 1976, pp. 45–6.

95. Sabine Von Dirke, *All Power to the Imagination!* (Lincoln: University of Nebraska Press, 1997), p. 163.

96. Michael Kramer, *Pantomime und Clownerie: Geschichte der Clownerei von der Commedia dell'arte bis zu den Festivals of Fools*, 2nd edn (Offenbach: Burckhardthaus-Laetare, 1986), p. 107.

97. Von Dirke, *op. cit.*, p. 160.

98. Elizabeth Manners, *The Vulnerable Generation* (London: Cassell, 1971), p. 27.

99. John Cage, *A Year from Monday* (London: Calder & Boyars, 1968), p. 9.

100. John Lydon, *No Irish, No Blacks, No Dogs* (New York: St Martin's Press, 1995), p. 152.

101. Simon Reynolds, *Blissed Out* (London: Serpent's Tail, 1994), p. 72.

102. *Ibid.*, p. 137.

103. *Ibid.*, p. 187.

104. Dave Stewart, quoted in *Daily Telegraph*, 13 June 1996.

105. Ben Watt, quoted in Jennifer Kabat, 'Jungle fever', in *Utne Reader*, November–December 1996, p. 98.

106. Jeremy Sams, quoted in Heather Neill, 'Talking over the asylum', *The Times*, 13 May 1997.

Arrested Development

107. Ginsberg, quoted in Barry Miles, *Ginsberg: A Biography* (New York: Simon & Schuster, 1989), p. 212.

108. *Ibid.*, p. 43.

109. Spike Milligan, interviewed by Sean O'Hagan in *Observer*, 3 December 1995.

110. Kerouac, quoted in Gerald Nicosia, *op. cit.*, p. 627.

CHAPTER 6

Spirit

Contemporary spirituality sanctifies the individual and at the
same time desecrates his potential.

As told in Barry Miles's biography of the original Beat poet, in the
summer of 1948 Allen Ginsberg underwent what he described nearly
forty years later as 'the only really genuine experience I feel I've had,
something that seemed like a complete absorption of all my senses into
something totally authentic as an experience'.[1] What was this 'totally
authentic' experience? This is how Miles tells it:

> *The summer heat was on. Allen lay on his bed by the open window,
> reading William Blake. The book was open to the poem 'Ah! Sunflower'
> from* Songs of Innocence *and* Songs of Experience. *Allen had his
> pants open and was absent-mindedly masturbating while he read; he had
> just come, when he heard a deep, ancient voice, reading the poem aloud. He
> immediately knew, without thinking, that it was the voice of Blake
> himself, coming to him across the vault of time. The voice was prophetic,
> tender . . . He described it: 'The peculiar quality of the voice was something
> unforgettable because it was like God had a human voice, with all the
> infinite tenderness and mortal gravity of a living Creator speaking to his
> son' . . .*
>
> *He suddenly had a deep understanding of the meaning of the poem and
> he realized that he was the sunflower. Simultaneous with the auditory
> vision came a heightened visual perception: The afternoon sunlight
> through the window took on an extraordinary clarity. The sky was
> ancient, the gateway to infinity, the same deep blue universe seen by
> Blake himself, and Allen knew this was the 'sweet golden clime' itself.*

Arrested Development

He was already in it. 'I suddenly realized that this existence was it'!, he said. 'This was the moment I was born for. This initiation, this consciousness of being alive unto myself. The spirit of the universe was what I was born to realize.'[2]

After this revelation, which closely resembles Aldous Huxley's experience under the influence of mescaline as told in his essay 'The doors of perception', Ginsberg went on to the fire escape outside and told two girls in the neighbouring flat that he had seen God. They shut the window in his face. According to Miles, he rang his former analyst and announced, 'It happened. I had some kind of breakthrough or psychotic experience' (note his readiness to equate spirituality with psychosis).[3] But the therapist hung up on him. His father was equally unsympathetic, as were his professors. Yet this was the one moment above all others when Ginsberg felt in profound sympathy with the entire universe, and he regarded it as the turning-point in his life: 'From now on I'm chosen, blessed, sacred, poet, and this is my sunflower, my new mind. I'll be faithful the rest of my life, and I'll never deny it, and I'll never renounce it.'[4]

Self-love

If we discount, for the moment, the possibility of divine intervention, what else could have occasioned this experience? It is surely no coincidence that Ginsberg's spiritual awakening occurred at a time when he was living in isolation – from college, from friends and from his family. This was an experience which was entirely peculiar to him, and a non-event to everyone else. Indeed, if it were judged by any empirical criterion, there was nothing exceptional there to be experienced. Nothing happened. Nevertheless for Ginsberg it was the defining moment of his life.

Ginsberg's inspirational moment – the one moment he felt truly, authentically alive – was also a moment in which his existence was neither challenged nor verified by external circumstances. Indeed the temporary suspension of the outside world might well have been the fountainhead of Ginsberg's inspiration, in which case the deity with which Ginsberg thought he was communing was perhaps not so much the Blakean spirit of the universe as a projection of himself, which his mind's eye had expanded to fill the infinite space that, in his state of isolation, was temporarily available to it. This would mean that

Ginsberg was really worshipping himself, just as he had been sexually pleasuring himself only a few seconds before.

So Ginsberg's spiritual moment was essentially self-centred. But what kind of self was being worshipped here? It is not a self defined by doing or by thinking. It simply *is*. In Gingsberg's spirituality, this – whatever this is – is it; and the sublime consists of the recognition that this is it. Thus having put the self on a pedestal, Ginsberg's spirituality proceeds to dismantle the active self, in that its definitive expression is a moment which is bereft of any self-defining activity.

Isolation and absence of activity seem to be the most prominent characteristics of Ginsberg's spiritual affirmation. But affirming an existing self of passivity and isolation is ultimately to deny the potential self of engagement and activity. Thus Ginsberg's spiritual moment is the negation of the poet Browning's insistence on aspiration and ambition, to wit, that 'Man's reach must exceed his grasp, else what is Heaven for?'

None of which would matter very much if it was confined to the personal history of one Allen Ginsberg. The trouble is, however, that thousands and even millions of young people have experienced very similar moments in the half-century since Ginsberg thought he had found God. Indeed, throughout this period the Ginsberg experience, along with that of Huxley, has been something of a model, and likewise the negation of ambition has turned out to be one of the strongest elements in contemporary spirituality.

Beautiful losers

By their very name the Beats announced their renunciation of ambition – a renunciation which they imbued with a spiritual quality. A few months after Ginsberg's revelation, Kerouac spoke to John Clellon Homes, author of the first Beat novel, *Go*, about the meaning of Beat. Kerouac explained it as an inward-looking expression of weariness: 'It's a sort of furtiveness ... an inner knowledge there's no use flaunting on that level, the level of the "public" ... and a weariness with all the forms, all the conventions of the world ... so I guess you might say we are a beat generation.'[5]

'Furtiveness' and 'weariness': these are words that correspond to the isolation and passivity of Ginsberg's mystical experience. Indeed Kerouac, like Ginsberg, went on to canonize these characteristics, so as to make Beat 'beatific' as well as 'beaten'. Initially impressed with petty criminal Herbert Huncke's usage of 'beat' to mean tired and beaten, Kerouac added a second, religious meaning. As described by his biographer Ann Charters, Kerouac was 'thinking about how down and out he felt' when he 'suddenly realized that beat had another meaning, a religious interpretation. Beat meant beatitude or beatific.'[6]

From then on, 'beat' contained a double meaning: beaten and beatific. Moreover, in the one term the two words were conjoined, so that to be beaten was also to be beatific. As described by another Kerouac biographer, Gerald Nicosia, 'in the symbol of beat Jack realised he had the perfect mixture of blues and "mystic signification"'.[7] Likewise Nicosia suggests that Ginsberg's spirituality was a consequence of his 'having been to the ends of the earth and accepted every humilation'; hence he 'was ready for something really new'.[8]

Kerouac's 'perfect mixture' of beaten and beatific was predicated on an image of the Beat as an essentially inactive individual, as 'the man who wandered the stars and could only look up at them, wishing he could fly'.[9] It would never occur to the Beat to do what the Wright Brothers did; indeed, if the world had always been populated by Beats, the aeroplane would never have been invented. Perhaps for the first time since the end of the Middle Ages and the beginning of the Renaissance, a notion of individuality was emerging among the Beats in which human activity does not figure, as it did, for example, in Browning's memorable line, as the mediation between heaven and earth.

In an outlook such as this in which there was no available means to make humanity's dreams into reality, the world itself took on a dreamlike, unreal quality: 'the dreamlike nature of reality, the reality of dreams', as Kerouac described it.[10] But for the Beats this was no bad thing. For them the point was neither to understand the world nor to change it. They thought of change, if at all, as an objectified process which comes about organically. For them the deepest insight was the realization that the world is not subject to human comprehension or appropriation. Neither doers nor thinkers, their mission was merely to be, and their only orientation to the world was to ride through it with an awed expression, as worn by Kerouac's crew in *On the Road*, or subsequently by Ken Kesey's Merrie Pranksters.

Theirs was a notion of self as receptor, not actor – a notion which necessarily eternalized and deified what is, and demonized the human spirit for bringing about change, namely ambition, which the Beats redefined as greed and 'Moloch'. Under the terms of such a passive outlook, 'this is it' became an eternal truth and a self-fulfilling prophecy. For if humanity is no longer the active agent of its own future, then, truly, this is as far as it goes.

Submission

There was a third element in Beat spirituality which is even more degraded. Nicosia has it that the poet Gary Snyder added another connotation to the term *beat*, namely 'the prospect of being beaten by the Zen master's stick'.[11] Along similar lines Charters explains that Kerouac used his writing as a kind of confessional, and that 'he never stopped thinking like a penitent': 'Kerouac often said his prose method stemmed from his background as a Catholic, confessing his sins to the priest as a boy every week, clearing himself of guilt by a full account of what he had done.'[12]

It might be couched in terms of Zen Buddhism, Catholicism, Judaism or Hinduism, or in an eclectic mixture drawn from every religion under the sun. But however it was expressed, submission was a constantly recurring element in Beat spirituality: the submission of the novice to the guru, the submission of the sheep to the shepherd. Its corollary was the abdication of individual autonomy, in that the individual who submits to the word of God, expressed through priest or guru, is necessarily giving up the final say in his or her own activity.

Twenty years later the Beatles went through a similar process of self-renunciation when they sat at the feet of the Mahareshi. They may have been more famous than Jesus Christ, and they may have rattled the jewellery of the British establishment. But their rebellion took the form of finding a new deity to subordinate themselves to. The fact that they concocted their own idea of God does not alter the essentially submissive element in their spiritual journey.

Among the Beats and those that followed them the act of giving up autonomy was experienced as a form of release or a state of grace, in that it provided an escape from the soul-destroying effects of the 'rat race' and the pressure to imitate the already discredited notions of individuality which the British poet Michael Horovitz later vilified as the '007 lifestyle/TV way of life'.[13] The new spirituality promised release from alienation and union with the whole of creation. None the less it was itself a form of alienation from the progressive idea of the active, history-making subject.

Divorcing humanity from its own activity, as the Beats and others have sought to do, necessarily means alienating oneself from the idea of humanity as the subject of history. Since, however, the subject in history, whether in the form of the bourgeois project or the working-class revolution, had patently failed to maintain its progressive impetus, alienating oneself from subjectivity took on the appearance of an act of liberation. It is no coincidence, therefore, that the turn to spirituality, often in the form of a return to 'the wisdom of older cultures', occurred at a time when, in the words of one former editor of the underground paper *IT*, 'Western society had plainly failed, Western values were transparently corrupt, and Western thought was in receivership'.[14]

Communal degradation

As well as alienating themselves from redundant notions of society, the Beats also engendered a sense of holy communion among themselves. The founding moment of the Beat communion in San Francisco came when someone passed round a bottle – a chalice that was both sacred and profane – among the audience at the poetry reading where Ginsberg recited *Howl* for the first time. But what was Ginsberg's audience being invited to commune with if not the communal acceptance of a diminished role in the world? The sense of togetherness in Beat arose from a shared willingness to alienate the self from subjectivity. Concomitant with self-imposed separation from history, to share in the holy togetherness of Beat meant participation in the negation and degradation of the active individual.

The simultaneous elevation and degradation of self, submission and the abdication of autonomy, and communion in self-alienation – these are the themes which recur throughout fifty years of spiritual meandering since Ginsberg kissed God.

DIY spirituality

In 'The Return of the Sacred', a recently published analysis of New Age attitudes, the Marxist critic Lynn Revell approached contemporary spirituality as an expression of individuation:

> *The assumption that the individual is God is a recurring theme throughout New Age thinking ... it is not involvement or engagement with society that enriches the self, but the championing of the self above society that the new sacred embraces.*[15]

Revell went on to contrast the inwardness and complacency of the

new spirituality with the outgoing virtues associated with Protestant-
ism, which when codified in the work ethic had the effect of elevating
activity into a sacred duty. Noting that 'there is no process of
developing new understanding and new knowledge – instead there is
the elevation and celebration of what already exists', Revell observed
that in modern mysticism 'what distinguishes the New Age sacred is
not merely the emphasis on the self, but the rejection of virtues and
perfection outside of the self as an illusion'.[16]

This is the world of DIY religion, where beliefs are not transferable
from one person to another; rather they are concocted at the
convenience of the believer, and they function not in the traditional
role of religion as an aspirational framework for society as a whole, but
as disposable accessories in the creation of a highly individuated
identity.

In this context there is no requirement for one's beliefs to be true, in
the sense of appertaining to anyone else. On the contrary, as *Times*
journalist Nigella Lawson explained in a column on astrology and
holistic medicine, non-verifiable beliefs are regarded as somehow
superior:

> *Anyone who believes in star signs (or iridology or homeopathy or whatever)*
> *believes that to have their particular belief denounced as unscientific is to its*
> *and their credit.*
>
> *That's how stupid it all is: if it cannot be proved it must, in the higher*
> *scheme of things, be right, is the form of unreasoning followed.*[17]

Such is the individuation of belief today that believers no longer feel
able to say that their religion is the true faith, only that 'it is true for me'.
This is the diminished sense of belief which Bob Dylan expressed when
he announced, 'you gotta read the *I Ching* . . . it's something to believe
in. Of course I don't believe in anything.'[18] In other words it is no
longer possible for society as a whole to believe in anything, least of all
itself; on the other hand we all need our own spiritual crutch to help
prop up our alienated individuality.

Stale spirits
Back in the late 1960s Theodore Roszak noticed the hippies' habit of
sampling Zen Buddhism and rejigging it to fit their own individual
purposes. He wrote of Zen's

unusual vulnerability to what I have called 'adolescentization'. That is to say Zen, vulgarized, dovetails remarkably with a number of adolescent traits. Its commitment to a wise silence . . . can easily ally with the moody inarticulateness of youth . . . Similarly, Zen's commitment to paradox and randomness could be conveniently identified with the intellectual confusion of healthily restless but still unformed minds.[19]

The mentality which Roszak could be forgiven for thinking was fresh and 'healthily restless' in the 1960s now looks stale and morbid in the 1990s. In the intervening period pop culture has been remade in the image of the counterculture, and disbelief in anything but the inner visions of the individual self has become a fixture. Those disposed to Zen have, as Roszak indicated, spiritualized their own day-to-day concerns. In effect they have taken religious beliefs which were originally derived from nature's domination over a primitive society and re-worked them into a grandiose expression of the sense of impotence experienced today by individuals who find themselves without the tools with which to appropriate reality. In place of a system of ideas we have the idealization of empty-headedness expressed in the form of contemporary spirituality.

The rise of Zen and its corollary, the demise of the philosophical tradition which originated in the Enlightenment, were both welcomed by the drama critic Martin Esslin. He explained the 'recent rise of interest in Zen in Western countries' as the correlate of 'the same tendencies that explain the success of the Theatre of the Absurd – a preoccupation with ultimate realities and a recognition that they are not approachable through conceptual thought'.[20]

For Esslin the recognition of the limits of conceptual thought was 'a profound mystical experience'.[21] Noting that 'Zen-Buddhism bases itself on the rejection of conceptual thinking itself', he observed that

in facing man's inability ever to comprehend the meaning of the universe, the great mystics experienced a sense of exhilaration and liberation. This exhilaration also springs from the recognition that the language of cognitive thought and logic cannot do justice to the ultimate nature of reality.[22]

Esslin went on to say that:

The dethronement of language and logic forms part of an essentially mystical attitude towards the basis of reality as being too complex and at the

*same time too unified to be validly expressed by the analytical means of
ordered syntax and conceptual thought . . .*

*The mystical experience of the absolute otherness and ineffability of
ultimate reality is the religious, poetic counterpart to the rational recognition
of the limitation of man's senses and intellect.*[23]

Esslin noted that the Theatre of the Absurd had renounced 'arguing
about the absurdity of the human condition, it merely *presents* it in
being'.[24] The same goes for modern mysticism. The point is for the
individual neither to attempt to overcome nor even to try to
comprehend the senselessness of society as it is currently constituted,
but merely to represent it and to project it onto a fictitious relationship
between the impotent individual and the ineffable deity.

Inactivity

Themes similar to Esslin's were explored in more detail by Alan Watts
in *The Way of Zen*, a book which was subsequently carried by thousands
of long-haired 'rucksack revolutionaries' on the 'hippy trail' to
Afghanistan.

Watts reported that 'Taoism, Confucianism and Zen are expressions
of a mentality which feels completely at home in this universe'.[25] But
for humanity to feel at home with what it is, as recommended by Watts
and countless others, it must alienate itself from the aspiration to
something better. This too Watts felt at home with, when he declared
that 'there is no purpose because there is no victory to be won, no end
to be attained'.[26] The Zen experience, he added, 'does not imply any
specific course of action, since it has no purpose, no motivation'.[27]

Moreover the novice must be trained out of the habit of pursuing
self-interest through contestation, because, as Watts described it,
'conflict is always comparatively superficial'.[28] The novice must also
be taught to suspend his or her capacity for rational choice:

*Much of Zen training consists in confronting the student with dilemmas
which he is expected to handle without stopping to deliberate and 'choose'.
The response . . . must follow with the immediacy of sound issuing from the
hands when they are clapped.*[29]

In this kind of 'training', there is no right or wrong answer. Negation of
discernment is the only response which is required. In this respect the
individual is called upon to deny his or her self-interested individuality.

Arrested Development

In a study of D. H. Lawrence published in the early 1960s the literary critic Graham Hough referred to this denial as 'the mystic's joy in the extinction of his personality'.[30]

Inactive activity

Modern mysticism is at once the elevation of the individual and the renunciation of rational self-interest on the part of the individual. To find themselves, individuals must throw off the capacity to re-make themselves. Hence, in their relationship with God they are really communing with the amplification of their own sense of impotence. Jeff Nuttall summed up this processes as 'the exemplary self-destruction of the young, many of whom now espouse that limp concern for pure spirit that is as life destroying as square materialism'.[31] The irony is that much of the radical and supposedly uplifting activism associated with the 1960s was really an attempt on the part of initiates to bring everyone else down to what Nuttall dubbed their 'life-destroying' level.

In *The Campus War*, a contemporary account of student unrest, John Searle observed a 'religious quality' in student activism which 'was further brought home to me in the liturgical style and ritualistic character of the great demonstrations'.[32] Searle concluded that campus radicalism was tantamount to a 'ritual exorcism of the devil of the Establishment'. And what was it about the establishment that seemed so devilish to the young radical of the 1960s? The draft and the anti-drugs laws spring most readily to mind. But underneath those particular issues was a more general sense in which the counterculturalists objected to the establishment's continuing belief in its own power and authority. Not only were they protesting at the way in which power was being exercised, they were also against its very existence. In this respect they were for the renunciation of power and the celebration of impotence.

When Ginsberg encouraged protesters to chant 'om' at the police, as he did in Chicago during violent demonstrations outside the 1968 National Democratic Convention, or when he attempted to levitate the Pentagon by means of meditation, in performing new rituals he was indicting the establishment for the hubris of believing in its own secular authority. Governments, as far as the new mystics were concerned, spent too much time trying to be in control, and as a consequence paid insufficient attention to the mysteries which, as Church of England clerics would have it, 'passeth all understanding'. The governing principle of the new mystics was the inadequacy of humanity in the face of the ineffable, and they sought to impose their newly discovered sense of inadequacy on everyone else. In this respect they were far more backward – and may even turn out to have been more destructive of the human spirit – than the nuclear scientists who invented the atom bomb.

Searle also commented on the religious inactivity of the counter-culture's radicals. 'The saddest feature of the hippie existence', he wrote, 'is its uncreative quality ... conscientiously doing nothing day after day.'[33] Theirs was an outlook which viewed all activity as deeply suspicious, except that which was loose and unorganized enough to be described as play. 'Hurry, and all that it entails, is fatal', declared Alan Watts, who aspired to a life of 'sitting quietly, doing nothing'.[34] To the new generation of mystics, of whom Watts was among the most prominent, the progressive aspiration to produce more, faster, better, was a kind of sacrilege.

In the 1990s, the renunciation of human activity is most clearly expressed in the work of Terence McKenna, who has gone so far as to propose 'that we should adopt the plant as the organisational model for the twenty-first century'.[35] McKenna insists that this will bring about a more harmonious existence, on the basis that 'the closer a human group is to the gnosis of the vegetable mind – the Gaian collectivity of organic life – the closer the connection ... to the partnership style of social organisation'.[36]

As might be expected from an anti-humanist, McKenna is also anti-democratic. On the question of how best to introduce the population to psychedelic drugs, he expressed a preference for the patrician approach of Aldous Huxley rather than the populism associated with Dr Timothy Leary. 'I think Huxley's approach was much more intelligent, not to try to reach the largest number of people, but to try to reach the most important and influential people ... especially the psychotherapists.'[37]

McKenna went on to describe psychedelic drugs as 'the greatest boon to psychotherapy since dreaming', in that 'psychedelics are to psychology what telescopes in the sixteenth century were to astronomy'. From this it can be seen that McKenna has adopted a quasi-medical model for the spread of allegedly life-enhancing psychedelics, in which it is not for the rational individual to decide whether to experiment with the suspension of his or her own rationality. Such experiments would presumably take place in a therapeutic environment, with a therapist or guru guiding the quasi-patient through the psychedelic experience. In McKenna's prognosis, therefore, the subject is invited to surrender not only to the drug but also to the guru or therapist. On both counts the mystical experience of the 1990s turns out to be the antithesis of personal autonomy.

Manipulation

McKenna's elevation of the guru–therapist over the non-autonomous individual is in keeping with the traditions of the counterculture and its mystical wing. For all the talk of oneness with God, the counterculture has introduced a host of new professionals with the quasi-priestly role of standing between humanity and God, and advising believers on how to realize their individual spirituality. Apart from gurus and therapists, the new priest-professionals include Tarot-card readers, macrobiotic food advisers, faith healers and practitioners of holistic medicine. Many counsellors, especially those from organizations such as Susie Orbach's Antidote, which claims to teach 'emotional literacy', seem also to fit into this category. Even Timothy Leary, who advocated taking LSD to the people, emphasized that converts should not be allowed to take the hallucinogenic sacrament into their own hands; rather they should sit at the feet of 'guides' who would shepherd them through the psychedelic experience. Leary prophesied 'a new profession of psychedelic guides' who would 'supervise these experiences', with an eye towards 'crowd control'.[38]

The relationship between modern gurus and their disciples is not unlike that of social workers and their clients. (How appropriate, then, that the first guru of the counterculture, Allen Ginsberg, should have been described by Leary as its 'social worker'.[39] In both instances the believer or client is expected to submit his or her experiences for verification by the guru or social worker. By the same token, unverified experience is spiritually invalid, and autonomy, by implication, is superseded by professional manipulation. All of which brings to mind the contentious point made by the maverick British essayist Paul Barker, namely that 'the Underground and Richard Nixon' (Tricky Dicky of Watergate fame) were united in their tendency towards 'manipulation'.[40]

The readiness of 1960s counterculturists to surrender to professional manipulation is now writ extra-large in the 1990s with the advent of the 'life coach', a growing Stateside phenomenon described in *The Times* in the following terms:

Part mentor, therapist, business consultant, best friend and nagging mum, a life coach advises on strategies for dealing not only with your boss but your parents, siblings, your spouse. They want to know how well you're eating. If you're exercising. Whether you're flossing every day. If you're up-to-date with bills. If your bed is comfortable – even if your bed is made.[41]

Surrender

In the canon of pop culture the surrender of personal autonomy continues to be regarded as a spiritually uplifting exercise. During the course of an interview with pop critic Simon Reynolds, Kurt Ralske of the avant-garde band Ultra Vivid Scene associated his music with surrender to God. 'An act of surrender', Ralske said, 'can be as liberating as an act of gaining control. The idea of surrender is connected to mysticism, giving in to a visitation of God's will.'[42] Reynolds suggested that other bands of the late 1980s were equally prone to 'give up the ghost'. He cited 'My Bloody Valentine on "I Believe"' as just one example.[43]

These bands may be the most explicit in their renunciation of autonomy, but it should be noted that the desire to 'surrender to the rhythm' is a constant feature of the pop music experience. In its quasi-religious effects pop music has always been the soundtrack to the suspension of rationality. 'You drowned in noise', is how Nik Cohn described the experience of a Rolling Stones concert in his account of the emerging pop sensibility, *Awopbopaloobopawopbamboom!*[44] This is an experience totally unlike the epic theatre of Bertolt Brecht, which depends on the audience applying its intelligence to the play. It is also contrary to the emotive force of a composer like Beethoven, whose music works to confirm rather than undermine the rational individual.

Various commentators have compared pop and 'progressive rock' to a mystical communion. Radical critic Paul Goodman called it 'the sacramental use of noise'.[45] Writing in the *San Francisco Oracle* in the year of the 'summer of love', Chester Anderson described 'rock' as 'a tribal phenomenon' which 'engages the entire sensorium' and 'constitutes what may be called a twentieth century magic'.[46] In the mid-1970s William Burroughs described 'rock' as 'one attempt to break out of this dead and soulless universe and reassert the universe of magic'.[47] In the 1980s Kate Dierson of the B-52s maintained that 'pop music provides … the new spirituality'.[48] In the 1990s dance culture has been imbued with a significance both mystical and communal.

Arrested Development

Ravers, like their hippie predecessors, come together in ritual fashion to divest themselves of their human intelligence. Arriving at a trance-like state – a form of mindlessness – is regarded as a spiritual sacrament which is shared among communicants in a resolutely non-verbal culture in which the term 'mindless' is not necessarily regarded as an insult.

Representing inadequacy

The new mysticism is both a response to a sense of inadequacy on the part of the human subject and a representation which thereby confirms that sense of inadequacy. It begins with a profound cynicism about humanity and goes on to canonize that cynicism in the naive re-affirmation of a personalized God.

Thus Douglas Coupland's first book, *Generation X*, described a cohort of young people who presumed that the only active sense of self they could muster would be woefully inadequate compared to the drag-effect of living in today's complex society; hence their cynical preference for inactivity. Coupland's second book was a collection of short stories entitled *Life after God*, in which the protagonist re-invented his own God in compensation for feelings of personal and social inadequacy. The cynicism of the first book may seem out of kilter with the naivety of the second. In fact they are united in the negation of history-making humanity.

In such circumstances even the affirmation of God has essentially negative consequences. In the final story of *Life after God* Coupland confessed 'my secret is that I need God – that I am sick and can no longer make it alone'.[49] But the construction of a privatized notion of the deity can only confirm the sense of being alone, and belief in a personalized God is itself an expression of lack of faith in humanity, thus underlining the feeling that we 'can no longer make it'.

Coupland's sentiments are by no means confined to the fashionable literati; they are as mainstream as the most popular television soap opera. Patsy Palmer (Bianca in *EastEnders*) told *The Face*, 'I've really got into reading books on spirituality. I feel that I've got a hole inside me, you know?'[50] The same cloud of incense has also settled over the White House since Bill Clinton took up residence there. Investigative journalist Bob Woodward has reported that 'while Clinton discussed with Al Gore how he could transcend himself, Hillary wrote a bestseller with the help of her gurus'.[51]

Dangerous

More than half a century ago, Karl Mannheim warned against official rigidity towards mysticism:

> As regards the modern movements of mass ecstasy, an entirely negative policy towards them would be futile ... the problem ... is rather to find new forms of spiritualisation than completely to deny the potentialities inherent in the new forms of group existence.[52]

The starchiness which Mannheim warned against was still a recognizable element in government policy as recently as the anachronistic Criminal Justice Act (1994), which outlawed the unlicensed amplification of music with 'repetitive beats'. But it looks as if the new power generation of politicians has finally taken heed of Mannheim's advice. Among the new intake into the corridors of power there are many who subscribe to mystical notions and personalized deities. Like the rest of us, they turn towards the divine creatures of their own fertile imagination in the hope of transcending the limits of today's barren society. Instead they arrive at a spirituality which is personalized but also self-alienated – a fantastic projection, indeed, of a society which is both individuated and stagnating. Moreover, as individuals who jointly constitute the new political elite, in their hands the negative trends within the new spirituality will have an even more forceful and destructive effect on the true spirit of human aspiration.

Journalist and television presenter Catherine Bennett has issued a pertinent warning about where these trends can take us, especially when they are taken up by those in positions of power and influence. If we abandon 'rational inquiry' in favour of the mystical, noted Bennett, 'we are at the mercy of dogma, unfounded scares, and anyone with a vested interest in ignorance'. She then concluded her piece with a reference to one of this century's most influential and pernicious mystics: ' "We stand at the end of the age of reason. A new era of the magical explanation of the world is rising." The speaker? Adolf Hitler.'[53]

Notes

1. Barry Miles, *Ginsberg: A Biography* (New York: Simon and Schuster, 1989), p. 104.
2. *Ibid.*, pp. 99–101.

3. *Ibid.*, p. 102.

4. *Ibid.*, p. 103.

5. Conversation between Kerouac and John Clellon Homes in November 1948, as reported in 'This Beat generation', *New York Times*, 1952, and quoted by Ann Charters in *Kerouac: A Biography* (London: Picador/Pan, 1978), p. 162.

6. Charters, *op. cit.*, p. 189.

7. Gerald Nicosia, *Memory Babe: A Critical Biography of Jack Kerouac* (London: Penguin, 1986), p. 273.

8. *Ibid.*, p. 209.

9. *Ibid.*, p. 273.

10. *Ibid.*, p. 448.

11. *Ibid.*, p. 524.

12. Charters, *op. cit.*, p. 336.

13. Michael Horovitz (ed.), *Children of Albion: Poetry of the Underground in Britain* (Harmondsworth: Penguin, 1969), Afterwords, p. 316.

14. Roger Hutchinson, *High Sixties* (Edinburgh: Mainstream, 1992), p. 115.

15. Lynn Revell, 'The return of the sacred', in Suke Wolton (ed.), *Marxism, Mysticism and Modern Theory* (London: Macmillan, 1996), p. 127.

16. *Ibid.*

17. Nigella Lawson, *The Times*, 13 November 1996.

18. Bob Dylan, quoted in Anthony Scaduto, *Bob Dylan* (London: Abacus, 1972), pp. 220–1.

19. Theodore Roszak, *Making of the Counter Culture* (London: Faber & Faber, 1971), p. 134.

20. Martin Esslin, *The Theatre of the Absurd* (Harmondsworth: Penguin, 1971), p. 417.

21. *Ibid.*, p. 416.

22. *Ibid.*, p. 417.

23. *Ibid.*, pp. 417–18.

24. *Ibid.*, p. 25.

25. Alan W. Watts, *The Way of Zen* (1957) (Harmondsworth: Penguin, 1962), p. 194.

26. *Ibid.*, p. 194.

27. *Ibid.*, p. 168.

28. *Ibid.*, p. 194.

29. *Ibid.*, p. 168.

30. Graham Hough, *The Dark Sun: A Study of D. H. Lawrence* (Harmondsworth: Pelican, 1961), p. 296.

31. Jeff Nuttall, *Bomb Culture* (London: Paladin, 1970), p. 241.

32. John R. Searle, *The Campus War* (Harmondsworth: Penguin, 1972), p. 61.

33. *Ibid.*, p. 52.

34. Watts, *op. cit.*, p. 154.

35. Terence McKenna, *The Archaic Revival* (San Francisco: Harper, 1991), p. 218.

36. *Ibid.*, p. 219.

37. *Ibid.*, p. 9.

38. Dr Timothy Leary, quoted by Jay Stevens, in *Storming Heaven: LSD and the American Dream* (London: Paladin, 1989), pp. 264–5.

39. Leary, quoted in the video *The Life and Times of Allen Ginsberg* (director: Jerry Aronson), Visionary Communications Ltd.

40. Paul Barker, *Arts in Society* (London: Fontana, 1977), p. 13.

41. Tessa Souter, 'A word in your ear', *The Times* Weekend, 22 March 1997, p. 1.

42. Simon Reynolds, *Blissed Out* (London: Serpent's Tail, 1994), p. 146.

43. *Ibid.*

44. Nik Cohn, *Awopbopaloobopawopbamboom!* (London: Paladin, 1970).

45. Goodman, cited by Bernice Martin, in *A Sociology of Contemporary Cultural Change* (Oxford: Blackwell, 1981), p. 160.

46. Chester Anderson, in the *San Francisco Chronicle*, 6 November 1967.

47. Burroughs, quoted in Joe Kohut and John J. Kohut (eds), *Rock Talk: The Great Rock'n'roll Quote Book* (London: Faber & Faber, 1994).

48. Dierson, quoted in *ibid.*

49. Douglas Coupland, *Life after God*, (New York: Simon and Schuster, 1994), p. 359.

50. Patsy Palmer, interviewed in *The Face*, January 1997, p. 88.

51. Bob Woodward, in *Sunday Times*, 7 July 1996.

52. Karl Mannheim, *Diagnosis of Our Time* (London: Kegan Paul, 1943).

53. Catherine Bennett, 'Would you believe it?', *Guardian*, 14 June 1996.

CHAPTER 7

Irony

**The paradox between aspiration and fatalism finds its
contemporary expression in the ironic condition.**

In London in the 1990s a number of upmarket clubs sprang up which
specialized in 'easy listening'. The DJs at these clubs were enthusiastic
revivalists who played smooth 'lounge' music, often involving strings as
well as a jazz line-up, which first came to prominence in the 1950s and
early 1960s when it was aimed primarily at an American market of
college students and young professionals.

In its original incarnation 'easy listening' was the last musical genre to
be invented for young people before the cult of the child kicked in, and
many of those who bought it did so because they wanted to appear
older and more sophisticated than they really were. Today, as we have
seen, the reverse is the case, with many record-buyers acting much
younger than they really are. At first sight the 'easy listening' revival,
and the re-emergence of 1950s-style cocktail bars in which to hear such
music, appear to buck this trend. One is tempted to assume that such
developments are the expression of a desire for sophistication and
adulthood. But on closer inspection it becomes clear that these trends
are part of a wider process which is pushing adulthood even further off
limits.

The fact is that young people at 'easy listening' clubs are playing at
being adults. They are dressing the part, and acting it out, just as they
did when as children they played games like doctors and nurses. On the
one hand, the fact that they have chosen this game suggests that they
really would like to be adult; on the other hand, they are also sending
up adulthood, and confirming the idea that it cannot be taken seriously.

The overall effect is rather like that when girls under eleven used to walk down the street in their mothers' high-heeled shoes. Yes, it showed that they wanted to be grown-up like their mums; but to any observer the sight of their small feet in such big shoes also emphasized how far they still had to go.

In the revival of 'easy listening', being an adult has been ironized. The cult of 'easy listening' involves dressing up as an adult and simultaneously looking at oneself in that costume and enjoying the incongruity of it. What's being expressed is at once the desirability and undesirability of adulthood, and the impossibility of realizing it in the first place. 'Easy listening' is a paradoxical display, which builds up an image of adulthood only to knock it down. The paradoxical character of this performance is what makes it ironic.

'Irony' said the eighteenth-century German philosopher Friedrich Schlegel, 'is the form of paradox ... Paradox is the condition *sine qua non* of irony.'[1] But what kind of paradox? Or, what is the particular paradox which underlies the contemporary ironization of adulthood? The Marxist critic Georg Lukács may have shed some light on the question when he suggested that 'irony gives form to the malicious satisfaction of God the creator at the failure of man's weak rebellions'.[2] Combining Schlegel's insights with Lukács's observations, one might suggest that contemporary irony is the form of the paradox between human rebellion and God's supremacy; or, to secularize these metaphors, the paradox expressed here is between the historical development of humanity and the apparently insuperable obstacles to further social development.

Moreover, the modern idea of an adult connotes an individual who is mature enough to play a full part in society and its continuing development. But what happens to adulthood when there is no clear path of social development for the would-be adult to participate in? Perhaps when there is no movement towards social development with which to engage, there can be no adulthood either. This is the paradoxical situation in which adulthood is necessarily ironized today.

The absurd

For the artist and critic Jeff Nuttall, writing at the end of the 1960s about the counterculture of the previous decade and a half, it was the very process of social development which had brought humanity to a point where further development was no longer possible or even conceivable. In particular the development of the atom bomb had in turn resulted in the development of 'bomb culture', predicated on the assumption that death is permanently hanging over us and progress is therefore at an end. In such a context, all we can do is act out its inherent absurdity, thus: 'The future is a void ... [which] reveals the fallacy of logic and rationality. The void is infinite and thus absurd. Consequently the only human activities which can be of any use ... are absurd practices.'[3]

At the end of the 1960s Nuttall was reviewing a fully fledged sensibility which had developed in the shadow of such sentiments. This orientation, already prevalent among a section of young people by the time Nuttall wrote *Bomb Culture*, had been prefigured by writers such as Joseph Heller and, a quarter of a century earlier, Albert Camus.

Heller published *Catch-22* in 1961. It is a novel of the Second World War which depicts officers and men at the mercy of the absurd machinations of the military establishment, most notably the epony-mous Catch-22:

> *There was only one catch and that was Catch-22, which specified that concern for one's own safety in the face of dangers that were real and immediate was the process of a rational mind. Orr was crazy and could be grounded. All he had to do was ask; and as soon as he did, he would no longer be crazy and would have to fly more missions. Orr would be crazy to fly more missions and sane if he didn't, but if he was sane he had to fly them. If he flew them he was crazy and didn't have to; but if he didn't want to he was sane and had to. Yossarian was moved very deeply by the absolute simplicity of this clause of Catch-22, and let out a respectful whistle.*[4]

In *Catch-22* there is no escape from the paradox that to report one's own insanity is itself the action of a sane man. By the same token, there is no let-out from war, and, by implication, the destruction of our humanity. All the protagonist can do to reassert his humanity is to appreciate the absurdity of the situation. (In this instance by means of 'a respectful whistle'; the standard response, now something of a cliché, would be what is generally described as 'an ironic shrug of the shoulders'.)

During the Second World War, while Paris was under Nazi occupation, Albert Camus had begun to explore a new 'feeling of absurdity'. He linked the advent of the absurd to the end of an established way of life, which had always been explicable in terms of rationality:

> *A world that can be explained by reasoning, however faulty, is a familiar world. But in a universe that is suddenly deprived of illusions and of light, man feels a stranger . . . deprived of memories of a lost homeland as much as he lacks the hope of a promised land to come. This divorce between man and his life, truly constitutes the feeling of Absurdity.*[5]

The sense which Camus articulated of being expelled from the world of 'reasoning, however faulty' was in his case probably prompted by the fall of France and the subsequent Nazi occupation. But when the Nazis in turn were expelled from Paris, the world of 'reasoning' was never fully restored, not least because, with their emphasis on race and nation, all traditional ideologies were tainted by their indelible connection with fascism.

Expelled from the realm of ideological certainty, Camus and the generations that came after him have experienced considerable difficulty in identifying a past ('a lost homeland') or a future ('a promised land to come') for themselves. Like Vladimir and Estragon in Samuel Beckett's *Waiting for Godot* (1955), we have been transfixed by a society that is simultaneously humanizing, dehumanizing and, since the beginning of the end of ideology, inexplicable. Hence we have tended to empathize with the sense of estrangement and ironic absurdity which Camus was among the first to express.

The ironic condition

In response to a stream of apparently inexplicable paradoxes which have surfaced during the past half century we have confirmed our inability to explain them, still less resolve them, by designating them 'absurd'; and we have responded in kind with an 'ironic shrug of the shoulders', or the equivalent thereof. Now that this response has become generalized throughout society, we are suffering from a condition in which every experience tends to be viewed ironically. Welcome to the ironic condition, in which rape, murder and dismemberment are regularly ironized, as in the gore-fest novel *American Psycho* by Bret Easton Ellis.[6] But in amongst all the ironic send-ups it is our own subjectivity which comes in for the ultimate put-down.

Arrested Development

Snapshot: 'Mong-ing'

On one occasion, instead of walking in front of a lorry which was waiting to turn out of a side-road, I crawled underneath it, in deliberate disregard of the fact that it could have moved off at any moment – with me underneath the back wheels. When I emerged, thankfully unscathed, I told my companion that 'it wouldn't make any difference whether I live or die'. It was all part of what we used to call 'mong-ing', as in *mongoloid*: speech and behaviour which was a self-conscious dumbing down of our capabilities; and all because there was nothing we felt we could apply our intelligence to.

Sometimes the punning and joking and self-deprecation would induce a feeling akin to nausea. How I wished I could find something to be serious about. Then I would be able to take myself seriously also. I remember walking along the road to school and saying to a close friend, 'What our generation needs is a Spanish Civil War.' Instead we felt we were condemned to live through the prism, and in the prison, of the ironic condition.

The Mods were the first popular youth cult to emphasize the absurd. Not to be confused with the revivalist notion of Mod and its fixation with scooters and parkas, original Mods recall that they 'were always intellectual ... one did read Camus'.[7] One of the earliest Mods defined the scene as 'existentialism and rhythm and blues. Amphetamines, John Lee Hooker and Sartre'.[8] Pete Shertser, founder-member of an early Mod gang called The Firm. reckoned there was a surrealist element to their vandalism, although Dada might be a more accurate point of comparison. Remembering his days as a Modernist vandal, Shertser said: 'We used to enjoy a bit of wrecking ... We'd cement a Hoover to a bath. Very Magritte influenced, Man Ray, all that kind of thing.'[9] Clearly there was a trickle-down effect whereby notions of the absurd and the ironic derived from high culture came to be expressed in youth subcultures such as Mod and, latterly, in mainstream pop culture.

The Mods and their progeny, swinging London, introduced an element of camp into pop culture. Thus Nigel Waymouth, co-owner of one of the first psychedelic shops in London, Granny Takes a Trip, defined it 'in pop jargon' as 'very camp'. Waymouth went on to define 'camp' as 'kind of taking the mickey out of sex by being theatrical'.[10] In *Revolt into Style* George Melly detected a similar ambience in and around the pop scene; and in 'Notes on camp', published in 1964, the

American intellectual Susan Sontag observed that 'in the last two years popular music ... has been annexed' by camp.[11]

Swinging camp

There is more to the question of camp in pop culture than the supposedly homoerotic narcissism of the first Mods, who are alleged to have spent many boys-only evenings together, drinking whisky and coke and posing in front of a mirror. True, the origins of the mannerisms associated with camp are to be found in the homosexual *demi-monde*. What is remarkable, however, is that camp transcended its background and made its way into pop. Furthermore, it did this not in the way that gestures and mannerisms associated with homosexuals had previously entered the mainstream, i.e. as the occasionally permitted exception which thereby validated the rule of family values. In this instance camp was an essential character trait of the new model personality which emerged alongside pop culture.

In the early 1960s when he first came to prominence, the young painter David Hockney was both gay and pop. In *The Young Meteors*, the contemporary account of swinging London written by Jonathan Aitken (the recently discredited former minister in the Conservative government), Hockney was noted for 'his whimsical "camp" attitude' that 'extends even to his own appearance'.[12] That this description would have been equally applicable to any of the early Mods indicates that camp had made its way into a largely heterosexual youth culture. It also suggests that the sections of the young generation which took camp to heart must have had something in common with the older homosexuals who spawned it.

In the mid-1960s the American critic Susan Sontag was moved to write an essay on the coming of camp into mainstream culture. Noting that 'to emphasize style is to slight content', Sontag described camp as 'one way of seeing the world as an aesthetic phenomenon'. She also observed that 'the Camp sensibility is disengaged, depoliticized – or at least apolitical'. It was, she added, 'the sensibility of failed seriousness' which 'sees everything in quotation marks'.[13]

It is tempting to dismiss camp as a pseud's version of trainspotting in which players score points by spotting artefacts which contain the right/ wrong combination of good/bad taste and therefore qualify for inclusion in the ever-expanding canon of camp. But why would anyone make such a pastime the defining element of their sensibility?

Arrested Development

Sontag's identification of camp's 'failed seriousness' gives us a clue. It is surely no coincidence that this lightweight orientation to a heavily aestheticized world was developed among a highly privatized social group, namely homosexuals, that was denied access to the public realm of all things serious. Devoting one's life to spotting the camp quality in artefacts is perhaps the knee-jerk response of those whom the rest of the world has refused to take seriously. This would mean that, in decreeing certain objects absurd but also endearing, camp sensibility is an expression of self-respect on the part of those who have been judged absurd by society. 'Seeing everything in quotation marks' would serve, therefore, as both a badge of exclusivity and a protection against exclusion.

Black camp

Surprisingly, given the traditional enmity between gays and blacks, there is a strong element of camp in much of the music and literature produced by black artists. For example, when his serious novel *If He Hollers Let Him Ago* failed to penetrate the American literary scene to any great extent, Chester Himes moved to Paris and turned to crime novels, set in Harlem, in which the combination of the garish and the absurd constituted a hard-edged kind of camp.

A similar hard-edged camp had long been in evidence in blues lyrics. It was further emphasized in the self-parodying rhythm-and-blues numbers written for a roster of black recording artists by the Jewish-born songwriters Jerry Leiber and Mike Stoller. In the early 1960s it also began to figure in the new Jamaican music of bluebeat and ska. Once again a camp-like sensibility was developed by a social group – in this instance, the blacks (with back-up from two Jews) – that was systematically excluded from the serious business of mainstream society and thereby came to know the experience of 'failed seriousness'. It was this common ground which enabled the white, homosexual writer Jean Genet to write one of the most successful plays about the condition of being black, simply entitled *The Blacks*.[14]

Shrinking subjectivity

In their adoption of camp, white heterosexual Mods took on the connotation of 'failed seriousness'. While camping it up, they played down the notion of individuals as active agents. In aestheticizing the world, they wilfully made themselves into minor critics rather than actors on the stage of history. The paradox in Mod is that it originated in the fast pace of modernization during the postwar boom, while at the same time representing an objectified sense of change in which the individual's active role was limited to questions of style and what to do at the weekend. Mod bands like The Action put quotation marks around the notion of activity, while the Mods' preference for amphetamines was both a reflection of the perceived speed of social change and a recognition that movement was something to be experienced passively, in the manner of a drug-induced high, rather than something which people, acting individually or collectively, might expect to bring about themselves.

Previous generations had enjoyed a wider field of vision; they assumed that, however long it took, they themselves would make the world anew. The 1960s generation was not sure whether it would change the world or make a pop record, and in the end it fell back on the forlorn hope that making a record would be enough to change the world. This contradiction, between an expanding sense of objectified change and a diminished sense of subjectivity, is what made Mod amenable to camp, the absurd and the ironic. Mods adopted these characteristics as the representation of what they saw as the 'failed seriousness' of the society in which they lived.

Towards the end of the 1960s, the Mod scene split into two opposing camps: the trend towards the hippies, via psychedelia; and the trend towards skinheads, via Hard Mod. The latter were a reaction against the pace of change, experienced by the skins as an alien process which they subsequently identified with the influx of non-white 'aliens'. They attempted to re-establish the boundaries of what they regarded as traditional, white working-class communities; and in order to achieve this they dressed in a pantomime costume which combined elements reminiscent of working clothes such as heavy boots and braces, together with an exaggerated image of working-class respectability incorporating Sta-Pressed trousers (not like the crushed and crumpled 'velvet loons' which hippies were just getting into) and short, neat hair (not long and matted), cropped to the point of absurdity.

In short, skinheads may have been brutal but they also ironized the brutal aspects of traditional working-class life; and they put quotation marks around middle-class youth culture by appearing as its reversed-out image. Furthermore, the skins presented an absurd image of themselves which recognized and reflected their lack of clout in the wider world. Even in their aggression they were still suffering from the ironic condition.

Meanwhile the skinheads' opposite numbers, the hippies, made inactivity into a camp lifestyle. They exaggerated their own 'laid-back' laziness. Rather than risk the experience of 'failed seriousness', they avoided applying themselves seriously to the external world, although they did insist that this avoidance was itself a serious threat to a work-oriented society. But when the authorities took them at their word, and set about attacking the counterculture, the hippies turned into yippies, who attempted to use irony and absurdity as their primary weapons of subversion.

Shock to schlock

In his study of the connections between pop, rock and radicalism, Robin Deneslow observed that 'the Yippies believed in creating a street theatre of the absurd'.[15] Deneslow explained how the yippies tried to top the absurdity of officialdom with a self-conscious absurdity of their own making: 'The [Vietnam] war was absurd, they argued, and so they too should be absurd, in the wildest possible fashion.'[16] As with the re-presentation of madness by the likes of Spike Milligan, the aim seems to have been to break the vicious circle of Catch-22 by re-rendering it in such a way as to highlight its absurdity.

There is a subversive moment in such a process; and when the yippies nominated a pig for president in 1968 they caused genuine outrage. But, thirty years later, the shock value of a joke election candidate has turned to schlock – no student union hustings would be complete without one; and, with hindsight, it is questionable whether anyone ever really expected that highlighting the absurdity of the existing world would be sufficient to bring us into another one.

From the vantage point of the 1990s we can now see that the ironic take on politics in the 1960s had little to do with reaching for a new radicalism. The use of humour was more like a defence mechanism which would protect the user from the imminent failure of his own seriousness. In other words, making a joke out of political contestation was a way of taking the sting out of losing – which was assumed to be inevitable, in the face of the crushing absurdity of *Godot* or *Catch-22*.

Snapshot: Radical?

My life as a radical teenager:

Campaigning, protesting, angry, enthusiastic: six months.

Cynical, ironizing, angry, passive: six years (plus another six years in my twenties).

Exam fever: six months.

That's all, folks!

Once again, even in a period associated with radical activism, there was a widespread assumption that events were ultimately beyond our control; and irony came into play both as a reflection of apparently irresolvable contradictions and as a form of protection against a mounting sense of powerlessness.

Having crossed over into white, heterosexual Mod culture in the 1960s, in the 1970s camp came up from the underground into mainstream society. According to Nik Cohn, what would previously have been regarded as 'drag' was 'within a few years ... worn by teenagers, suburban swingers, middle-aged tourists from Idaho'.[17]

In the 1960s Carnaby Street was full-on camp, but it was one of the relatively few places in Britain where you could buy into a sensibility based wholly on paradox and self-parody. But in the 1970s advertisements promoting mainstream products took on an ironic tone, and this gradually took over from the more assertive techno-babble of the previous decade. At about the same time astute observers like Leslie Fiedler and S. J. Perelman noted 'the transformation of Surrealist gallows humour into commercial entertainment'.[18]

In many respects the early 1970s were an absurd re-presentation of the 1960s: flared trousers ballooned outwards; cuban heels became stack heels; and drum breaks grew into interminable solos. Glam rock ironized stardom; and then punk came along and ironized glam rock with the glamour of degradation. As Dick Hebdige put it, 'punk's rhetoric was steeped in irony ... an addendum designed to puncture glam rock's extravagantly ornate style'.[19] By the end of the decade the literary critic and novelist Malcolm Bradbury felt engulfed in irony:

There are bohemians on every street corner, self-parodists in every boutique, neo-artists at every discotheque ... if there is a dominant feature, it is surely an element of in built provisionality: an instinct indeed towards parody and self-parody.[20]

Arrested Development

Ironization carried on apace throughout the 1980s. The New Romantics carried camp to new extremes. In the dealing rooms of the City yuppies played out a cocaine-driven camp drama of decadent capitalism, over-dressed in shoulder pads and red braces. The decline of collectivity, with trade union membership halved since 1979, was matched by a growing preoccupation with individual strength. But this too was ironized in the cult of bodybuilding, as represented in Arnold Schwarzenegger films, where the protagonist's musculature is as overblown as his vocabulary is minimal; and the overall effect is simultaneously powerful and laughable.

In the 1990s pop culture has endlessly re-worked its own past, ironizing everything – if it was not already ironic – in the process. So in 1996 when veteran music journalist Roy Carr set about compiling a second edition of *The Hip*, his encyclopedia of cool, he was moved to complain that 'everything's turning into self-parody'.[21]

In the 1950s cool cats might have identified themselves, in their own mind's eye and to others, by virtue of their ironic detachment. Their sense of irony would have been proof of their powers of observation and evidence of a refusal to engage in any project other than their own disengagement. But this mindset can no longer serve as an identifying mark, and Stanley Cohen and Laurie Taylor have noted that it is now a common or garden feature of suburban existence: 'But when the door is shut against the night, and the two children are safely in bed, husband and wife turn to each other and laugh. They are subscribers to the new self-consciousness.'[22]

The ironic condition is now as ubiquitous as Marks & Spencer's underwear; or, as journalist Tom Junod wrote in the American edition of *GQ* magazine, 'everyone aspires to be hip and therefore no one is'.[23] Moreover, the 'failed seriousness' inherent in ironic detachment and its resistance to engagement is now compounded by a new generation's failure to live up to earlier, cool images of ironic detachment and 'failed seriousness'. In this respect the ironic condition is like a spiral which expands while subjectivity shrinks: growth in the former necessarily implies a commensurate loss of the latter.

Anti-ironists
Since the emergence of the new sensibility in the 1950s various commentators have pointed out the shortcomings of ironic detachment. In his initial exploration of the new alienated, Kenneth Keniston

noted that 'in all their wanderings', they were destined to 'remain observers but not participants – or rather, their participation consists of observation'.[24] Keniston's observation is a poignant indication of the diminution in subjectivity – from active to passive participation – which has accompanied the rise of the ironic condition.

Novelist Ralph Ellison was concerned about the self-deprecating retreatism which he observed in the newly ironic jazz of the 1940s. He regarded 'bop' as 'a word which throws up its hands in clownish self-deprecation before all the complexity of sound and rhythm and self-assertive passion which it pretends to name; a mask-word for the charged ambiguities of the new sound, hiding the serious face of art'.[25] Writing about bebop Ellison came close to Sontag's notion of 'failed seriousness' in camp. He concluded that bop was a kind of assertive self-deprecation which ultimately represented 'retreat from the wartime tensions'.[26]

In an essay on Thelonious Monk jazz critic Raymond Horricks compared the reclusive pianist and composer to Gully Jimson, the protagonist of Joyce Cary's novel *The Horse's Mouth*. Horricks quoted Cary's description of Jimson as an artist who 'makes a joke out of life because he dare not take it seriously ... he is afraid that if he does not laugh he will lose either his nerves or his temper'.[27] Here the suggestion is not of 'failed seriousness' but of seriousness withheld on the basis that, if applied, it would be bound to fail.

In *Generation X*, written on the cusp of the 1990s, some thirty years after Horricks's essay, Douglas Coupland described the application of virtually the same safety-first approach as a 'a life-style tactic', which he dubbed 'derision pre-emption', and defined as 'the refusal to go out on any sort of emotional limb, so as to avoid mockery from peers. Derision pre-emption is the main goal of knee-jerk irony.' Coupland further defined 'knee-jerk irony' as 'the tendency to make flippant ironic comments as a reflexive matter of course in everyday conversation'.[28]

A real-life but nevertheless extreme example of 'derision pre-emption' is to be found in the public life and private conversations of the late-lamented comedian Peter Cook, of whom one of his closest colleagues once said that he never spoke in his own voice but always took on the voice of one or another of his comic characters. This meant that Cook could never be held to account for anything that came out of his mouth: he could always fall back on the disclaimer that it was only the character talking. The fact that a man who is thought to have been one of the most talented of his generation seems to have devoted his whole life to the defensive 'life-style tactic' of 'knee-jerk irony' speaks volumes about the lack of confidence and aspiration among the generation which came of age (but never, it seems, to full maturity) in the early 1960s.

Snapshot: Showing off

My schoolboy band The Southside Greeks were due to play for the last time at the Sixth Form Centre. Having grown out of our previous aspiration to play 'progressive rock', we now modelled ourselves on The Faces (The Small Faces with Rod Stewart instead of Steve Marriott as lead singer), and adopted a pose which suggested that, in the words of one of their songs, having a 'real good time' was the only thing that mattered in life. Of course we knew that was not really the case, and so, we suspected, did The Faces; moreover, aged seventeen we did not even know how to have a real good time. But what else could a young man say, at a time when it seemed there was nothing else to be said?

So, the last number in our last set was to be a rendition of the old Bobby Womack rhythm and blues song 'It's All Over Now', recently re-recorded by Rod Stewart. The Stewart version featured a series of instrumental breaks which appeared at the end of the track: each member of the band had four bars in which to show off, with a rousing chorus between successive instrumentalists. We had decided to copy this arrangement, and on the night everything went as we had rehearsed it, until it came to my bass break. Instead of playing the fiddly bit that I had practised, and which some people had already commented favourably upon, when the moment for my solo arrived I took the fingers of my left hand off the fretboard and with my right had hit the four open strings at random. The result was a splurge of indistinguishable sounds. But I heard it as a deliberate anti-solo which was meant to express my contempt for the idea of 'youthful promise' in a society which, as I saw it at the time, promised nothing in the way of advance and enlightenment.

With hindsight, it looks more like an attempt to make a virtue out of my own insecurity at the thought of embarking upon life as an adult.

Apart from those who assumed an air of 'failed seriousness', and those who have used irony as protection against failure, there are those who have lived out the ironic condition by making a paradoxical success out of their failure. In *The Holy Goof*, a biography of Neal Cassady (aka Dean Moriarty in Kerouac's *On the Road*), William Plummer wrote that 'wordy failure was always Cassady's most creative element'.[29] According to the comparative religion professor at San Quentin, Cassady 'was at his most sublime in prison ... shining with earthly fire'. Both descriptions tend to confirm that one of the first role models of the counterculture lived the latter part of his life within the confines of the ironic condition.

Snapshot: Intellectual slumming

At my school there was a fashion for the brightest, most personable boys to take up with one or two individuals who were more or less social inadequates. On the part of the bright students this was meant as an ironic rejection of being groomed for success. Hanging out with the losers was also meant to indicate that everyone was valuable and important in their own way. The added irony, however, is that the juxtaposition of the young man most likely to alongside the young man least likely to had the effect of intensifying the discrepancy between them. We knew we were being ironic, but we did not appreciate that our little ironies tended to confirm the very paradox we thought we were transcending.

Self-preservation/self-destruction

All these variations in the avoidance of seriousness are derived from the contemporary contradiction between humanity's achievements and the apparent impossibility of making any further progress. The resulting paradox promotes a mood of resignation in which irony functions as the vestigial remains of subjectivity. It is the sweetener that softens the bitter taste of defeat and preserves the self from obliteration.

Discussing the work of Joseph Heller and Kurt Vonnegut, Malcolm Bradbury noted the correlation between 'comic anarchy' and 'ironic resignation': 'Heller's vision of innocence lost, of modern man denatured by the system and falling into ironic resignation, brings his work close to that of another novelist of historical pain, resigned passivity and comic anarchy, Kurt Vonnegut.'[30]

Snapshot: Ironic circles

End of year one at university. Just could not bear the thought of going through another round of exams. 'Forgot' to apply for another year in my hall of residence even though it was the best in the city. Skipped classes, retired to a distant spot in the college grounds. To read Heller's *Catch-22*, of course. All set to leave university, but then again, everywhere else I go there is going to be a Catch-22 so I guess I might as well stay here. Sat the exams. Got close to a first. Stayed for another couple of years and completed my degree (2:1). That's the funny thing about irony, it leaves you right where you started, only more so.

Perhaps the 'pain' of history, combined with our new-found inability to imagine ourselves overcoming it, is what gives rise to the anarchic comedy of ironic resignation. This hypothesis seems to be borne out in the work of William Burroughs, which is at once a scream of outrage, as Bradbury observed, and also a scream which must remain unanswered in so far as his novels contain no representation of the human subject capable of answering it, except perhaps with louder screams and more intense outrage.

It seems pertinent, therefore, that Bradbury should have described Burroughs's books as satires without control:

> *Drawing on 'junk' in two senses, of drugs and cultural rubbish . . . Burroughs has called his books satires, but this suggests a control which their form denies. They see and challenge a world of oppressive, authoritarian systems . . . and in this sense satirize a distorted, plot-ridden, science-managed age; but at the same time Burroughs has described himself as a 'cosmonaut of inner space' and his fictional world . . . coincides with his own inner fantasies. The result is a satirical grotesquerie in which there can be no stable object of indignation, only a condition of outrage . . .*
>
> *His books are post-humanist, unstable and volatile texts attempting to penetrate . . . a world . . . in which the human subject is dissolved, by an imagination in much the same condition.*[31]

Here Bradbury touched upon the corrosive character of Burroughs's irony. He is a satirist, but without the expectation that the object of his criticism will ever be superseded by anything better. Instead of being directed outwards, his writing therefore takes on an inward dynamic, with the result that its ultimate target is the integral human self, the subject. The American literary critic Leslie A. Fiedler seems to agree with Bradbury's assessment. In Burroughs and his epigones he detected 'a weariness with the striving to be men. It is the end of man which the school of Burroughs foretells, not in terms of doom but of triumph. Let the experiment be over; let the focused consciousness blur into cosmic night.'[32]

Fiedler seems to have been suggesting that it is the human subject which suffers most from Burroughs's verbal bombardment, more so even than the 'science-managed age' or the narrative tradition. In this respect, irony, which originated as an expression of the defeat of the self, comes to be even more self-defeating.

Along similar lines, the Polish poet and critic Czeslaw Milosz observed that 'irony often corrodes the hand which wields it'. He also noted the element of desperation in irony and its proximity to submission: 'from what is a desperate protest masked with a smile to nihilistic acquiescence is but one step.'[33] Milosz concluded that 'irony is the glory of slaves'.[34]

The American critic Christopher Lasch observed that 'ironic detachment dulls pain but also cripples the will to change social conditions'.[35] Noting that in pop culture 'threat and menace evaporate in the camp giggle',[36] the British sociologist Bernice Martin seemed to agree that irony is the antithesis of confrontation.

More recently the columnist and novelist Julie Burchill has pointed out that irony is a kind of compensation for the impotent: 'those who can, do; those who can't, spoof.'[37] Style journalist Dylan Jones located the ironic condition among 'a nation of adults that still consumes as teenagers', suggesting that irony has become a way of life for those who cannot grow up.[38]

Ironic humanism?

Irony has its champions, however. The American philosopher Richard Rorty holds that the 'ironist', as one who 'faces up to the contingency of his or her own most central beliefs and desires', is on the side of humanity: 'liberal ironists are people who include among these ungroundable desires their own hope that suffering will be diminished, that the humiliation of human beings by other human beings may cease'.[39]

Rorty isolates three conditions which must be fulfilled for the person concerned to be designated an 'ironist':

(1) she has radical and continuing doubts about the final vocabulary she currently uses, because she has been impressed by other vocabularies,

vocabularies taken as final by people or books she has encountered; (2) she realizes that argument phrased in her present vocabulary can neither underwrite or dissolve these doubts; (3) insofar as she philosophizes about her situation, she does not think that her vocabulary is closer to reality than others.[40]

For Rorty the ironist is someone who is alive to the fact that there are different points of view which contradict each other, without expecting these contradictions ever to be resolved; rather (s)he makes the unlikelihood of resolution into a principle of sorts.

Rorty realizes that the stance he is describing is akin to Sartre's notion of the 'meta-stable' in which the bearers are 'never quite able to take themselves seriously because always aware that the terms in which they describe themselves are subject to change, always aware of the contingency and fragility of their final vocabularies, and thus of their selves'.[41]

But Rorty maintains that, for all its fragility, this is what the intelligent self must become, at a time when 'since the end of World War Two, the course of events has made it harder to tell a convincing story of social progress'.[42] For Rorty the provisionality of the ironists is historically justified; moreover, he claims it provides them with 'autonomy' rather than 'affiliation to a power other than themselves'.[43]

In Rorty's defence of irony, as in its emergence historically, there is a rebellion against ideological absolutism, and in particular against what had been held to be the absolute truth of social progress. The ironic condition should therefore be seen as part of the overall trend towards relativism; and, at a time when the establishment itself was holding on to its absolute beliefs, although experiencing increasing difficulty in doing so, there was an anti-establishment element in this trend. But now that absolutism has been disestablished even among the establishment, the ironist's provisionality (translated as 'pragmatism' in current political jargon) is the new orthodoxy, and disaffiliation from 'a power other than themselves' turns out to be an affiliation to powerlessness.

If irony is the playful recognition of paradox, in the absence of the historical subject it can lead only to the proliferation of paradox and the further diminution of the potential for history-making subjectivity. As with the work of William Burroughs, society is the ostensible target of ironic criticism but it is the subject, i.e., the human potential for changing society, which is ultimately dissolved by it.

Spiralling irony/subsiding subjectivity

The proliferation of irony and its debilitating effect is demonstrated by the critical intent and ultimate failure of *The Modern Review* under its first editor, Toby Young. (The journal has now been revived, under the aegis of Julie Burchill and Charlotte Raven.)

With financial backing and editorial input from Julie Burchill, Young set up *The Modern Review* in 1991 with the slogan 'low culture for highbrows'. Despite its small circulation, *The Modern Review* was widely admired for attempting to analyse society through pop culture (although relations with cultural studies academics were sometimes fraught, presumably because the latter considered this to be their exclusive terrain).

After a few months without closely identifying its mission in life, except to repeat the long-accepted notion that Bob Dylan can be as profound as Keats (only in a world which makes everything superficial, I am tempted to add), *The Modern Review* hit upon a campaign against the ironic condition as its *raison d'être*.

In the issue for December 1992 to January 1993 the anti-irony campaign was launched with a front-cover story entitled 'Irony in the soul', co-written by Young and Ed Barrett, who went on to become commissioning editor at *Arena* magazine. Noting that 'there is no longer good and bad, only ironic and unironic', Young and Barrett mocked what they dubbed 'the quotation generation' – their contemporaries – for its obsessive retreat into trivia:

> They would know, for instance, that the narrator of The Magic Roundabout was Emma Thompson's father ... It goes without saying that such earnestness can only ever be applied to the most meaningless of details. When it comes to anything more serious than which of Spock's parents was human, the preferred style is one of Wildean detachment ...
>
> Being ironically detached is ultimately to be nowhere ... Perhaps the ironist will reply that he is simply biding his time, waiting for a genuinely authentic source of identity to come along. In the meantime he'll sit it out in the uncontaminated space between two quotation marks. Yet all this irony has an annoying habit of seeping into other areas of your life until there is nothing left to ground yourself in. For all their brattish arrogance, the Quotation Generation are in danger of being left in the waiting room of history.[44]

Arrested Development

Snob irony

Young and Barrett also recognized the snobbery inherent in the quotation generation:

> Your social standing is determined not by your income but by how ironically detached you are ... Indeed the entire point of putting words like 'swanky' in air quotes is to demonstrate their superiority to those prehistoric enough to use them unironically – like their parents ... Theirs is a two-class society in which you're either the kind of chump who thinks that Ralph Lauren polo shirts are up-scale, or else you think they're 'up-scale'.[45]

In a subsequent issue Young's close colleague Cosmo Landesman identified irony as the acceptable face of English chauvinism: 'for the chattering classes – who usually consider patriotism a nasty vice – irony is a source of national pride ... the English are almost earnest about their sense of irony'. Landesman went on to say that in his opinion irony is 'over-rated': 'it is the nervous tic of those too timid to hold convictions'. He concluded that 'the trouble with the English is: they have no culture, only the quotation marks of irony'.[46]

Consuming irony

The crusade against irony soon spread beyond the pages of *The Modern Review*. In January 1994 Landesman explained the significance of anti-ironism to the readers of the *Sunday Times*: 'This is not some small aesthetic dispute, but is part of a wider disenchantment with modern life. The dandyish delight in ironic distance now fills many with disgust.'[47] In May 1994 *Sunday Times* columnist Mark Edwards echoed the Landesman–Young–Barrett thesis, in his observation that 'irony is a great excuse for anything ... in short, irony allows anyone to avoid responsibility for their actions and attitudes.' But one of the main culprits identified by Edwards as hiding behind the skirts of irony was none other than Julie Burchill, columnist and mentor of *The Modern Review*. An over-abundance of irony, Edwards noted, allowed Burchill to 'write books in a trashy genre and retain her reputation as a really clever person because she knows it's a trashy genre'.[48]

Edwards's criticisms of Burchill are equally applicable to *The Modern Review* as a whole. This was a magazine which set out to challenge the cowardice of its contemporaries, exposing their obsession with trivia as a retreat from reality, and castigating the playful recognition of contradiction – exemplified in the obsessive use of quotation marks, compulsive punning and other ironic wordplay – as an exercise in superficiality and complacency. But these same tendencies were also characteristic of *The Modern Review* itself.

In its subtitle, 'low culture for highbrows', *The Modern Review* dedicated itself to the over-serious pursuit of the trivial, while, in the manner of ironists everywhere, excusing this mismatch with an ironic quip. While Young indicted the quotation generation for their voyeurism and dilettantism, he produced what purported to be a review of modern times which concerned itself almost exclusively with matters of personal taste. Under the rubric of *The Modern Review* matters of substance were deemed substantial, i.e. warranting space in the magazine, only in so far as they impinged upon the likes of *Baywatch*, *The Clangers* and *Star Trek*. Not only an aestheticization of the world, this was a reading of reality through the prism of the trash aesthetic.

Young castigated the quotation generation for consigning themselves to the waiting-room of history and using irony as a substitute for activity. But he seemed not to realize that his own paper's fixation with the intricate details of pop culture was itself an expression of the same anti-subjectivity which was and is the fountainhead of the ironic condition. Instead of challenging the passivity and superficiality which Young correctly identified as component parts of the ironic condition, he compounded the condition by confirming one of its other components – the 'failed seriousness' inherent in the aestheticization of experience, which represents an inability to approach reality in anything other than the narrowest and least threatening terms.

Young as good as admitted that he had been unable to transcend the ironic condition when he wrote a follow-up article entitled 'The end of irony?' His own failure of nerve was exposed in the following declaration: 'The only alternative to irony is naive idealism ... we may not be able to go forward and we may not be able to go back. But I'd prefer to remain where I am than jump into the abyss.'[49] Thus, rather than being an antidote to irony, *The Modern Review* soon became an exercise in high camp – a junior version of the *Spectator*; and, when this paradox showed no signs of abating, Young closed down the magazine and took up residence in the United States of America. On shutting the office door for the last time, presumably he shrugged his shoulders and walked away like a true ironist.

Arrested Development

Spontaneously reproducing

At the end of the 1990s irony is often frowned upon, as if it were one of those excessive accessories associated with the 1980s. But the ironic condition is more deep-seated than that, to the point where even those who want to be rid of it will find themselves reproducing it anyway. The inescapability of irony (according to Martin Amis, 'irony is what the twentieth century is all about'[50]) and its intensification during the past half-century are derived from the paradox between the continuing existence of the human potential and the current implausibility of creating a context in which that potential can be realized. As long as this paradox remains unresolved, pop culture will continue to be adversely affected by the ironic condition.

Not only pop culture, but politics also. In some respects the 1997 general election campaign was a replay of the *Modern Review* conundrum, with Tony Blair in the Toby Young role. Blair invited the electorate to reject the hollow cleverness associated with the ironic capitalism personified by the yuppified Tories of the 1980s. There would be no easy money, Blair said, but by reclaiming values such as honesty and decency we could build ourselves a New Britain under New Labour. Blair milked the widespread moral revulsion against the too-clever-by-half Tories, just as Young had suggested that the ironic condition was morally reprehensible, in so far as it is superficial, dishonest and cheap.

However, just as Young felt unable to transcend irony and the mode of passive commentary, so Blair was unable to offer an active programme of social transformation. In fact the contradiction between the fervour of Blair's rhetoric and the timidity of New Labour's economic programme (adopting the budget of the outgoing government, for example) was itself a kind of ironic paradox. Moreover, it was accepted as such by an electorate, which is itself well versed in the ironic condition. That is to say, voters' likes and dislikes are probably as strong as ever, but they no longer expect programmatic dynamism or ideological coherence from their politicians. In 1997 Blair embodied the paradox between the desire for 'social justice' and the 'new realism' that survival is all we can expect – an embodiment which the electorate was well able to relate to.

In 1949 the critic Cleanth Brooks described irony as 'the most general term that we have for the qualification which the various elements in a context receive from the context'.[51] Blair is perhaps the first British prime minister to preside over a fully ironized political context, in which the activity of government is held to be so tightly constrained by contemporary circumstances (the 'global economy' and 'globalization' are terms which are said to show the futility of economic programmes devised by mere nation-states; likewise in ideological terms the consensus that 'there is no alternative' is said to constitute proof that there cannot be an alternative). Previously government was understood to be the attempt to transform the context in which it came into office, but this definition would be entirely incompatible with what can only be described as the new political ironism of New Labour.

When context overwhelms the individual, or is perceived so to do, then the subject becomes abject. Thus the ironist ultimately sees himself or herself as a victim of circumstance; or, as described by Northrop Frye, 'the archetype of the incongruously ironic is Christ ... the innocent victim'.[52] This is the key to the further irony which Blair personifies. The Prime Minister invites us to commune with an idea of ourselves as innocent Christlike victims, while playing cynically on the fact that the electorate is so disillusioned with society that it expects little or nothing positive from politicians. In the politics of New Labour, humanity is at once the highest of the high and the lowest of the low; and in this paradox Blair is once again in tune with the ironic condition that made its way into politics via the pop culture which both he and we know so well.

Notes

1. Peter Firchow (ed.), *Friedrich Schlegel's Lucinde and the Fragments*, 1971.

2. Georg Lukács, *The Theory of the Novel*, trans. Anna Bostock (London: 1971), p. 92.

3. Jeff Nuttall, *Bomb Culture* (London: Paladin, 1970), p. 67.

4. Joseph Heller, *Catch-22* (London: Pan, 1962), p. 63.

5. Albert Camus, *Le Mythe de Sisyphe* (Paris: Gallimard, 1942), p. 18.

6. Bret Easton Ellis, *American Psycho* (New York: Random House, 1991).

7. David May, quoted in Jonathon Green, *Days in the Life* (London: Minerva, 1989), p. 35.

8. Steve Sparks, quoted in *ibid.*, p. 35.

9. Pete Shertser, quoted in *ibid.*, p. 37.

10. Nigel Waymouth, interviewed by Jonathan Aitken, *The Young Meteors* (London: Secker & Warburg, 1967), pp. 24–5.

11. Susan Sontag, 'Notes on camp' (1964), in *A Susan Sontag Reader* (London: Penguin, 1983), p. 107.

12. Aitken, *op. cit.*, p. 199.

13. Sontag, *op. cit.*, pp. 106–16.

14. Jean Genet, *The Blacks*, 1955.

15. Robin Deneslow, *When the Music's Over* (London: Faber & Faber, 1989), p. 79.

16. *Ibid.*

17. Nik Cohn, 'Carnaby Street part one', in *Today There Are No Gentlemen* (London: Weidenfeld and Nicolson, 1971).

18. Humorist S. J. Perelman, cited by Leslie Fiedler, *Love and Death in the American Novel* (London: Paladin, 1970), p. 452.

19. Dick Hebdige, *Subculture and the Meaning of Style* (London: Methuen, 1979), p. 63.

20. Malcolm Bradbury, 'A dog engulfed by sand. II: Abstraction and irony', *Encounter*, January 1979, pp. 39–40.

21. Roy Carr, quoted in Roger Tredre, 'No "hip" replacements for old jazzers', *Observer*, 2 June 1996.

22. Stanley Cohen and Laurie Taylor, *Escape Attempts: Theory and Practice of Resistance to Everyday Life*, 2nd edn (London: Routledge, 1992), p. 53.

23. Tom Junod of *GQ America*, quoted by Tredre, *op. cit.*

24. Kenneth Keniston, *The Uncommitted* (New York: Harcourt, Brace, 1960), p. 93.

25. Ralph Ellison, 'Morals and manners at Minton's', *Esquire*, 1959, p. 108.

26. *Ibid.*

27. Raymond Horricks, 'Thelonious Monk', in *These Jazzmen of Our Time* (London: Jazz Club, 1959), p. 27.

28. Douglas Coupland, *Generation X* (London: Abacus, 1992), p. 150.

29. William Plummer, *The Holy Goof*, quoted in Jay Stevens, *Storming Heaven: LSD and the American Dream* (London: Paladin, 1989), p. 317.

30. Malcolm Bradbury, *The Modern American Novel* (Oxford: Oxford University Press, 1984), p. 167.

31. *Ibid.*, p. 152.

32. Leslie A. Fiedler, *Waiting for the End* (Harmondsworth: Penguin, 1967), p. 185.

33. Czeslaw Milosz, introduction to *Post-War Polish Poetry*, quoted in D. J. Enright, *The Alluring Problem: An Essay on Irony* (Oxford: Oxford University Press, 1988), p. 20.

34. Milosz, quoted by Christopher Hitchens, 'Hooked on ebonics', *Vanity Fair*, March 1997.

35. Christopher Lasch, *The Culture of Narcissim* (London: Abacus, 1980), p. 96.

36. Bernice Martin, *A Sociology of Contemporary Cultural Change* (Oxford: Blackwell, 1981), p. 181.

37. Julie Burchill, quoted by Dylan Jones in 'Will of irony: the tribulations of ironic existence', *Arena*, September 1989.

38. *Ibid.*

39. Richard Rorty, *Contingency, Irony, Solidarity* (Cambridge: Cambridge University Press, 1989), p. xv.

40. *Ibid.*, p. 73.

41. *Ibid.*

42. *Ibid.*, p. 86.

43. *Ibid.*, p. 97.

44. Toby Young and Ed Barrett, 'Irony in the soul', *The Modern Review*, December 1992–January 1993.

45. *Ibid.*

46. Cosmo Landesman, 'American myths no. 1: Americans have no irony', *The Modern Review*, April–May 1993.

47. Cosmo Landesman, *Sunday Times*, 15 January 1994.

48. Mark Edwards, 'Communication breakdown', *Sunday Times*, 2 May 1994.

49. Toby Young, 'The end of irony?', *The Modern Review*, April–May 1994.

50. Martin Amis, speaking at Books Etc, Charing Cross Road, to promote *Time's Arrow* (London: Jonathan Cape, 1991).

51. Cleanth Brooks, *The Well-wrought Urn: Studies in the Structure of Poetry* (New York: Harcourt Brace, 1949), p. 191.

52. Northrop Frye, *The Anatomy of Criticism* (Princeton: Princeton University Press, 1957), p. 42.

CHAPTER 8

Wiggas

The embrace of black culture has always been seen as a sign of the counterculture's good faith. But is hard to see how pop culture's romance with diversity has significantly improved the position of blacks in society. Moreover, the phenomenon of whites identifying with an erroneous idea of being black is indicative of a degraded selfhood rather than the progressive identity with which it is traditionally associated.

In the 1920s white society took up the habit of visiting black nightclubs. According to Neil Leonard in *Jazz and the White Americans*, among the visitors to Harlem, the primarily black district of New York, were 'intellectuals' such as Eugene O'Neill, Theodore Dreiser and Dorothy Parker. Trips to black clubs, said Leonard, 'titillated the sensibilities of well-to-do members of slumming parties'.[1] Once the evening was over, with one or two exceptions these visitors tended to go straight back to the well-to-do districts whence they came.

From the 1940s onwards, however, white visitors came upon black culture with a more serious purpose. They came in search of a way of life which would be earthy, vigorous and above all authentic, as opposed to the dissemblance and artifice which tainted their own existence, or so they believed. And they wanted not only to look at this way of life, as their predecessors had been largely content to do, but also to live it out for themselves. These were the first white negroes, or wiggas as they have subsequently become known.

In other words since the 1940s young white tourists have come looking for roots that they themselves do not have. But, in seeking to identify with the perceived rootedness of blacks, they have ascribed to blacks the very same characteristics which were previously projected on to them by 'scientific' racists. Except that where the latter put a cross, the new bohemians put a tick; and congratulated themselves for being 'broad-minded' in doing so.

The reformulation of racism in the counterculture's approach to blacks will become apparent if the following passages are compared:

> *Jazz music causes drunkenness . . . a continuous whirl of impressionable stimulations to the brain . . . Reason and reflection are lost and the actions of the persons are directed by the stronger animal passions.*[2]

> *At lilac evening I walked with every muscle aching among the lights of 27th and Welton in the Denver colored section, wishing I were a Negro, feeling that the best the white world had offered was not enough ecstasy for me, not enough life, joy, kicks, darkness, music, not enough night . . . wishing I could exchange worlds with the happy, true-hearted ecstatic Negroes of America . . . There was excitement and the air was filled with the vibration of really joyous life that knows nothing of disappointment and 'white sorrows' and all that.*[3]

The first quotation is from an appraisal of jazz and its effects cited by Leonard and written by a New York physician, Dr E. Elliot Rawlings. Published in the 1920s, Rawlings was railing against the influence of jazz and its allegedly decivilizing tendencies. The second passage is from Jack Kerouac's *On the Road*. This piece was published in 1957, and its author was recommending blackness, as he saw it, as an antidote to the white man's 'disillusionment'. But note that both authors subscribe to essentially the same conception of what it means to be black: drunkenness/ecstasy; animal passion/joy; impressionable stimulations/joyous vibration; 'reason and reflection are lost/life that knows nothing of disappointment'.

What Rawlings disapproved of in the 1920s Kerouac was in awe of in the 1950s. But, in praising where previously there was blame, the latter has maintained the caricatured image of blackness devised by the former – a caricature which is still prominent in pop culture today. Moreover, in investing the non-rational with higher status than Rawlings's 'reason and reflection', Kerouac necessarily removes the possibility of employing rational means in order to overcome racism and the caricatures to which it gives rise. Blacks are thereby condemned to eternal 'ecstasy'. Whites meanwhile are exhorted to spend their lives in search of a similarly one-dimensional mode of existence.

Arrested Development

Seen in this light the counterculture's celebration of black music needs to be re-examined. It may even come to be recognized as a contributing factor to the continuance of particular oppression, and as an element in the new degradation of the self which is fast becoming universal.

Black therapy for whites

Although Albert Camus commented half-enviously on the facility shared by Arab youths for living exclusively in the present moment, among the existentialists it was Jean-Paul Sartre who first identified the therapeutic powers of blackness. In the novel *Nausea* (1949) his narrator found temporary relief from the sickening sensations which beset him while listening to a blues record by a negro woman. Sartre's protagonist reported that 'I felt my body harden and the nausea vanish' as he felt the song enter into him, to the point where 'I am the music'.[4]

In the following decade, the 1950s, Norman Mailer explored the 'wedding of the white and the black' in his essay 'The white negro'. Mailer noted that 'it was the Negro who brought the cultural dowry'.[5] This dowry, according to Mailer, included the ability to live in the present as the existentialists dreamed of doing, and an intensity of experience bordering on savagery, in that 'the Negro (all exceptions admitted) could rarely afford the sophisticated inhibitions of civilization'.[6] In the *ménage à trois* between the bohemian, the juvenile delinquent and the negro, Mailer said, the dowry brought by the latter became the cultural currency of their joint offspring, 'the hipster'.

'The white negro' found many adherents, among them Colin MacInnes, the Australian-born writer who took up residence in London, where he became the unofficial liaison officer between blacks, teenagers and bohemians. In a biography of MacInnes, *Inside Outsider*, Tony Gould recalls that 'towards Mailer his attitude was reverential'.[7]

MacInnes was one of the first London-based intellectuals to divest himself of what had previously been regarded as the white man's burden to civilize the rest of the world. In a remark which hints at the white man's new quest for authenticity in black culture, MacInnes declared, 'we should stop trying to teach, and begin to learn again from Africa and Asia'.[8] While MacInnes was writing, the Beatles and The Rolling Stones constituted themselves, in their original incarnation, as straightforward imitators of black rhythm and blues, with particular reference to record labels such as early Tamla Motown (the Beatles) and Chess (The Rolling Stones).

In his novel *Absolute Beginners* MacInnes described a coterie of negrophile teenagers in late 1950s London. These were the prototypes for the Wardour Street Mods of the early 1960s. In *The Meaning of Mod* Dick Hebdige referred to these Mods as 'the first all-British white Negro'.[9] Interviewed by Charles Hamblett and Jane Deverson for the book *Generation X*, a Mod teenager confided that 'At the moment we are hero worshipping the spades.'[10] Hebdige subsequently pointed out that, for the Mod, 'the Black Man was a constant, serving symbolically as a dark passage ... where another order was disclosed'.[11]

American counterculturists of the mid- to late 1960s were equally captivated by the idea of being black. When the US authorities came down hard on student demonstrations towards the end of the decade, a pamphlet started circulating on the West Coast with the title *The Student as Nigger*. Meanwhile the Diggers of San Francisco claimed that students were not authentic enough to be niggers; they came up with the slogan 'Diggersareniggers' instead.[12] A few years later John Lennon and his new-found feminist partner Yoko Ono sought to dignify the plight of women worldwide with a polemical track entitled 'Woman Is The Nigger Of The World'. At around the same time Janis Joplin became the first white negro woman singer of the counterculture.

Roots

Punks hated hippies but retained the latter's affection for blacks together with an affectation of what they saw as black mannerisms. When a riot occurred at the Notting Hill carnival in 1976, The Clash wanted in on the action and lead singer Joe Strummer cried out for a 'white riot, a riot of my own'. Richard Hell, who with Tom Verlaine founded the New York band Television before fronting his own outfit, Richard Hell and the Voidoids, echoed the phraseology of the 1960s when he claimed that neither students, nor hippies nor women but 'punks are niggers'.[13]

Interviewed in *Woman's Own*, the mother of a British punk seemed to endorse Hell's claim when she remarked that 'seeing those chains and the dog collar round the neck' reminded her of 'the TV series *Roots*',[14] which was shown in Britain in the early 1970s. Taken from Alex Haley's novel about a black American visiting the African continent of his ancestors, *Roots* described the voyage of self-discovery which he experienced there.

Hebdige later described the 'blackness' of 1970s reggae as

'proscriptive ... an alien essence'.[15] He also suggested that in identifying, as in the notion of a punky reggae party, with a form of blackness that was so deliberately alienated from British society, the punks were committing 'a symbolic act of treason' in their 'blatant disavowal of Britishness'.[16] This is an extravagant claim, especially considering that the Two-Tone bands, who were the most accomplished in combing Jamaican rhythms with a punkish ethos, attracted a significant racist element among their wider following. Hebdige was on safer ground in describing the punk aesthetic as a 'white "translation" of black "ethnicity"'.[17] It was a translation which continued the love/hate relationship with its model, as in previous and indeed subsequent incarnations of the white negro.

In the 1980s white audiences picked up on the new black music such as rap and hip-hop. In 1993 the Los Angeles rapper Ice-T released a controversial album, *Home Invasion*, the cover of which featured a young white suburban kid surrounded by all the paraphernalia of black street culture, and fantasizing about a black man making love to a white woman. On the title track Ice-T rapped about white America losing control of its progeny, which, he said, was coming increasingly under the influence of black artists such as himself. Following the controversy surrounding his rock-rap track 'Cop Killer' which in the presidential election year of 1992 attracted adverse criticism from both Republican and Democrat politicians, *Home Invasion* and its cover may have cost Ice-T his record deal with Time Warner.

Despite gloomy predictions of draconian censorship, the furore over Ice-T's *Home Invasion* probably raised the status and sales potential of rap among young white suburbanites looking for a way to offend their parents. It was around this time that the white disciples of rap came to be known as 'wiggas', in place of the term 'white negro' which sounded increasingly harmless and even quaint. 'Wiggas' was a follow-on term derived from black rappers and their frequent use of the word 'niggas' to connote both brotherhood and brutalization.

It is easy to poke fun at wiggadom, as when Notting Hill trendies affect dreadlocks and Jamaican patois, or when an all-white band dubs itself the Young Black Teenagers and declares, 'the way we choose to use black has nothing to do with a skin shade, it's a state of mind'.[18] But these are the absurd extremes of a commonplace process whereby 'black culture has become the most pervasive influence on popular culture' – as Michael Bane, author of *White Boy Singin' the Blues,* once said.[19]

From Radio Two to the soundtrack of television adverts to the music that is played in supermarkets, in the 1990s every facet of popular culture has been coloured by the young white folks' desire to be black. Unfortunately the blackness so highly prized today has little to do with the real experience of living as a black person. For, as Bane also pointed out, 'white America has created a carefully constructed mythology of the American Black';[20] and it is this mythology which is the stuff of white negro fantasies.

Mythologies

The best deconstruction of the myth-making which surrounds both blacks and the white negro was accomplished even as their union was first consummated. Indeed it is striking that in the intervening years the cultural relations between black people and white youth have tended to become more rather than less opaque.

In 1946 the man who could lay claim to be the first white negro, Jewish-born instrumentalist Mezz Mezzrow, published an account of his life entitled *Really the Blues*. The book was ghost-written by Bernard Wolfe, one-time bodyguard of the exiled Trotsky, who also provided an afterword in which he addressed a new generation of negrophiles concerning the vexed relationship between black performers and the whites who try to imitate them. 'Negrophilia and Negrophobia are not, or are not *just*, polar opposites', cried Wolfe. 'We may have to see them ... as the two sides of one coin, a coin we're forever flipping.'[21]

Wolfe noted that 'Negrophiliac whites prefer to see the Negro as a pre-social creature in whom the romping subjective is king'.[22] They envied the negro because 'he evades all the pressures and batterings to which one is subjected at the centre and which are lethal to the "inner spark" ',[23] not realizing that this evasion is one and the same as the negro's status as a 'pariah', i.e. his oppression. Moreover, Wolfe recognized that black performers are straitjacketed in the notion of 'romping subjectivity' which is projected on to them by whites:

> The 'creative' Negro, far from being his own spontaneous self, may actually be dramatising the white man's image of the 'spontaneous' Negro 'as he really is' ...
>
> What we take, in the singing and dancing Negro, for his own self-portrait may very well be a composite portrait which the white world has

slapped together haphazardly out of its emotional leftovers and flung over the Negro.[24]

Wolfe described New Orleans jazz as 'largely an accommodation to the mask' placed over blacks by white society, whereas bebop was 'a partial jibe at the mask', and also the expression of 'an overpowering lust for respectability'.[25] He portrayed white and black in a dissembling dance of reflexivity, predicated on false notions of authenticity:

> *Their [the Negrophiles'] eyes cue the performance. The more they relish the Negro on stage as 'authentic', blinding themselves to the degree of calculation in the performance, the more the Negro must cling to the mask which they take for real faces ... The truth about the Negro performer is that he is required to be a Negro impersonator ... The apparent creator is most typically only a middleman between the white as tyrannical psychic impresario and the same white as passive sidelines consumer.*[26]

If Wolfe was right, then the white negro has never imitated blacks, but only the image of being black that he himself originated. Moreover, much of 'black culture' is the acting out of the white fantasy of being black, with blacks as merely the medium for a performance which is scripted for them in advance. Borrowing from the eminent author Gunnar Myrdal, Wolfe described the 'proliferating irony' of this mutual deceit as 'the tyranny of expectancy'.[27] (It is a tyranny which black rappers have recently tried to manipulate to their own financial advantage, only to see it backfire in the killing of Tupac Shakur and Biggy Smalls. The chequered career of boxer Mike Tyson is another case in point.)

Smothered subjectivity

The negro artist, Wolfe added, must battle to stop himself being squeezed out of his own performance by society's expectation of him: 'the self he tries to focus on is ... often crowded offstage entirely by the Other.'[28] Noting that 'the social fringe can become a bohemia only for those who gravitate there out of choice, surfeited with the sober life behind', he distinguished between the negrophile dalliance with life on the edge, and the plight of those 'exiled there from birth because of alleged insecurities'.[29]

Wolfe also noted that 'Negro song and dance are, in their innermost frames, laments for the *smothered* subjective'.[30] In recognizing that the real black experience is defined not by 'romping' but by the limitations imposed on activity, Wolfe hit upon – but did not draw out – the reason why so many whites gravitate towards that experience (even if, in coming towards it, they redraw it in their own image, thus making it more opaque and pushing it further away).

The cult of the primitive is not peculiar to our own epoch. The jazz critic Francis Newton observed that 'the search for the pure, the innocent, the "natural" counterpart to modern Western bourgeois society is as old as that society itself, for it reflects the permanent awareness of its fundamental flaws'.[31] However, awareness of flaws has hitherto coexisted with an even more powerful recognition of the benefits of civilization. The cult of the primitive was thus a minority interest which, when other contemporary currents are taken into account, tends only to emphasize the confidence in progress which was widespread until recently. But now that progress is thought to be at an end, and civilization is sometimes said to have been a mistake from day one, the fetish for blackness has acquired a novel significance.

The American sociologist Alvin Gouldner was on the right lines when he suggested that 'at the bottom of the modern plea for authenticity' is 'the failure of successful conformity to produce gratification'.[32] But more sorely felt than the lack of gratification is the absence of aspiration or a sense of ourselves as aspirant beings, either individually or collectively. In any case, the failure to which Gouldner refers is now so far advanced that 'successful conformity' no longer exists. More often than not, success is now correlated with socially acceptable forms of difference rather traditional modes of conformity.

In today's context, then, the preoccupation with the work of 'authentic' black artists is essentially an expression of the decline of subjectivity. There is a sense of closure articulated in the blues, for example, which originates in the experience of being consigned to the fringes of society. Large numbers of whites, who continue to enjoy access to all areas of society, nevertheless have come to identify with the sense of closure in the blues. They have done so at a time when the prospect of making history seems remote and when all alternatives to existing society are closed off.

In other words, whites have picked up on the sense of closure derived from the boxed-off experience of a particular form of oppression, and adapted it to sum up the fatalistic sentiments which stem from the unprecedented consciousness of limits which has been growing steadily throughout the second half of the twentieth century to the point where it is now almost universal, This adaptation has been most assiduously performed, as in the British blues boom of the late 1960s, by young, white, middle-class males, precisely the group of people who in previous historical periods would have expected to venture furthest and achieve the most, and who therefore feel the current sense of closure most acutely.

In the absence of subjectivity, therefore, the blue notes transcend the particular experience upon which they resonated originally, and provide us all with the soundtrack to our general abject-ivity. If we all wannabe black, that is because, in the sense that society no longer seems open to our intervention, we are the niggers of history.

Crow Jim

It is half a century since Wolfe unravelled the cultural cloth of the white negro. A decade after Wolfe, Ned Polsky wrote a riposte to Normal Mailer which wove a similar pattern. 'Even in the world of the hipster', Polsky pointed out, 'the Negro remains essentially what Ralph Ellison called him – an invisible man.'[33] He went on to explain how the Negro was called to play a role already mapped out for him by the new bohemia: 'The white Negro accepts the real Negro not as a human being in his totality but as the bringer of a highly specified and restricted "cultural dowry", to use Mailer's phrase. In so doing, he creates an inverted form of keeping the nigger in his place.'[34]

In certain circles the 'inverted form of keeping the nigger in his place' was known as 'Crow Jim'. In an essay on the Beatniks in and around Greenwich Village at the end of the 1950s Polsky explained how putting blacks on a pedestal may not have been as brutalizing as Jim Crow, the quasi-official system of apartheid operating in the South; nevertheless it definitely had the effect of restricting rather than liberating black people:

> Although the white beat grants the Negro a fuller role than other white 'pro-Negro' groups do, he does it merely by compounding the limited roles those groups demand. For the white beat, the Negro fulfils the liberal's demand that he entertain plus the radical's demand that he symbolize the results of reactionary oppression plus the Harlem thrill-seeker's demand that he act out the primitive in all of us.[35]

Polsky stressed that, under the terms of the 'white beat' outlook, the 'one thing the Negro must not try to do is try to be white'.[36] Given the tortuous career of Michael Jackson in recent years, pop culture (the culture which emerged from the popularization of Beat) seems to have re-enacted, on a grander scale, Polsky's prognosis in respect of Beat culture.

As the white negroes have become more numerous, comments on them, as a cultural phenomenon have tended to be less penetrating, though not without interest. Referring to a negrophile passage by Kerouac, the black novelist and essayist James Baldwin quipped, 'I would hate to be in Kerouac's shoes if he should ever be mad enough to read this aloud from the stage of the Apollo theatre.'[37] In *Inside Outsider* Tony Gould cites the recollections of a friend of Colin MacInnes by the name of Victor Musgrave. MacInnes, it seems, was wont to stroll at night through certain districts of London, stopping 'every few yards to strike up conversations with passing black men – "like an unofficial MP in his constituency"'.[38] Gould also admits, somewhat grudgingly, that MacInnes, who was gay, could be even more patronizing in his sexual encounters with blacks: 'dispassionate whites may observe, from a comfortable distance, that Colin's behaviour towards blacks was reprehensible and patronising, if not hypocritical, and, in the sexual arena, downright exploitative.'[39]

Albert Goldman, in his reconstruction of the life of comedian Lenny Bruce, made a useful distinction between the upwardly mobile black hipster and the deliberately downward drift of the Beat. The hipster, according to Goldman, was typically 'a dandy' who affected 'a very cool, cerebral tone', and who aspired 'to the finer things in life' – whereas 'the Beat was originally some earnest middle class boy like Kerouac, who was stifled by the cities and the culture he had inherited and who wanted to cut out for distant and exotic places'.[40]

Eric Clapton's biographer Christopher Sandford has allowed backing musician Ben Palmer to explain how adulation for ageing bluesmen was not enough to extricate them from second-class status while on tour with their white imitators: 'Here was Muddy [Waters], 63 and in bad health, stuck in the back of the coach with the roadies. There was something odd about the white musicians sitting like King Tut in the dining car while the blacks got boxed lunches.'[41] Confirming Wolfe's observation that negrophilia is the reflex of negrophobia, Sandford contextualized Clapton's infamous onstage statement, 'I think we should vote for Enoch Powell', by saying that 'most of the people Clapton admired were black, most of the people he vilified were black too'.[42]

Arrested Development

In *Crosstown Traffic*, a retrospective account of the career of Jimi Hendrix from the vantage point of the late 1980s, Charles Shaar Murray explained that, in Hendrix, the white counterculture at last found a black musician it could do business with:

> When 'hip' and 'radical' white youth sought a musical and political rapprochement with black culture but found the problem of relating to real live black people virtually insuperable, Hendrix was there: a black man of their own generation who understood them, shared their rhetoric and actively courted their favour. [43]

Snapshot: Who's fooling whom?

It was one of those tours in the early 1970s when obscure, ageing bluesmen, some of whom had never before been out of their home state, were brought over to Britain to strut their stuff and satisfy the cravings of young white students. The venue was the Lanchester Polytechnic students' union in Coventry, and I was at the front of the audience when the (white) rhythm section started playing. Then an elderly black man was helped on stage and guided to the piano, and I turned round to the schoolfriend standing beside me. We grinned. This was the real thing. Here was an authentic black man, who was real in a sense that we did not feel ourselves to be. We were not sure if the man on stage, who went by the name of Boogie Woogie Red, was actually blind, like some other blues singers we had heard of; but he was certainly black, and that was enough to be going on with.

Boogie Woogie Red grinned back at us. We assumed we were witnessing Red's spontaneous joy at playing his own music. Maybe we were. Or maybe he knew what we expected of him, and he grinned because he knew he could match our expectations with his eyes shut – and get paid for it.

Jeff Greenfield displayed a healthy scepticism towards the counter-culture's courting of black radicals. For the counterculturists, Green-field said, 'the Black Panthers were a kind of updated manservant. Instead of cleaning up the young gentleman's room for him, they would kill a pig [police officer] for the young gentleman.' [44] Tom Wolfe, besides berating New York's high society for the 'radical chic' of their dilettantism towards the Panthers, observed that the white negroes always dressed up in the wrong costume: '[they] never bothered to look at what the brothers on the street were actually wearing'.[45] Presumably because, like inverse missionaries, the white negroes came upon blacks with a preconceived idea of what they should be like.

At around the same time, a black writer by the name of Calvin C. Hernton made a pointed attack on blacks trying to live up to society's clichéd expectations of them:

> *Surprisingly (or is it to be expected?), there are Negroes who are afflicted with the white man's mythological concept of Negro sexuality. Their behaviour around white women is strictly sexual. They prance around, jump up and down, gyrate their pelvises, and nearly every word they speak has a sexual reference. It is not simply a matter of trying to exploit the white man's sex image of the Negro. No! Such Negroes would have us believe that they live entirely in their sex, and, like raving cripples, they do! These Negroes are diseased by the racist's grotesque sex image of them, which, after all, is nothing more than a myth.*[46]

Nearly twenty years later a musician from Minneapolis by the name of Morris Wilson echoed these sentiments in his remarks to the first British biographer of Prince. Wilson claimed that Prince had compounded the white stereotype of sexually obsessed blacks, and he complained that black musicians 'almost can't get a [recording] contract unless you're writing that kind of trash. They kind of wanna keep you in that bag. That's the stereotype that you have and they want to keep you there. Prince and all of them, they fall right into line with that.'[47]

Snapshot: Anthropology

Early summer 1976. Bristol University Rag Ball. A sizeable part of the entertainments budget had been spent in bringing Toots and The Maytals and The Heptones over from Kingston, Jamaica, to make their British debut. But reggae and ska had yet to catch on with middle-class students and there was plenty of empty space in the Anson Room when the rude bwoys took the stage.

I was standing near the front, accompanied by a friend from Coventry who later went on to play a key role in Two-Tone Records. The two of us kept turning, looking at each other and grinning; half in awe and, it must be said, half-laughing at the reggae musicians for the way they twisted 4/4 rhythms and made them into something which seemed to us both authentic and idiosyncratic.

We had reacted in much the same way a couple of years earlier when we went to see the newly released Jamaican feature film *The Harder They Come*, and caught our first sight of a Rastafarian with what looked like a tree on top of his head.

It would be dishonest to claim we were laughing with the figure on screen, or the men on stage. We laughed at them on account of their native eccentricity, and we laughed at ourselves because, for all our supposedly superior schooling and middle-class upbringing, they could take themselves seriously in a way which we could not bring ourselves to do.

These were not straightforward feelings of superiority, and we would have reacted angrily to any white person who expressed such sentiments. For my part (I cannot speak here for my companion), I recall feeling both inferior (I could never play like that, I could never be as cool as that) and superior (if my identity was not as strong, neither was it as fixed and narrow as theirs). I suppose the best way to explain my viewpoint is that I was something like an anthropologist spying on the mannerisms of a group of human specimens. I thought I was being non-judgemental, but really I had discovered a way of being patronizing and right-on at the same time.

Different drums

Michael Bane emphasized the divergence between black aspirations during the 1960s and the self-deprecation which white negroes sought to verify in reference to certain types of black music. Bane quoted record producer Norman Drayton explaining how whites grafted themselves on to the blues just at the time when blacks were trying to leave them behind: 'The blues and R&B were rapidly falling out of favour with the black community ... Things were upward and mobile and hip, and they didn't want to hear pain ... guttural accents and primitive sorts of things.'[48] Likewise, Bane noted that in their political protests blacks eschewed the pranksterish mentality of the radical counterculture in favour of more serious demands: 'The Kerner Commission on Civil Disorders found that black protests throughout the sixties were aimed more at getting a fair piece of the pie than throwing the pie in somebody's face.'[49] This contrast was further represented in diverging musical trends: 'so while white music ... continued in the smash-the-beer-bottle tradition, black music got straighter and straighter.'[50]

Bane was wise to the depoliticizing dynamic of the counterculture.

'The danger involved', he warned, 'is that the cultural revolution will ultimately result in social autism: a kind of hedonistic quietism that will represent less a Great Refusal than a Great Cop-Out.'[51] He also recognized the element of self-degradation in the white negro, quoting the statement by S. I. Hayakama that 'white liberals . . . in their hunger for humiliation, will take as revealed truth anything an angry black man says'.[52] But this hunger does not preclude the further humiliation of blacks, as Bane was quick to point out with reference to the pantomime blackness acted out by the all-white Blues Brothers: 'Imitation is not only a safe refuge, it allows you to vent emotions that are not usually held in check. It's a good joke – them funny-looking guys imitating niggers and all. But they're white – get it?'[53]

Bane was writing at the beginning of the 1980s. In the late 1980s and early 1990s Simon Reynolds was one of the few writers who tried to get behind the relationship between black and white music. Whites, noted Reynolds, were enjoying 'an exotic flirtation with the Other, a pop foray into a perceived heart of darkness'.[54] White musicians were turning 'beige' in their elaboration of 'blackness . . . as a model of oneness with your body, of being in touch with your emotions . . . Beige vocalists admire and envy the "blacks" for being more in touch with their emotions, their bodies, the unfettered ignorance of their self-expression.'[55]

Meanwhile, as Reynolds noted, black musicians were straining on the leash and trying to move in the opposite direction, to the point where 'hip-hop' was by no means concerned with empathy and personal warmth but rather comprised a kind of 'soul on ice, a survivalist retreat from engagement' which resulted in the 'frozen shells of a minimal self'.[56]

Reynolds's observations recall Goldman's distinction between the upward mobility of the hipster and the downward drift of the Beat. Except that by now the reflexive 'tyranny of expectancy' referred to by Myrdal and Wolfe has reached the *n*th degree, so that it becomes increasingly difficult to ascertain to what extent the alienation expressed in hip-hop and rap is an expression of ingenuous disengagement by blacks, and to what extent it is a calculated rendition of the alienated sensibility which blacks have copied from disenchanted whites, who as white negroes then go on to recycle the black version of their own alienation.

Thus when rapper Snoop Doggy Dog said of the gangsta lifestyle that 'it's a movie for white kids'[57], he was telling the truth – on one level; but on another level the truth of his statement is also part of another 'movie' in which rappers play the gangsta's part which was invented for them by white boys – a part which is then sold back to suburban whites as the authentic black street culture of the inner city.

Nowadays predominantly white bands play reggae in the shadow of black sessionmen from Jamaica who rate all-white rock bands among their highest musical influences. The interlocking circles of homage and imitation are often referred to as 'cross-pollination' and taken as a sign of healthy interaction between black and white. Among musicians themselves this may well be the case. The old adage that pop music is the art of knowing what to nick still holds good. But when it is considered not for its aesthetic qualities but as a phenomenon which expresses trends in society, 'cross-pollination' is by no means the sign of a healthy dynamic. Rather it is the function of a stagnant society in which blacks are incarcerated in larger numbers than ever before, whether in urban ghettos or in prison; while increasing numbers of whites no longer envisage society as a vista which is open to them, hence their identification with the music of closure and abject-ivity which was previously the preserve of those who had been shut out of mainstream society and forcibly distanced from its progressive momentum.

If there is an equality here, it is an equality derived from the tendency for whites to feel as degraded by an alien society and as excluded from objectified history as only blacks used to be. This is the equality of mutual degradation, and the white negro or wigga is the expression of the tendency for black and white to unite around a shared sense of powerlessness.

Jean Genet, in his introduction to *Soledad Brother: The Prison Letters of George Jackson*, declared that 'prison serves no purpose ... the time for blues is over'.[58] In one sense he was right. Nothing can be gained from singing the blues over and over again. To do so is to revel in our current impotence. As a forecaster, however, Genet could not have been more wrong. The blues are deeply embedded in our times, to the point where our craving for the culture of closure now forms an integral part of the self-limitation in which we are all incarcerated.

Notes

1. Neil Leonard, *Jazz and the White Americans* (Chicago: University of Chicago Press, 1964), pp. 70–2.

2. Dr E. Elliot Rawlings, quoted in *ibid.*, p. 33.

3. Jack Kerouac, *On the Road* (1957) (London: Penguin, 1972), pp. 180–1.

4. Jean-Paul Sartre, *Nausea*, trans. Lloyd Alexander and John Lehmann, (London: Hamish Hamilton, 1949), p. 34.

5. Norman Mailer, 'The white negro', *Dissent*, summer 1957.

6. *Ibid.*

7. Tony Gould, *Inside Outsider* (1983) (London: Allison and Busby, 1993), p. 164.

8. Colin MacInnes, 'Sterilities and virilities', *Encounter*, November 1963.

9. Dick Hebdige, 'The meaning of Mod', mimeographed paper for the Centre for Contemporary Cultural Studies, Birmingham.

10. Charles Hamblett and Jane Deverson, *Generation X* (London: Tandem Books, 1964), quoted in Hebdige, *Subculture: The Meaning of Style* (London: Methuen, 1979), p. 54.

11. Hebdige, *op. cit.*, pp. 53–4.

12. Abbie Hoffman, *The Best of Abbie Hoffman* (New York: Four Walls Eight Windows, 1989), p. 22.

13. Richard Hell, quoted in *NME*, 29 October 1977.

14. Punk's mother featured in *Woman's Own*, October 1977.

15. Hebdige, *op. cit.*, p. 64.

16. *Ibid.*

17. *Ibid.*

18. The Young Black Teenagers, quoted in Peter Clark, 'Wiggas wannabe black', *Evening Standard* (London), 21 March 1994.

19. Michael Bane, *White Boy Singin' the Blues* (Harmondsworth: Penguin, 1982), p. 15.

20. *Ibid.*, p. 15.

21. Bernard Wolfe, Afterword to Mezz Mezzrow, *Really the Blues* (1946) (London: Flamingo, HarperCollins, 1993), p. 400.

22. *Ibid.*, p. 401.

23. *Ibid.*

24. *Ibid.*, pp. 393–4.

25. *Ibid.*, pp. 395, 402.

26. *Ibid.*, pp. 395–6, 401.

27. *Ibid.*, p. 395.

28. *Ibid.*, p. 402.

29. *Ibid.*, p. 403.

30. *Ibid.*, p. 403.

31. Francis Newton, *The Jazz Scene* (Harmondsworth: Penguin, 1961), p. 256.

32. Alvin Gouldner, *The Coming Crisis of Western Sociology* (New York: Basic Books, 1970), p. 424.

33. Ned Polsky, 'Reflections on hipsterism', *Dissent*, winter 1958.

34. *Ibid.*

35. Ned Polsky, 'The Village Beat scene: summer 1960', in *Hustlers, Beats and Others* (Harmondsworth: Penguin, 1971), p. 182.

36. *Ibid.*

37. James Baldwin, *The Black Boy Looks at the White Boy*, quoted in James Campbell, *Paris Interzone* (London: Secker & Warburg, 1994), p. 258.

38. Gould, *op. cit.*, p.111.

39. *Ibid.*, p. 220.

40. Albert Goldman, *Ladies and Gentlemen, Lenny Bruce* (London: Picador/Pan, 1976), p. 278.

41. Christopher Sandford, *Eric Clapton – Edge of Darkness* (London: Gollancz, 1994), p. 227.

42. *Ibid.*, pp. 99–100.

43. Charles Shaar Murray, *Crosstown Traffic* (London: Faber & Faber, 1989), p. 16.

44. Jeff Greenfield, *No Peace No Place* (New York: Doubleday, 1973), p. 217.

45. Tom Wolfe, *Mauve Gloves and Madmen* (New York: Clutter & Vine, 1977), p. 188.

46. Calvin C. Hernton, *Sex and Racism* (London: Paladin, 1970), p. 71.

47. Morris Wilson, quoted by Dave Hill, in *Prince: A Pop Life* (London: Faber & Faber, 1989), p. 3.

48. Bane, *op. cit.*, p. 191.

49. *Ibid.*, p. 208.

50. *Ibid.*

51. *Ibid.*, p. 229.

52. S. I. Hayakawa, quoted by Bane, *op. cit.*, p. 210.

53. *Ibid.*, p. 247.

54. Simon Reynolds, *Blissed Out* (London: Serpent's Tail, 1994), p. 80.

55. *Ibid.*, pp. 156, 82.

56. *Ibid.*, p. 156.

57. Snoop Doggy Dog, quoted in Clark, *op. cit.*

58. Jean Genet, Introduction to George Jackson, *Soledad Brother: The Prison Letters of George Jackson* (Harmondsworth: Penguin, 1971).

CHAPTER 9

Limits

It has been perceived as a limitless carnival of self-expression,
but by positing self-expression as the furthest reach of human
experience, the counterculture was always imbued with a
sense of limitation.

In 1996 there appeared on British television a striking advertisement for
Rimmel cosmetics. With a soundtrack taken from the first hit single by
Supergrass ('we are young . . .'), the advert showed young women using
the advertiser's products to develop and extend their identities; and it
ended with the slogo 'there are no limits'.

The Rimmel advert was the encapsulation of what many
commentators have said about pop culture, in their descriptions of it
as a limitless terrain for unending self-expression. Peter York, for
example, in *Modern Times* (his preview of the 1980s, not to be confused
with his retrospective television series on the decade) contrasted the
liberating range of self-expressive styles currently available to the
discerning consumer with the bad old days when 'there was no
alternative' to the dictates of the fashion houses.[1]

In a similar vein cultural critic Frank Mort describes today's society
as one of 'extravagant and aggressive pluralism'.[2] Likewise anthropologist Ted Polhemus has distinguished between the days when 'trickle-
down' fashion was a singular model imposed from above, and the street
styles that nowadays 'bubble up' from below in all their limitless
diversity. 'The bubble-up process', said Polhemus, 'has made us a fully-
fledged creative democracy in which talent isn't thought to be limited
by class or race or education or how much money you've got in the
bank.'[3]

But is lifestyle really limitless? Is it the litmus test of an open-ended society? Polhemus seems confident that it is; nevertheless he noted that, unlike fashion, which 'celebrates change and progress', style is 'inherently conservative and traditional and it is for this reason that it often makes use of permanent body decorations'.[4]

Perhaps it is rather the case that today's supermarket of style holds out a false promise of limitlessness. It might be more accurate to say that, in today's carnival of identities, you can have any colour you like so long as you accept the essentially conservative proposition that life is limited to style. Furthermore, perhaps this sense of limitation is further reflected in what Polhemus has identified as the inherent conservatism of style. If so, the sentiment expressed recently by *Guardian* columnist Linda Grant to the effect that 'limiting human activity is a definition of what we mean by society',[5] might have been informed more by the style warriors of the counterculture than by the Cold War warriors of recognized conservatism.

Rebellion as limitation

Contrary to the surrounding aura of unrestrained self-expression, the founding documents of the counterculture are imbued with a sense of the necessity of limitation. In *The Rebel* (1951), for example, the French existentialist Albert Camus averred that humanity must learn to limit its aspirations. Moreover he argued that learning to limit oneself was the mark of the rebel: 'In order to exist, man must rebel, but rebellion must respect the limit it discovers in itself – a limit where minds meet and, in meeting, begin to exist ... Each tells the other that he is not God.'[6]

For Camus it was the establishment and the established left that represented limitlessness and its associated dangers. His refusal of the grand narratives of communism, fascism and bourgeois democracy meant refusing their expectation of unlimited progress. 'The errors of contemporary revolution', wrote Camus, 'are first of all explained by the ignorance or systematic misconception of the limit which is inseparable from human nature and which rebellion accurately reveals.'[7]

Instead of open-ended development the rebel would seek to put 'a limit to history and at this limit the promise of a value is born'.[8] Camus defined genius as 'a rebellion which has created its own limits'.[9] If rebellion has a philosophy it 'would be a philosophy of limits'.[10] The adoption of limits would also require the renunciation of the attempt to accomplish wholesale social transformation, at a time when, according to Camus, 'to transform is to act, and to act, nowadays, is to kill while it still does not know if murder is legitimate'.[11]

The sense of necessary limitation first articulated by Camus was repeatedly expressed throughout the counterculture. Thus the prominent American anti-Vietnam-War activist Tom Hayden later recalled that he had 'experienced what Camus called the "temptation of hate" ', but Hayden drew back from the edge at the vital moment: 'In the end I was fortunate to reach a point of return, of personal and political reintegration.'[12] In Hayden as in Camus the defining characteristic of the rebel is that he or she refuses mainstream society and also refuses to go all the way in his or her renunciation.

Overwhelmed

Camus sought to take the notion of the subject in history and redefine it as a new subjectivity which enables humanity to live in harmony with its own limitations. However, some critics recognized this as tantamount to the end of subjectivity and the development of an idea of the individual as essentially the object of circumstances beyond their control.

Thus Norman Mailer observed that 'Hip sees the context as generally dominating the man'.[13] Describing the 'rebel without a cause', Dr Robert Lindner depicted a rebellion constrained by circumstances: 'forced from without to conform, and from within to rebel, he rebels within the confines of conformity'.[14]

George Melly noted that '[James] Dean represented the defeated teenager'.[15] Julie Burchill, taking the release of *Reality Bites* as an opportunity to look back at rebel teen films in the 1950s, said of 'Dean's big two bolshie films' that 'they both yearn back towards a time when families were more solid and traditional, less prone to collapse and mutation'.[16]

Likewise Michael Bracewell, writing in the *Independent*, cited 'characters who, faced with the traditional rites of passage, would sooner not bother'.[17] Where Burchill described the Dean movies as 'conservative' and suggested that their protagonist was defined by an inability to cope with change, Bracewell seemed to identify rebel conservatism as the submission of the self to the apparently final enormity of existence: 'Central, therefore, to the literature of teenage disaffection, is the iron curtain of apocalyptic dread (a sense that the world has already ended).'[18]

Arrested Development

In their various ways all three writers defined Hollywood's disaffected teenagers as the prisoners of circumstance. Jeff Nuttall described the origins of the counterculture in much the same way: 'moral shame, moral absurdity, moral paradox and moral outrage had frozen us at a point of almost total negativity'.[19]

On the other side of the Atlantic the first comedian of the counterculture, Lenny Bruce, also declared that 'all my humour is based on destruction and despair'.[20] Likewise Paul Goodman talked about a psychology of impotence: 'People believe that the great background conditions of modern life are beyond our power to influence ... [There are] inevitable tendencies of history ... Our psychology, in brief, is that history is out of our control.'[21]

According to Nuttall, the question facing his generation was 'how best could one go about the business of waiting in humiliation for the end of man?'[22] In *Reflections on the H Bomb* Gunther Anders had already prefigured Nuttall's thesis of a 'bomb culture' in which humanity's options are severely restricted by the enormity of our own creation:

*Because we are the first Titans, we are also the first dwarves or pygmies ...
In fact the helplessness with which contemporary mankind reacts – or fails
to react – to the existence of the superbomb bespeaks a lack of freedom the
like of which has never before existed in history ... We have indeed reached
the freezing point of human freedom.*[23]

Two American commentators, Sheldon S. Wolin and John H. Schaar, spoke of society's 'powerlessness' being mirrored by the voters' 'apathy, despair and impotence'.[24] Moreover, the counterculture was not immune from the general sense of powerlessness which they described, but tended to express it more intensely. 'The campuses', said Wolin and Schaar, 'shared with the rest of society the growing sense of collective and individual impotence.'[25] Meanwhile the British sociologist Mike Brake complained that the earliest manifestation of the counterculture revolved around 'a life style' which expressed the 'existential values of the futility of action'.[26]

The limited sense of self, and the sense of self overwhelmed by context, are equally discernible in the seminal music of the counterculture. Music critic Richard Williams has described the album *Birth of the Cool*, featuring Miles Davis, Gil Evans and Gerry Mulligan, as 'a title that came to stand for an entire genre, a whole generation and others beyond them'.[27] It is perhaps significant, then, that the only vocal track on the record, featuring singer Kenny Hagood, was a renunciation of erstwhile aspirations entitled 'Darn That Dream'.

The renunciation of the aspirant self and the embrace of a self defined by limits have been constant themes throughout the counter-culture and its popular progeny. Forty years on, Greil Marcus heard the sound of an extremely limited and even degraded sense of self, clearly audible in the instrumental mix as well as the lyrics of Kurt Cobain's *Nirvana*:

> It might be months on the radio or MTV before you begin to catch what's being said in Nirvana's songs – 'sell the kids for food', 'I don't mind if I don't have a mind', 'I feel stupid and contagious', 'I'm neutered and spayed' . . . but the feeling of humiliation, disintegration and defeat by some distant malevolence is what the music says by itself.[28]

This is the negativity at the root of what has come to be known as 'attitude'. Ostensibly a form of rebellion which is also an assertion of subjectivity, the real function of 'attitude' in today's context is to proclaim one's own limitations loudly and to dismiss the possibility of ever going beyond them.

Power, no thanks

One of the characteristics of the newly limited sense of self has been withdrawal from the quest for power. Camus advocated the 'affirmation of a nature common to all men' outside ('which eludes') the 'world of power'.[29] Graham McCann observed that the rebel males of the 1950s (Clift, Brando, Dean) seemed to express the notion that 'the quest for power in all aspects of life is inherently self-defeating'.[30] The Beatles summed up the renunciation of power in the phrase 'All you need is love', which was echoed in the early 1970s by a young radical writer by the name of Mark Gerson, in his declaration that 'I don't need power when I'm hypnotised' by love.[31]

For once the Cold War warrior George Kennan may have been right when he observed in the student activists of the late 1960s not the contest for power but an apprehensive attempt to dispense with power altogether:

> One senses not so much a fear directed to the question as to where governmental power is to reside, but rather a fear of power itself – an insistence on its fragmentation in the interests of its harmlessness; a

determination not to see it gathered, unified, and made real, even in the hands of an electoral majority.[32]

Noting that hostility to power itself was typical of a conservative tradition 'rooted in Burke and Gibbon', Kennan went on to explain that in refusing power rather than seeking to acquire it, the student revolutionaries of the 1960s were hardly living up to the traditional definition of 'revolution':

> *One wonders whether those who use the term 'revolution' this way really know what it traditionally means. That it means, in their minds, to defy power is clear; but that it means to replace power and above all to shoulder responsibilities that go with it, is not clear at all.*[33]

In the 1990s the renunciation of power continues to be seen as a good thing, especially in conjunction with what some critics look upon as an emerging ecology of naturalized technology. In 1994 Kevin Kelly, who was the founder and publisher of the *Whole Earth Review* before becoming editor of *Wired* magazine, published a book, *Out of Control*, in which he argued that our lives would be more rewarding if only humanity gave up striving for control and learnt to live in harmony with a new generation of self-proliferating machinery: 'Even without the control we must surrender, a neo-biological technology is far more rewarding than a world of clocks, gears and predictable complexity.'[34]

Limited terrain

Some critics were always able to see through the aura of limitlessness and to recognize the emergence of the counterculture as a relocation of young people's endeavour to a more limited terrain of self-expression and personal growth, rather than social transformation and development. Writing in the 1960s the American essayist Granville Hicks discerned a diminution in the scale of the subject matter chosen by new novelists. Unlike the writers of his generation – the 1930s – Hicks complained that:

> *The typical writer of the past 20 years seldom deals with large political or economic issues. His characters are not figures in business or government or leaders of social revolt. They are almost always offbeat persons: a kid in a carnival, an adventurer in Africa, a storekeeper in Brooklyn. And they are not seen, as a rule, against a broad social background but in some small and isolated area of life.*[35]

In 1956, the year of the Suez Crisis and the Angry Young Man, film-maker Lindsay Anderson wondered out loud about the limited character of contemporary protest: 'how then are we to explain the prevalence of cynicism, the baffled idealism and the emotional fatigue? Why are so many young voices resentful and defeatist rather than pugnacious and affirming?'[36]

A year later, in the magazine *Encounter*, Colin MacInnes suggested that the teenagers' indifference to politics left them marooned in a 'kind of happy mindlessness'.[37] Ten years after that, MacInnes observed that, by a kind of transubstantiation, the limited range of youth's concerns had come to be seen as a positive virtue:

Much about the attitudes of the young, however picturesque and superficially attractive, seems to consist in trying to transform, by some self-persuasive alchemy, the mere inclinations they have into sacred principles: 'we like to do this or that, therefore it's right we do it.'[38]

For the American critic G. Legman the hippie revolt was a self-indulgent fake which represented cowardice rather than contention: 'A hippie or beatnik is a frantically self-advertising coward and parasite, all tired and "beaten" by a struggle in which he somehow never engaged.'[39] The 'cool-cat', Legman added, was restrained by his own 'frightened narcissism'.[40] Likewise, in a campus debate with Jack Kerouac, the latter's opponent James Weschler (described by an eye-witness as 'the optimistic liberal') was moved to declare 'there is no valour in the Beat's flight and irresponsibility'.[41]

Radical quietism

With Allen Ginsberg, acceptance of the limited terrain of human activity acquired radical connotations. According to Ginsberg, 'the problem is that the problems ... are insoluble, the world situation is "hopeless" ... the right action is patience, generosity, observation, not to be afraid of death, not to be afraid of Apocalypse'.[42]

It seems as if Ginsberg succeeded in redefining inactivity as 'the right action'. A similar attempt is discernible in the poet Michael McLure's contribution to the 1967 San Francisco Be-In, one of the defining moments of the counterculture. McLure, reports Jay Stevens, 'recited a long alliterative play on the line "this is it, and it is all perfect"'.[43] The idea that 'this is it' had previously been the touchstone of conservatism, in its insistence that this is the best of all possible worlds and that the impact of humanity on nature and society must go no further. But in the 1960s the prospect of going no further came to be associated with radicalism.

The alleged radicalism of inactivity was encapsulated in Ken Kesey's formula 'just walk away and say fuck it',[44] and embodied in the version of the *Tibetan Book of the Dead* produced by Timothy Leary and friends. David Zane Mairowitz, whose own book *The Radical Soap Opera* captures the bathos of the counterculture, described this volume as 'a sort of communist manifesto of the interior economy' which preached against external activity: '[It] stresses a state of inaction or passive integration with the world that encounters you ... The obvious corollary is that *action* is the property of an *acting* (and, by inference, unhappy) ego.'[45]

In the Leary definition, explained Mairowitz, 'an external action, if not a product of expanded consciousness, was "robot behaviour"'. By 'expanded consciousness', Leary and his disciples meant agreement with their notion of the primacy of contemplation. In their extremely limited outlook, therefore, the only laudable activity was that which facilitated a passive orientation to the world.

Mairowitz went on to explain that the 1960s notion of a 'cultural revolution' (not a social revolution) was a 'historic admission' in that it already implied a diminishing scale of social change. Moreover, the antipathy to action inherent in this notion was itself a form of self-limitation, as expressed in the San Francisco Be-In. Noting that 'some 30,000 humans gathered to demonstrate for no purpose whatever', Mairowitz described it as 'a pure carnival of zero' which articulated 'a certain hope and ecstasy for a revolutionary future', but which conformed to the Camus definition of genuine rebellion in that it 'did not revolve around any notion of *act*'.[46]

The first guru of such radical quietism was the English novelist and essayist Aldous Huxley, whose account of taking mescalin, *The Doors of Perception*, from which the band The Doors took their name, offered a motivation for becoming motiveless, and for limiting one's role in life to primarily that of passive receptor. This is how Huxley welcomed the suspension of will under the influence of mescalin:

> *Though the intellect remains unimpaired and though perception is enormously improved, the will suffers a profound change for the worse. The mescalin taker sees no reason for doing anything in particular and finds*

most of the causes for which, at ordinary times, he was prepared to act and suffer, profoundly uninteresting. He can't be bothered with them, for the good reason that he has better things to think about.[47]

From his account it is clear that the suspension of will is not a major cause of concern to Huxley. The drug-taker has 'better things to think about' such as the folds in his trousers: 'Those folds in the trousers – what a labyrinth of endlessly significant complexity! And the texture of the grey flannel – how rich, how deeply, mysteriously sumptuous!'[48]

It all sounds innocent enough, if a bit daft. But, mindful of the active claims made by left- and right-wing champions of progress, Huxley declared that this passive orientation to the world was a sign of devilish rebellion:

'This is how one ought to see' I repeated yet again. And I might have added 'These are the sort of things one ought to look at'. Things without pretensions, satisfied to be merely themselves, sufficient in their suchness, not acting a part . . . in Luciferian defiance of the grace of God.[49]

But if Huxley was seeing 'things without pretensions, satisfied to be merely themselves', this means that he was also satisfied that 'things' should remain themselves, without interference from him. In his notion of 'Luciferian defiance' it is Huxley who has renounced the possibility of 'acting', limiting himself instead to the role of enlightened observer; and like Camus he believed that enlightenment would be brought about by virtue of such self-limitation.

On the 'errors' inherent in this point of view, the pillar of the establishment George Kennan was more progressive than either Camus or Huxley:

One of these errors – and it is one that affects particularly those who take drugs, but not those alone – is the belief that the human being has marvellous resources within himself that can be released and made available to him merely by the passive submission to certain sorts of stimuli . . . It is only effort, through doing, through action – never through passive experience – that man grows creatively.[50]

Many among the New Left of the 1960s would formally have agreed with Kennan on this point. But, as Theodore Roszak explained, the political wing of the counterculture managed to redefine activism through the prism of aesthetic contemplation. Recognizing 'the easy transition from the one wing to the other of the counterculture', Roszak demonstrated the links between them: 'Beat-hip bohemianism may be too withdrawn to suit New Left radicalism; but the withdrawal is in a direction the activist can readily understand. The "trip" is inward, toward deeper levels of self-examination.'[51] Thus, added Roszak, 'when the New Left calls for peace ... the hippie quickly translates the word into *shantih*'. Even Marxism came to serve as an adjunct to self-expression. According to Roszak, 'It is rather as if the Neo-Marxists are attempting to usher Marx into the contemporary world on the coat-tails of existential artists.'[52]

Alienation as limitation

Thus the counterculture designated a narrower range of human activity than previous generations would have expected of themselves. This is apparent not only in its celebration of passive contemplation but also in the disdain for association with other people, i.e. collectivity, a disassociation which necessarily implies a narrower range of possible activity and potential outcomes.

The great chronicler of life in America Studs Terkel once remarked to Bob Dylan that 'what you stand for, you belong to nobody but yourself'.[53] In one sense this was a radical repudiation of existing networks and their failings; but from Dylan's own pronouncements it becomes apparent that his belonging to nobody but himself was also a form of self-limitation designed to offset the effects of apparently futile engagement with other people:

> *Going to college and learning why things happen is ridiculous in the face of the realization that things are going to happen whether you know why they're happening or not ... what Joan Baez is doing, and all those people demonstrating, they're not going to save the world ... None of it's real. Just slogans.*[54]

Dylan's turn away from the last vestiges of collectivity associated with folk music and protest songs towards the existentialism of his second period (followed by a third period in which he crawled into the womb of religion) amounted to a trade-off between the narrowness of the alienated sensibility and the seemingly inevitable failure of collective action. Like many of his generation and those that have followed, Dylan chose the former rather than risk the latter. In doing so he prefigured the arch-conservative Margaret Thatcher's declaration to the effect that there is no such thing as society, as when he explained that 'I don't think in terms of society because society just fights among itself. I'm part of the me, the me that's inside, not part of society in any way.'[55]

Dylan's preference for such an intensely limited point of entry into society was later echoed in John Lennon's lyric: 'I believe in me/Yoko and Me/And that is reality.'[56] Reviewing Dylan's career and that of his contemporaries, Roszak was moved to observe that 'the task of remodelling themselves ... rapidly takes precedence over the public task of changing institutions or policies'.[57] In other words the stage where such figures played out their dissent was distinctly limited compared to the more expansive politics of previous generations which had dared to attempt the full-size tasks of 'changing institutions or policies'.

Diminishing dissent

The diminution of dissent was a form of gradual retirement from politics, which was itself presented as a new kind of post-political radicalism. Thus John Hopkins, one of the co-founders of *International Times* (*IT*), has said that he 'gave up politics' after the Labour prime minister 'just dumped disarmament as soon as he was elected' in 1964.[58] Two of the sharpest commentators on British politics in the 1960s, David McKie and Chris Cook, entitled their book *The Decade of Disillusion*, recognizing that 'the optimistic assumption that most problems could be resolved if only men of goodwill could be brought together round a table was badly mangled by the end of the sixties'.[59] In his contribution to the volume edited by McKie and Cook, Hugo Young (latterly a senior columnist for the *Guardian*) saw in 'the futile history of CND' a premonition of the radicalism of the late 1960s. Both of these, Young averred, were predicated 'perhaps more than anything else' on 'disillusion with the Labour Party'.[60]

The new dissent was thus a reaction against the limits to growth and social transformation in mainstream politics. But for the most part it acceded to those limits and, by limiting dissent to matters of personal behaviour, constructed itself around them. The Mods, for example, according to their chronicler Dave Laing, 'no longer believed in the idea of work, but had to submit to the necessity of it'.[61] The way in which they expressed their disbelief in the work ethic was therefore limited to what they wore after office hours. As the young Dick

Hebdige observed, such a limited form of dissent left the fundamental laws of society untouched:

> *The magical transformations of commodities had been mysterious and were often invisible to the neutral observer, and no amount of stylistic incantation could possibly affect the oppressive economic mode by which they had been produced.*
>
> *The state continued to function perfectly no matter how many of Her Majesty's colours were defiled and draped around the shoulders of skinny pill-heads in the form of sharply-cut jackets.*[62]

The 'incidental' revolution

At the time, however, there was some expectation that changes in consumer choice would lead, as one-time *IT* editor Roger Hutchinson subsequently said, to the 'creation of a new order incidentally, as the result of everybody eating much more brown rice, listening to The Grateful Dead, smoking hash rather than drinking beer'.[63] For a moment it seemed there was going to be an 'incidental' window of limitless opportunity.

'I really thought we were going to change the world', DJ John Peel later recalled, 'I thought we would be responsible for the moral advance that would match the technological advance of the previous 100 years.'[64] Likewise Jim Haynes, founder of the Arts Lab in Drury Lane, remembered thinking 'we could change the world. First and foremost it was going to be a world of mutual respect, mutual acceptance.'[65] But the radicalism of this putative transformation turned out to be very limited indeed. Another veteran of the counterculture, Richard Trench, put his finger on its constricted character when he recalled that 'I wanted the world to change ... Everybody would work less, everybody would become middle class like us, everybody would read poetry like us.'[66]

If Trench is correct, much of the radicalism of the 1960s would be best interpreted as an attempt by sections of the young middle class to make the world over in their own image; a kind of embourgeoisement with brown rice. Comments made by Wolin and Schaar even seem to suggest that the counterculture came about as the middle classes, recognizing that their previous social roles were no longer viable, searched for new roles to perform:

The sense of futility which pervades the campuses can also be understood as an expression of the plight of the middle classes today. Historically, the middle classes shaped their identity in demanding the release of human energy ... mobility, opportunity and progress were the watchwords ... Since technological society is the supreme achievement of the middle classes, the appearance of crisis will fall hardest on the progeny of the middle class.[67]

Wolin and Schaar concluded that for the middle classes, the 'pains and discontents of powerlessness' were now preferable to the traditional 'values and rewards of powerfulness'.[68] It seems fair to add that, henceforth, the middle classes would try to make the world over in the image of their own impotence.

Middle-class myopia

There were other commentators and participants who observed a kind of middle-class domesticity at the heart of the counterculture. Mike Brake noted that ' "doing your own thing" could be seen as a hippy "stretched value" of the middle class evaluation of individualism and self-growth'.[69] John Lennon told *Rolling Stone* editor Jann Wenner that the counterculture had resulted in nothing much more than 'a lot of middle class kids with long hair walking around in trendy clothes'.[70] Spencer Dryden described the yearning for security among the audiences of his band Jefferson Airplane, one of the most radical of the era: 'They don't want the discipline of the home, and yet they want the security. And the only thing that will give them security is to give them what they want.'[71]

The prison of the self

Dryden's fellow-band-member Paul Kantner thought that his audiences were asking to have limitations imposed upon them. 'People were looking for someone to tell them how to run their lives', he said.[72] Kantner's comment suggests that some participants in the counterculture were looking for the domineering father they never had. Moreover, most counterculturists were content to live entirely within a narrow range of acceptable activity and thinkable thought. Jack Newfield noted 'an appalling anti-intellectualism' among even the most radical American students. He reported that their knowledge of revolutionary politics was minimal, and the novels they read had all been published recently, 'and most dealt with the decadence or absurdity of life'.[73]

Paul Goodman, who was generally sympathetic to the counter-culture, was shocked by its self-limiting ignorance. 'I once taught at Black Mountain College', Goodman recalled, 'and to my astonishment I found that the students had never read the Bible, Milton, Dryden, Gibbon, etc. etc., nor did they feel – as a lack – that such things existed.'[74]

Goodman explained that the Beats used a deliberately narrow vocabulary as an expression of rebellion, which had the unfortunate side-effect of restricting their dissent to a form of self-indulgence:

> *the paucity of its vocabulary and syntax is for the Beats essentially expressive of withdrawal from the standard civilization and its learning. On the other hand, this paucity gives, instead of opportunities for thought and problem-solving, considerable satisfaction in the act and energy of speaking itself, as is true of any simple adopted language, such as pig-Latin . . .*
>
> *They regard talk as an end in itself, as a means of self-expression, without subject matter. In a Beat group it is bad form to assert or deny a position as true or false, probable or improbable, or to want to explore its meaning. The aim of conversation is for each one to be able, by speech, to know that he is existing and belonging. So among perfectly intelligent and literate young men, some movie or movie star will be discussed for an hour, giving each one a chance to project his own fantasies; but if someone in despair tries to assert something about the truth or worth of the movie, the others will at once sign off.*[75]

For all their desire to escape the limitations of the 'standard civilization', Goodman observed that the Beats were 'unable to make the jump to the great international humanist community because, simply, they don't know anything, neither literature nor politics'.[76]

Goodman also observed that the Beats were 'so hip and sure that society cannot be different'.[77] This meant that their politics – and politics is primarily a contest about doing things differently – were necessarily 'unimpressive'. Moreover, a world without contestation tends to lose sight of cause and effect. Thus, for Goodman, Beat literature suffered a lack of motivation which reflected and resulted from a way of life constrained by disengagement:

*The Beat novelist wants to say that we did leave Chicago and did go to
New York. But how would one know? When there is not much structure
for the experience – no cause to leave Chicago, no motive to go to New
York – these things become very doubtful and it is hard to make the
narrative solid. So incidents are multiplied without adding up to a plot;
factual details are multiplied that do not add up to interpretation or
characterisation . . . young Beats compile notebooks of poems and drawings,
but since there are no problems of art, these do not add up to a body of
work.*[78]

Goodman observed that the Beats had two equally limited ways of
being: 'cool and mask-faced experiencing little; or to be sent far out,
experiencing something'. The former implied limiting the impact of the
world on the self, while the latter suggested giving up the self to some
kind of external stimulus. As with the rave culture dichotomy between
dancing and chilling, in each case the open-ended potential of the self-
in-the-world is noticeable by its absence. Goodman must have had a
sense of the limitations inherent in these ways of being when he
concluded by ruminating as to whether 'ordinary growth in experience
would not be a more profitable enterprise and ultimately get them
much further out'.[79]

Radical retreat

Goodman felt that the contempt for the straight world expressed by the
counterculture was really an attempt to disguise insecurity. 'In general',
he opined, 'coolness and mask-face are remaining immobile in order to
conceal embarrassment, temper or uncontrollable anxiety.'[80] Nearly
twenty years later, at the end of the 1970s, Ralph W. Larkin saw the
same 'mask face' in American high school students: 'their lives seem to
be characterised by flight. Thus the "fun" orientation of the youth was
not so much a joyful expression of selfhood, but a bulwark erected to
screen out pain.'[81] Larkin also suggested that the young were seeking
'the refuge of the self' in response to the 'general decline in the
legitimacy of all social institutions'. He painted a picture of a generation
erecting a storm shelter and confining itself within its walls.

   Even at the high point of its radicalism, the counterculture can best
be understood in terms of its limitations, i.e. by what it did not dare to
think or do. For example, in England Frank Parkin saw the limitations
inherent in the spate of student occupations at the end of the 1960s:

'The occupation of the [university] premises may be regarded as a token seizure of the state. The student radicals in Britain in particular are bound to make do with ersatz conquests ... because real targets are quite beyond their reach.'[82]

Wolin and Schaar were particularly acute in their observation that the radical students' refusal to seek power meant that authority could be 'delegitimized' without being challenged: 'Its forms and grounds remain intact. The students have refused authority its proper reverence, but they have not seized much, if any, of its vital substance, power.'[83] Wolin and Schaar added that 'changes of this kind are entirely consistent with the democratic values and the "ethic of responsibility" which higher education is supposed to promote'.[84] They also observed that the counterculture was more of a mood than a coherent political movement; and that this mood was inherently limited by its hostility to theoretical development:

> *Rather it is a mood, a feeling of rage and revulsion which is increasingly impatient with theory, or even thought and argument. The anti-intellectual strain which was present in the movement from the beginning has triumphed. Theory on the New Left is now reduced to the vulgar Marxism and Maoism of Progressive Labor, or to the Weathermen view of white radicals as a suicide squad.*[85]

Noting the section in the 1970 State of the Union address where president Richard Nixon promised to 'make peace with nature, and begin to make reparations for the damage we have done', Wolin and Schaar contended that the limited character of student radicalism came even more to the fore with the turn to environmentalism in the early 1970s. They described the environment as 'an issue which can connect the energies and ideals of the young to the policies and machinery of the system ... when the disappointments and abrasions of political encounters become too much, it permits a full catharsis of moral indignation without seriously affecting the structure of power or the logic of the system'.[86]

In their new-found 'commitment to nature', said Wolin and Scharr, 'the confused minority of activists who had struggled for racial justice and economic improvement' were 'tacitly conceding that racial and economic injustice were ineradicable facts of American society'.[87]

Escape into style

On the cusp of the 1970s some sections of the counterculture became more explicitly escapist. 'You're just escapees', said one elderly inhabitant to the members of a commune which had recently established itself in his vicinity. 'Change America and you won't have to come to New Mexico.' But America had communes instead of communards, and even then, as the elderly citizen observed, 'there ain't no place to escape to'.[88]

Others tried to escape into the adjoining territories of cynicism and style. In Britain in the early 1970s Jeff Nuttall began to sense 'cynicism' among his students: 'their point was that cross-dressing is more important than being able to paint a fucking picture ... Okay it had been an audacious gesture in 1964 ... But in the early seventies it was just style.'[89]

From what Nuttall says, it seems that stylization was the corollary of a deradicalization, in which the bearers agreed to limit themselves further to questions of style in exchange for the space to arrive at their own answers, which in turn were restricted entirely to matters of style. This escapism is what Dick Hebdige saw in David Bowie's 'meta-message': 'escape – from class, from sex, from personality, from obvious commitment – into a fantasy past ... or a science fiction future'.[90] In this respect, Hebdige admitted, style is 'just so much graffiti on a prison wall'.[91]

Along similar lines, in their 'obituary' of rock'n'roll, Julie Burchill and Tony Parsons fulminated against the music as an agent of deradicalization: 'it made you into a consumer, a potential moron', they declared, before parodying The Rolling Stones with the line 'it's only rock'n'roll and it's plastic, plastic, yes it is!'[92] The young gunslingers at the *NME* were shooting down the bad reputation of rock'n'roll, pointing out that its radicalism was so limited that it had all been used up long ago. In fact the limitations of countercutural radicalism were its defining characteristic, to the point where the deradicalization which accompanied the retreat into style was always immanent within the counterculture.

Unlimited snobbery

Perhaps the only aspect of the counterculture that was not limited was its arrogance. There was more than a whiff of snobbery and even paternalism on the part of initiates towards the uninitiated. This much was noted by J. Eisen in an account of Altamont (the Rolling Stones concert that went badly wrong when the Hell's Angels, who had been taken on as stewards, got out of control and killed a black member of the audience): 'It was as though identification with the new culture, with long hair and serious differences with your parents, meant that somehow you possessed a superior way of life and a superior insight into the nature of the universe.'[93]

In *The Greening of America* Charles Reich also mapped out a missionary role for the counterculture, in his assertion that 'the task of the new generation is to be the teachers of their fellow men and women'.[94]

Lewis S. Feuer kept a sharp eye on the elitism inherent in 1960s radicalism. Noting that the sociologist C. Wright Mills had 'made the intellectual class into the historical elite',[95] Feuer contended that the New Left saw itself as 'the student infantry' of the 'intellectual elite', hence it was 'more elitist' than its predecessors.[96] He also noted that the New Left was 'disenchanted with the working class', and would have to look 'elsewhere to satisfy its need for a populist identification'.[97] Feuer saw the events of May 1968 almost entirely in terms of elitism:

> The events of 1968 suggested, however, that the French student movement of the future would oscillate even more between two extremes of elitism – one in which it saw itself as the chosen generation of future rulers, demanding all sorts of privileges within the system, and the other, an aimless, directionless protest against the system, as an embittered last stand of the children's world, the guardians of pure values against old men.[98]

Some of Feuer's prophecies were undoubtedly accurate, including his prognosis for the New Leftist of the 1960s: 'when he is rejected by his hoped-for lowly class allies, the New Leftist turns either to individual violence or individual withdrawal; the terrorist and the hippie are the commingling alternatives within the next stage of the New Left.'[99]

Feuer derided the students' call for 'participatory democracy' as 'the authoritarianism of the young intellectuals and their allies of the moment'.[100] Noting that 'the student intellectual, self-appointed as his people's liberator ... becomes his people's dictator',[101] he indicated that the fashion for irrationality among the student left would result in repression whenever and wherever they made their way into government. Kennan too recognized the anti-democratic prejudices of a culture in which, as he observed, 'majorities are not to be trusted' and 'minorities are to be the favoured children of society'.[102]

Snapshot: Snob

At fourteen my hair was long and I travelled across town to attend a direct-grant school and, on Saturday mornings, to the drama group sponsored by Coventry Cathedral. My taste in music, and that of my middle-class friends, was what used to be known as 'progressive' – Pink Floyd, Cream, Colosseum etc. But my family home was in a working-class district, not far from the decidedly tough area where my mother was brought up. The other teenagers at the local youth club which I sometimes went to wore their hair much shorter, and they listened to soul and reggae, not 'progressive' rock. With one foot in each camp, I took it on myself to act as some kind of a liaison officer between the two.

At school, in the debates in General Studies lessons, I drew on my proximity to working-class life in an attempt to sound more earthy and authentic. In the company of my working-class contemporaries, however, I tried to get them to improve themselves by listening to my kind of music. Not surprisingly, I was rebuffed; and I sometimes remarked that this was because they were not 'cultured' enough to appreciate my suggestions.

On one occasion I remember my mother asking me why I had not taken up an invitation to visit the home of a local boy with whom I was on friendly terms. When I demurred, shrugging my shoulders and muttering in what was then a uniquely teenage fashion, she gave me a withering look, and said: 'I suppose he's not *cultured* enough for you.'

I will never forget her scorn for the role of cultural missionary which I had adopted in relation to those of my contemporaries who came from the same social background as she did; and, ever since then, her contempt for my snobbishness has engendered in me an early warning system against those elements in pop culture who think they know what's good for everyone else.

Contempt for the masses has certainly featured in the mindset of some of pop culture's most radical protagonists. In Dave Rimmer's book on the 'new pop' of the 1980s he quoted John Lydon, formerly Johnny Rotten of the subversive Sex Pistols, as saying: 'And as for you poor little cows who buy Duran Duran records, you need serious help 'cause these people are conning you.'[103] The self-righteousness of this remark (you need someone like me to tell you when you have been conned) is 'basic to the practice of rock criticism', Rimmer claimed: 'Implicit in this attitude ... is the idea that some music is good for you, some music isn't and if all the "poor little cows" just stopped screaming for a minute and listened to those in the know, then they'd be a lot better off.'[104]

Social work

Recognizing that 'pop fans aren't stupid', Rimmer seemed to be suggesting that the 'the practice of rock criticism' has functioned as a kind of social work, in which critics and others set themselves up to train the primitive tastebuds of the young masses. This chimes in with the remark attributed to style journalist and radio host Robert Elms to the effect that 'the post-68 generation basically despised the material aspirations of the working class'.[105]

Some of the counterculture's pivotal moments have an air of 'we know what's good for you' about them. In the light of New Labour's ban on cigarette advertising in Britain, announced in 1997, it is interesting to recall that the front-runners of the counterculture in the Netherlands, the Provos, were, according to Richard Neville 'raised in the anti-smoking circuses of Robert Jasper Grootveld, who began by painting K (for Kancer) on every tobacco hoarding in sight'.[106] Likewise, the township of Christiana, established in Denmark in 1971 as 'an independent hippie city state' has since become a model village of the sort which would have gladdened Tony Blair's heart during his dalliance with communitarianism.

Interviewed by Alex Bellos in the *Guardian*, one resident of Christiana since its inception explained: 'we are very, very conservative really. It's very ironic. At first the only rule was that you could do anything you wanted as long as you didn't hurt anybody else. Now there are limits and rules.'[107] Perhaps it would be more true to say that the counterculture has always been about setting limits. It is just that now its constraining character is more clearly visible.

The therapeutic state

The state provided another avenue of escape for counterculturists coming down from the high of the late 1960s. Throughout the 1970s droves of New Leftists became radical social workers with a mission to raise the consciousness of their clients and convert them to what was fast becoming a doctrine of limitations. This was the stance mapped out by Peter Berger in *Pyramids of Sacrifice*: 'Trust those who evince consciousness of limits of action and of their own limits! Indeed, if the concept of "consciousness raising" has any merit, we would recommend that it be employed for any enterprise that teaches a consciousness of limits.'[108]

If the consumer could not be trusted to make the right choices, the 'counselling ideology of the personal service professions'[109] would be there to help them. And when former residents of communes made their re-entry into society as radical social workers, they encouraged their clients to share their willingness to limit consumption. In January 1970 a new publication entitled *The Modern Utopian* declared, 'the key ... is to reduce one's intake and outgo of material goods – to deal with the poverty of the world by rejecting America's materialistic standards'.[110] By the end of the decade, spreading this philosophy of limits was a priority for the new generation of social workers. The latter also sought to bring the alienated sensibility to the still-collectivized masses, as in the proposition that 'the primary purpose of social work is to individualise people in the mass urban society'.[111]

The relationship between countercultural freedoms and the doctrine of limitation, and the conversion of erstwhile counterculturists into an establishment-in-waiting, were closely observed by the American critic Christopher Lasch. In *The Minimal Self* Lasch averred that narcissistic self-expression is motivated by self-doubt and 'signifies a loss of selfhood',[112] reflected in turn in the 'newer literature of authorial self-abnegation', such as the work of William Burroughs.[113]

In *The Culture of Narcissism* Lasch highlighted the constricted viewpoint which prompts the preoccupation with feeling good about ourselves and our personal relationships: 'Having no hope of improving their lives in any of the ways that matter, people have convinced themselves that what matters is psychic self-improvement.'[114] He went on to expose the fatalistic acceptance of limits inherent in the fetish for personal growth:

> The cult of personal relations, which becomes increasingly intense as the hope of political solutions recedes, conceals a thoroughgoing disenchantment with personal relations, just as the cult of sensuality implies a repudiation of sensuality in all but its most primitive forms. The ideology of personal

*growth, superficially optimistic, radiates a profound despair and resignation.
It is the faith of those without faith.*[115]

Lasch appreciated that the 'minimal' self would also be fragile, with a
predilection for therapy (ostensibly bolstering the self but in reality
undermining it), and a propensity to abdicate autonomy in favour of the
therapist. Noting that 'even the radicalism of the sixties served as a form
of therapy',[116] and thereby making the necessary connection between
the two, Lasch abhorred the new dominance of what he dubbed 'the
therapeutic sensibility', which he envisaged displacing religion and
politics as the organizing frameworks of contemporary society.[117]

In the 1990s, as more of us come under the 'therapeutic' influence of
various practitioners of the 'rebel' philosophy of limits, it seems that the
prophecies of Christopher Lasch have come to ghastly fruition.

Notes

1. Peter York, *Modern Times* (London: Heinemann, 1984), p. 10.

2. Frank Mort, *Cultures of Consumption* (London: Routledge, 1996), p. 25, referring,
apparently favourably, to a point previously made by Jon Savage.

3. Ted Polhemus, *Street-style: From Sidewalk to Catwalk* (London: Thames & Hudson,
1994), p. 12.

4. *Ibid.*, p. 13.

5. Linda Grant, 'In search of cybersex', *Guardian*, 22 April 1997.

6. Albert Camus, *The Rebel* (1951), trans. Anthony Bower (Harmondsworth: Penguin,
1973), pp. 27 and 270.

7. *Ibid.*, p. 258.

8. *Ibid.*, p. 216.

9. *Ibid.*, p. 236.

10. *Ibid.*, p. 253.

11. *Ibid.*, p. 16.

12. Tom Hayden, *Reunion* (New York: Random House, 1988), p. xvi.

13. Norman Mailer, 'The white negro', *Dissent*, summer 1957.

14. Robert Lindner, *Must You Conform?* (1956), quoted in Graham McCann, *Rebel
Males* (London: Hamish Hamilton, 1992), p. 13.

15. George Melly, *Revolt into Style* (Harmondsworth: Penguin, 1970), p. 32.

16. Julie Burchill, reviewing *Reality Bites* in *Sunday Times*, 5 June 1994.

17. Michael Bracewell, 'Boys and girls come out to play', *Independent*, 2 March 1996.

18. *Ibid.*

19. Jeff Nuttall, *Bomb Culture* (London: Paladin, 1970), p. 129.

20. John Cohen (ed.), *The Essential Lenny Bruce* (St Albans: Granada, 1975), epigraph.

21. Paul Goodman, 'The psychology of being powerless', the second of two Massey Lectures transmitted by the Canadian Broadcasting Company, 1966, published as part of the A. J. Muste Memorial Institute essay series (New York), p. 23.

22. Nuttall, *op. cit.*, p. 105.

23. Gunther Anders, 'Reflections on the H bomb', in Eric and Mary Josephson (eds), *Man Alone: Alienation in Modern Society* (New York: Dell, 1962), p. 290.

24. Sheldon S. Wolin and John H. Schaar, *The Berkeley Rebellion and Beyond* (New York: Vintage, 1970), p. 12.

25. *Ibid.*, p. 14.

26. Mike Brake, *Comparative Youth Culture* (London: Routledge, 1985), p. 87.

27. Richard Williams, *The Man in the Green Shirt* (London: Bloomsbury, 1993), p. 53.

28. Greil Marcus, *Esquire*, August 1992.

29. Camus, *op. cit.*, p. 216.

30. Graham McCann, *Rebel Males* (London: Hamish Hamilton, 1992), p. 26.

31. Mark Gerson, *The Whole World Is Watching* (London: Pitman, 1970), p. 198.

32. George Kennan, *Democracy and the Student Left* (London: Hutchinson, 1968), p. 200.

33. *Ibid.*, p. 208.

34. Kevin Kelly, *Out of Control: The New Biology of Machines* (London: Fourth Estate, 1994), p. 607.

35. Granville Hicks, 'Writers in the thirties', in Rita James Simon (ed.), *As We Saw the Thirties* (Chicago: University of Illinois Press, 1967), p. 100.

36. Lindsay Anderson, *Sight and Sound* (London: British Film Institute, September 1956).

37. Colin MacInnes, in *Encounter*, December 1957.

38. *Ibid.*

39. G. Legman, *The Fake Revolt: The Naked Truth about the Hippie Revolt* (New York: Breaking Point, 1967), p. 22.

40. *Ibid.*, p. 43.

41. James Weschler, 'The optimistic liberal', quoted in Jack Newfield, *A Prophetic Minority: The American New Left* (London: Anthony Blond, 1966), p. 44.

42. Allen Ginsberg, quoted in Abe Peck, *Uncovering the Sixties* (New York: Panther, 1985), p. 307.

43. Michael McLure, cited in Jay Stevens, *Storming Heaven: LSD and the American Dream* (London: Paladin, 1989), p. 445.

44. Ken Kesey, quoted by Peter Buckman, *The Limits of Protest* (London: Panther, 1970), p. 229.

45. David Zane Mairowitz, *The Radical Soap Opera* (Harmondsworth: Penguin, 1976), p. 177.

46. *Ibid.*, p. 189.

47. Aldous Huxley, *The Doors of Perception* (1954) (London: Panther Granada), pp. 21–2.

48. *Ibid.*, p. 25.

49. *Ibid.*, p. 31.

50. Kennan, *op. cit.*, pp. 10–11.

51. Theodore Roszak, *The Making of a Counter Culture* (London: Faber & Faber, 1971), p. 63.

52. *Ibid.*, p. 94.

53. Studs Terkel, quoted in Anthony Scaduto, *Bob Dylan* (London: Abacus, 1972), p. 143.

54. Bob Dylan, quoted in *ibid.*, p. 220.

55. *Ibid.*

56. John Lennon, quoted in Ralph W. Larkin, *Suburban Youth in Cultural Crisis* (Oxford: Oxford University Press, 1970), p. 153.

57. Roszak, *op. cit.*, p. 63.

58. John Hopkins, quoted by Jonathon Green, *Days in the Life* (London: Minerva, 1989), p. 125.

59. David McKie, Introduction to McKie and Chris Cook, *The Decade of Disillusion: British Politics in the Sixties* (London: Macmillan, 1972), p. 5.

60. Hugo Young, 'Politics outside the system', in *ibid.*, p. 218.

61. David Laing, *The Sound of Our Time* (London: Sheed & Ward, 1969), p. 150.

62. Dick Hebdige, 'The style of the Mods', mimeographed paper for the Centre for Contemporary Cultural Studies, University of Birmingham.

63. Roger Hutchinson, *High Sixties* (Edinburgh: Mainstream Publishing, 1992), p. 124.

64. John Peel, quoted by Green, *op. cit.*, pp. 128–9.

65. Jim Haynes, quoted in *ibid.*, p. 129.

66. Richard Trench, quoted in *ibid.*, p. 129.

67. Wolin and Schaar, *op. cit.*, p. 15.

68. *Ibid.*

69. Brake, *op. cit.*, p. 83.

70. John Lennon, quoted by Jan Wenner, *Lennon Remembers* (Harmondsworth: Penguin, 1973).

71. Spencer Dryden, quoted in Joe Kohut and John J. Kohut (eds), *Rock Quotes* (London: Faber & Faber, 1994).

72. Paul Kantner, quoted in *ibid.*

73. Jack Newfield, *A Prophetic Minority: The American New Left* (London: Anthony Blond, 1967), pp. 120–1.

74. Paul Goodman, *Growing Up Absurd* (New York: Vintage, 1960), pp. 112–13.

75. *Ibid.*, p. 175.

76. *Ibid.*, p. 112.

77. *Ibid.*, p. 187.

78. *Ibid.*, p. 183.

79. *Ibid.*, p. 181.

80. *Ibid.*, p. 175.

81. Larkin, *op. cit.*, p. 48.

82. Frank Parkin, 'Adolescent status and student politics', in *Generations in Conflict*, Special issue of *Journal of Contemporary History*, vol. 5, no. 1 (1970).

83. Wolin and Schaar, *op. cit.*, p. 17.

84. *Ibid.*, p. 18.

85. *Ibid.*, p. 121.

86. *Ibid.*, p. 130.

87. *Ibid.*, p. 131.

88. Quoted in Jon Stewart, 'Truckin' towards Taos with Tootsie', *Organ* magazine, 1970.

89. Nuttall, quoted in Hutchinson, *op. cit.*, p. 188.

90. Dick Hebdige, *Subculture: The Meaning of Style* (London: Methuen, 1979), p. 61.

91. *Ibid.*, p. 3.

92. Julie Burchill and Tony Parsons, *The Boy Looked at Johnny* (London: Pluto Press, 1978), p. 96.

93. J. Eisen, *Altamont* (New York: Avon, 1979), p. 163.

94. Charles Reich, *The Greening of America* (Harmondsworth: Penguin, 1971), p. 246.

95. Lewis S. Feuer, *The Conflict of Generations* (London: Heinemann, 1969), p. 389.

96. *Ibid.*, p. 405.

97. *Ibid.*

98. *Ibid.*, p. 284.

99. *Ibid.*, p. 407.

100. *Ibid.*, p. 413.

101. *Ibid.*, p. 179–80.

102. Kennan, *op. cit.*, p. 200.

103. Dave Rimmer, *Like Punk Never Happened: Culture Club and the New Pop* (London: Faber & Faber, 1985), p. 108.

104. *Ibid.*

105. Robert Elms, cited in Mort, *op. cit.*, p. 41.

106. Richard Neville, *Playpower* (London: Jonathan Cape, 1970), p. 26.

107. Alex Bellos, 'Some kind of freedom', *Guardian*, 25 September 1996.

108. Peter Berger, *Pyramids of Sacrifice* (London: 1976), pp. 156–7.

109. Geoffrey Pearson, *The Deviant Imagination* (London: Macmillan, 1975), p. 137. Pearson is summarizing an argument made by Paul Halmos. The full sentence reads: 'Paul Halmos has argued that the counselling ideology of the personal service professionals is a potent agent of social change, one which brings about a "moral reformation" of political and industrial leaders.'

110. Dick Fairfield, 'We are all one vision', *The Modern Utopian*, vol. 1, no. 2 (January 1970).

111. Carol Meyer's 'proposition' cited by Pearson, *op. cit.*, p. 137.

112. Christopher Lasch, *The Minimal Self* (London: Picador, 1985), p. 57.

113. *Ibid.*, p. 134.

114. Christopher Lasch, *The Culture of Narcissism* (London: Abacus, 1980), p. 4.

115. *Ibid.*, p. 51.

116. *Ibid.*, p. 7.

117. *Ibid.*, p. 13.

CHAPTER 10

The End of Adulthood?

A new political order has emerged in which the victim is
supreme, and adults are treated more like children. Meanwhile,
many adults are more likely to think of themselves as victims,
or to identify with the motif of the authentic, innocent child.
The result is a convergence between on the one hand the
spontaneous development of a cultural personality which is
victimized and childlike, and on the other hand the remoulding
of the individual's relationship to the state in accordance with
his supposed immaturity. The convergence of these trends is
facilitated by the already existing non-adult language provided
by the counterculture and the pop culture which succeeded it.

The key question in such circumstances is whether adulthood will go into abeyance; or whether the end of adulthood
can be resisted by a critique of infantilism and the reclamation
of subjectivity.

'I draw most strength from the victims for they represent America to
me ... You are my heroes and heroines. You are but little lower than
the angels.'[1] So said Janet Reno, attorney general of the United States of
America, as part of her address to a victims' rights conference in August
1996. Reno's near-worship of victims ('little lower than the angels')
demonstrates the drastic change that has occurred in the *mores* of the
most powerful country in the world, which, as American critic James
Hillman has pointed out, used to be famous for its 'heroic culture'.[2]
The effusive praise for victims on the part of one of the most senior
officers appointed by the federal government also suggests that the
Clinton administration has adopted the victim as a model persona – the
kind of person it can do business with.

Arrested Development

A small number of American critics have noted and protested against the elevation of victimhood. 'The victim', observed Christopher Lasch, 'has come to enjoy a certain moral superiority in our society', to the point where competing interest groups now 'vie for the privileged status of victims'.[3] The conservative critic C. J. Sykes was equally unimpressed by the elevation of victimhood, which he correlated with 'the decay of American character'. Sykes was concerned that 'the claim that one is a victim has become one of the few currencies of intellectual exchange',[4] to the extent that the invocation of victim status is often sufficient to close down debate and prevent further interrogation of almost any controversial topic.

We're all victims now

Victims are everywhere; and, by the same token, it seems that everyone is involved in a relationship of victimization. In 1995 Channel 4 broadcast *Battered Britain*, an extensive season of programmes, most of them documentaries, which depicted British society as a nexus of abusive relationships. Writing in the *Observer* in the summer of 1996, Nicci Gerrard wrote a feature article entitled 'The monster inside us all' in which she claimed that 'some people are born bullies – others are born victims. Each of us has been one or the other.'[5] Gerrard's categorization of the general population into bullies and victims is now commonplace, with the added complication that bullies are often said to be responding in kind to an earlier phase of their lives in which they themselves were victimized. Experience of victimhood has come to be regarded as the common denominator which defines our humanity.

In *The Face*, meanwhile, Damon Albarn (the lead singer in the band Blur) saw through the perceptions of victimhood which Gerrard *et al.* seem to take at face value. Albarn recognized that our self-image has been re-oriented to the point where there is a tendency for all of us to see ourselves as victims, regardless of whether or not such an image is justified: 'If there's going to be an epitaph for the nineties, it will be "by the end, we all felt like victims".'[6]

This is the era in which celebrities, from footballers to princesses, cannot hope to retain their celebrity unless they come up with a story in which they play the role of the victim. Politicians can also expect to acquire extra kudos by virtue of their proximity to victimhood. During a pre-election television broadcast by the New Labour Party, Anita Roddick, co-owner of The Body Shop, was heard to say of Tony Blair

'I like the way he looks exhausted.' As noted by *London Evening Standard* columnist Peter Bradshaw, this remark must have been 'sanctioned, perhaps even encouraged by Labour's top PR brass' because it gave the desired impression that Blair was 'adorably vulnerable'.[7] Even the most powerful job in the land, that of prime minister, has been re-defined to incorporate the widely accepted assumption that we are all victims of the circumstances in which we find ourselves.

Top persona

Just as Adam Smith's *homo oeconomicus* (economic man) was the predominant self-image of the individual during the progressive phase of capitalism, so nowadays the victim is among the top personae in today's society. Moreover, it seems that the greasy pole which brought the victim to this position was none other than the axis which runs through pop culture all the way back to the counterculture which preceded it.

In the mid-1990s the figure of the pop star as self-made victim was updated by Richey Edwards, the lead singer of The Manic Street Preachers, who disappeared on the morning of 31 January 1995, never (yet) to be seen again. Before his unexpected exit, Edwards's lyrics had proclaimed that 'everyone's a victim', and he sang of 'the beautiful dignity in self-abuse'.[8] Edwards first made a name for himself when, in front of a journalist, he carved '4REAL' in his arm with a razor, and a photograph of him, bleeding but impassive, went to the *NME*. Edwards's enigmatic retreat from pop life provides an equally powerful image of victimhood, on which his current reputation now rests.

It would be fanciful to suggest that either Nicci Gerrard or Janet Reno is devoted to The Manic Street Preachers and the memory of missing band member Richey Edwards. Nevertheless both of them will undoubtedly have been touched by the pop sensibility to which Edwards is now a prominent contributor, and which itself contributed to the notion that everyone is a victim (Edwards/Gerrard) and to the image of the beautiful dignity of victims (Edwards/Reno).

Pre-adult

In today's society the other, equally powerful self-image is that of the child. Apart from the victim, pre-adulthood is the only other universal unit of cultural currency, while adulthood itself is about as welcome as negative equity. Hence the statement by William Eccleshare, chief executive of the leading advertising agency Amnirati Puris Lintas to the effect that contemporary advertising constantly utilizes images of the pre-adult in the knowledge that over-twenty-ones will identify with them: 'If all advertising seems to be directed at the young it's because we've found the most effective way to appeal to everyone is to make commercials which embody attitudes associated with youth.'[9]

The identification with the pre-adult on the part of most over-twenty-ones has led some commentators to talk about the end of the generation gap. In the *Sunday Telegraph* Alasdair Palmer remarked that 'it's hard to rebel when parents and their children dress alike, enjoy the same music and agree politically'.[10] At fifty Channel 4 newscaster Jon Snow sings in his own band, Four Play, and admits that 'I still wonder what I'll do when I grow up' – unlike his own father whom he remembers as old and white-haired at the same age.[11] Cultural anthropologist Ted Polhemus has predicted that youth may be about to disappear from a culture in which the old insist on staying young.[12]

Power and the image of powerlessness

The victim and the child are the two leading cultural personalities in today's society. Moreover they complement each other, in that they are joined together by the common element of powerlessness. Abused and defenceless, the victim and the child are attractive personae in that they represent life beyond the discredited struggle for power between competing, self-interested adults. How ironic, therefore, that the motifs of the victim and the child have been adopted by a new ruling elite in its pursuit of more power over individuals and society.

That the elevation of victimhood has a corrosive effect on adult autonomy is best illustrated by reference to the growing influence of Victim Support, the state-sponsored national charity which supports the victims of crime. Victim Support is now one of the key organizations in British society. The highest echelons attend its training programmes. As chief lobbyist for victims' rights, Victim Support had the ear of the previous Conservative government, and much of its agenda was endorsed by Tony Blair shortly after taking office as prime minister. Moreover, in its expression of an unprecedented sense of people being permanently at risk, Victim Support reflects the public mood. What began as a local support scheme in Bristol in the mid-1970s has mushroomed into a nation-wide federation with eight hundred paid staff, seventeen thousand volunteers and a Home Office grant of £12 million a year. According to its adherents, this is money well spent. They claim that Victim Support is answering a call for 'respect, recognition and support' which the criminal justice process has failed to meet.

Pledged to redress the current 'imbalance' in favour of the defendant, Victim Support has successfully campaigned for victims to be allowed to state how they have been affected by the crimes committed against them and for this 'victim statement' to be introduced into the deliberations of British courts. According to Victim Support, this is a step towards putting victims and defendants on an equal footing. But the campaign to improve the status of victims can have the effect only of denying the rights of defendants. Moreover, the Victim Support ethos substitutes the cultural personality of the victim, and the equally exaggerated persona of the bully, for the legal personality of the autonomous adult. Not only does this pose a threat to legal norms, it also constitutes an attack on the role of adulthood throughout society, and an extension of state power over us all.

In its statement of victims' rights (1995), which influenced the revised version of the Conservative government's Victim's Charter (1996), Victim Support argued for various measures which affect legal procedures: 'Victims should have the right to withhold their identity from the accused during the investigations.' This means that during the preparation of his or her case the defendant may not be allowed to know by whom he or her stands accused. Such secrecy, if it occurred elsewhere, would prompt British commentators to refer to it as the legal practice of a police state.

'Vulnerable witnesses should have the right to an alternative to giving evidence in open court.' This is an apparently benign demand for the protection of those such as rape victims who may have been traumatized by the assault perpetrated against them. But the move away from open court sets a dangerous precedent. Protecting the anonymity of 'vulnerable witnesses', which also features prominently in New Labour's criminal justice policy, could lead to a situation in which 'professional witnesses' elaborate and fabricate evidence against the accused.

'The questioning of victims and other witnesses should be carried out with respect for the dignity of the individual.' Again this seems like an innocuous request for the civilized treatment of victims. In fact it calls into question the whole basis upon which defendants may refute allegations made against them. If this became the guiding principle of cross-examination, it would mean that the interests of the alleged offender, traditionally served by aggressive cross-questioning in an adversarial setting, would be subordinated to a new etiquette which gives precedence to the feelings of the supposed victim.

There is more at stake here than a trade-off between supposed victim and alleged offender. Defendants' rights do more than protect the individual interests of the defendant. They are a necessary part of the procedure for arriving at the facts of the case. Downgrading defendants' rights means undermining the capacity of the criminal justice system for methodical investigation and objective judgement. By the same token, prioritization of victims' rights tends to elevate the feelings of the victim as interpreted by criminal justice professionals.

The merit of the traditional, adversarial trial lies in its function as a contest between opposing versions of events. Until these contrasting accounts have been tried and tested, they are granted little weight. Hence, in theory at least, the alleged offender is 'innocent until proven guilty'. But Victim Support insists that there is a prior duty to 'respect' the untested account of victims and prosecution witnesses. This goes against the legal basis of criminal justice, which requires that respect for any testimony must be earned by public verification in open court.

It also goes against the assumption that those who come into court, whether for the prosecution or on behalf of the defence, are independent adults who can put their case and answer for themselves. In the mind's eye of Victim Support, however, the courtroom is half-populated by those who are deemed incapable, either because they are victims traumatized by crime or because they are criminals who cannot control themselves. The other half of the courtroom is made up of professionals whose function is to compensate for the immaturity of the rest of the population, either by protecting victims from criminals or by protecting criminals from themselves. This ethos loses sight of the level playing field of adult autonomy, and replaces it with a two-tier set-up comprising those who are non-adult (the people) and those who are called upon to play a super-adult role (the professionals).

The wholesale reformulation of legal norms in the image of victimhood may sound like a tall order. But in today's context the substitution of the victim persona for the traditional legal personality is entirely plausible. The academic discipline of criminology has already been recast with the victim rather than the offender as its protagonist. In the 1960s and early 1970s criminologists, in the manner of 'appreciative' sociologists, carried out endless 'offender surveys' which were often mildly sympathetic to their subjects. Since the late 1970s, however, the emphasis (and the funding for research) has been on the victim, hence the plethora of 'victim surveys' which after nearly two decades shows no sign of abating.

Victims at work

The notion of victimhood is also coming into force in the workplace, where it has the capacity to engender a fragile sense of togetherness at a time when collectivity among employees is at an all-time low, and the leadership offered by employers is also at a low ebb. Against this background, in 1996 Victim Support convened a conference of union officials and managers (which I attended in my capacity as a journalist) under the title 'Violence in the workplace: action for employee care'.

At the conference there was a consensus in favour of 'corporate strategy' to 'recognize the effects of crime and provide appropriate responses to meet the needs of victims', possibly by implementation of one of a range of training programmes developed by Victim Support.

Why the sudden concern about victims of crime in the workplace? Helen Reeves OBE, the director of Victim Support, gave the impression that work is now a violent place, with 'one in four of all crimes of violence' occurring there. Yet, according to Dr Peter Graham, speaking in his capacity as director of the health and policy division of the Health and Safety Executive, there were no official figures for violence at work: 'we don't have hard data ... There are no national statistics.' The absence of 'hard data' did not prompt anyone to question the new-found concern over violence at work, however. Rather, the lack of statistical evidence gave added cause for concern because 'although we're all very concerned, there isn't as yet a strong grip on the level of violence, which makes it difficult to get awareness messages across to employers'.

Such is the consciousness of risk, and so strong is the image of ourselves as victims, that a cause for concern can now be plucked out of the air and into the realm of public policy; and, if there is no empirical evidence to back it up, this is no longer grounds for dismissing it as an exaggeration, but instead makes it even more of a cause for concern.

So this particular conference must have been motivated by something other than hard evidence of a rising tide of workplace violence.

Arrested Development

Perhaps, after a decade of corporate downsizing, managers came looking for a way to reinstate the company ethos in a form which would not excite derision from employees. It may be that concern for victims of violence, whether real or notional, offers managers the opportunity to distance themselves from the discredited 'slash and burn' techniques of the 1980s, and the chance to re-invent themselves as caring representatives of 1990s-style ethical capitalism. Focusing on victims at work enables them to pupate their own self-image from the clones of greedy Gordon Gekko in Oliver Stone's *Wall Street* to something like the butterfly touch of The Body Shop's Anita Roddick.

Of course if managers really wanted to alleviate the sense of vulnerability experienced by today's working population, they could offer more money, shorter hours and a job for life. Instead they are devising corporate strategies which depict work as a place where employer and employee are equally at risk from violent crime. The real effect of this fiction is to obscure the imbalance of power between employer and employee, and to disguise further the coercive element which is built into their unequal relationship.

Emotional appeal

In previous historical periods, when society felt more confident about itself, the attempt to engender togetherness by cultivating a shared sense of victimhood would surely have been regarded as superfluous, if not ludicrous. But this is no longer the case. Protecting the victim persona serves as a notional greater good in a society which dares not think big; and in today's uncertain atmosphere victimhood carries an emotional appeal which spans all sections of society.

The emotional appeal of victimhood is clearly visible at the annual national conferences of Victim Support. During one such event, on a hot afternoon in July 1996, I sat amongst a packed auditorium of Victim Supporters as they listened to the personal testimony of three victims of horrendous crimes. The first to speak was Julie Chimes, who explained how she was repeatedly stabbed by a woman she had invited into her home. Chimes reported that she also felt wounded by the apathetic response of passers-by, and the uncaring attitude of those in authority. The next person to speak was Merlyn Nuttall, who recounted how on 18 February 1992 she was 'abducted from a main road, sexually assaulted and left for dead'. The final contribution came from David Howden, whose nineteen-year-old daughter Tessa was murdered in the family home in 1986. Howden recalled that when 'confronted with the remains of my daughter', there was 'no friendly social worker or doctor'. Addressing the conference delegates, Howden concluded that 'only you can help' the victims of crime. In reply the assembled Victim Supporters gave him a standing ovation.

Only a Spock-like Vulcan could have remained entirely unmoved by these accounts of human suffering. What was extraordinary, however, was the delegates' assumption that, as Nuttall said of her ordeal, 'it could have been you'. In fact her testimony was moving precisely because so few people have undergone an ordeal like hers. If it was really commonplace, i.e. if it really could have been you, or me, or all of us, then her dreadful tale would have had little dramatic effect. But the audience of Victim Supporters wanted it both ways: they were moved by the drama of these singular events while interpreting them as confirmation of the idea that everyone is a victim in the making.

Howden was the most moving of the three speakers, and he concluded with an appeal for people to demonstrate their common humanity by caring for the victims of crime. It is a sign of the strange days in which we live that people find it relatively easy to come together around an idea of ourselves as victims, whereas the heroic strikes most of us as untenable, and ambition is usually redefined as 'greed' and regarded as undesirable.

In this context victimhood tugs at our emotions; and when many people are pulled the same way at the same time it can feel like a new kind of solidarity. But at events like these, and also in media coverage of tragic cases of fatal abuse, we are being invited to solidarize around a joint sense of weakness and vulnerability in the face of death – a morbid, psycho-social syndrome which the prescient social critic Frank Furedi has rightly described as 'mourning sickness'.[13] At best this is impracticable, in that helplessness hardly provides a firm basis for the redevelopment of collectivity. At worst, it means that we are united in self-alienation and become even more frozen in the repudiation of our potential to act forcefully and decisively upon the world. This is to deny, rather than confirm, what makes us fully human.

Children's rights? – wrong
As well as through the promotion of the victim, adulthood is being attacked from another direction. The growing demand for 'children's rights' may do little to improve the lives of children. But it serves to

undermine parents and their rights, while extending the authority of state-sponsored professionals.

With the Children Act 1989 the Conservative government put children's rights at the centre of social policy, and the New Labour government has followed suit. At first sight, the bipartisan emphasis on children's rights might seem progressive; comparable, perhaps, to the emancipation of women or blacks. But this very comparison is indicative of the fallacious character of 'children's rights'.

Women and blacks are adults who are denied equal rights in so far as they belong to specific social groups which are oppressed in society. Were it not for the fact that their rights have been withheld, they would be capable of exercising them fully. Children, on the other hand, are by definition not adults. They are still learning to be adults, hence they are incapable of exercising rights on an equal footing with already existing adults. Children are necessarily immature, in a way that women and black people are not. In this respect they can have no claim to equal rights.

Official emphasis on 'children's rights' cannot succeed in raising children to the same level of capability as adults, any more than you can legislate to put the amoeba and the monkey at the same point on the evolutionary scale. But the cause of 'children's rights' does have the effect of bringing adults, in official eyes, down to the level of children. It does this by putting children on a par with adults, as if they were no more and no less capable than adults in their dealings with society. The corollary is that adults are no more and no less capable than children. As a result we are all officially infantilized by means of the progressive-sounding language of 'children's rights'.

While adults are pulled back to the same level as minors who by definition cannot yet exercise rights for themselves, various state-sponsored professionals have raised themselves up to new heights of super-adult authority by promising to exercise rights on behalf of children. Under the Children Act 1989, for example, the state acts on behalf of the child to protect it from abuse. According to the liberatarian commentator James Heartfield, 'it is not the child that exercises the rights, but the state. The state steps in as a kind of super-parent, to lord it over those parents deemed to have failed in their responsibility to children.'[14]

The events at Waco, Texas, in April 1993 provide a graphic illustration of how the state's role as super-parent can go tragically wrong. Janet Reno, the aforementioned Attorney-General of the United States of America, was persuaded that the children in the compound of the Branch Davidian cult were at risk of abuse. As a lawyer who made her name in child-abuse cases, Reno may have been particularly sympathetic to such claims. In any case, she gave the FBI permission to move in. The authorities mounted a military-style operation which resulted in the death of eighty-six people, who were either gunned down or killed in the ensuing fire. Of these seventeen were children, of whom Heartfield says they were 'apparently killed in defence of their own rights'.[15]

Short trousers

The corrosion of adulthood does not usually take the form of charred bodies and outright carnage. But whatever form it takes, this process tends to destroy our sense of independence and to create a debilitating culture of dependence. Thus when Patricia Hewitt, speaking for the Institute of Public Policy Research in 1996, declared that in the interests of children 'we need a new statement of what parenting means',[16] she was really suggesting that the state, or a body close to it, should codify a model of parenthood and pressurize parents to adhere to it, thereby removing from them the opportunity to bring up their children as they see fit.

David Blunkett, the (then) shadow education secretary, picked up Hewitt's suggested when in January 1997, four months before taking office, he announced New Labour's plans for what the *Daily Telegraph* (23 January 1997) dubbed 'child-rearing lessons'.[17] It is extraordinary to think that parents now require lessons in order to accomplish what their forebears have succeeded in doing since time immemorial. As noted in an article by Tony Farsides in *The Face*, this is the ethos of an 'ever-more authoritarian state ... ironically, not on the back of some right-wing backlash, but with a look of concern and evening classes in good parenting'.[18] Moreover, by undermining the autonomy of parents the effect of the Hewitt–Blunkett trend is to put adults back in short trousers, in the comical style of the late Jimmy Clitheroe. For without autonomy our adult status becomes dubious, and we really are in danger of turning into overgrown children.

The child motif now looms large on the stage of national politics. When Tony Blair wanted to get the 'peace train' going in Northern Ireland, he posed on the steps of Number 10 with a twelve-year-old girl who had written and asked him to sort out the troubles there. Previous British prime ministers have stressed the inviolability of the Union, or banged on about the right of Ulster's majority to stay British (hoping meanwhile that the rest of us would not have caught on to the fact that the six-county province of Ulster was created artificially just so that British prime ministers could talk of protecting democracy when really they were protecting Britain's interests). But for Blair the trump card is neither the Union nor democracy but the protection of children, and the effect of his game is to turn politics into an upscale version of *Jim'll Fix It*. Ironically, this is a game that many Irish republicans have been playing for some time, with their notion of Britain as an abuser who has repeatedly violated Mother Ireland and her children since the great famine of 1847.

Writing in the *Spectator* the distinguished political columnist Bruce Anderson warned that 'if Mr Blair runs his government as a children's crusade, he will eventually get the bird'.[19] Anderson recalled that Jimmy Carter got short shrift from the electorate after he cited his daughter Amy's opinions about nuclear weapons during the American presidential election debates of 1980. He concluded, 'If Mr Blair goes on pretending to base his actions on children's advice, there will come a moment when the British people say "yuck".' Of course Anderson was right to point out the sickly sweet flavour of politicking with children. But he seems not to have recognized that the British as well as the American public has recently acquire something of a taste for it. Yes, it would have been considered absurd if Franklin Delano Roosevelt had posed with Shirley Temple to announce the New Deal. But in today's context it is the idea of a plan to deal with economic recession which strikes one as implausible, whereas the deployment of children is now an unfortunate part of the political furniture.

The twin personae of powerlessness, the victim and the child, have been brought together in a series of emotive panics about child sexual abuse. The insidious effect of this overheated concern was exhibited in a presentation to the Victim Support annual conference held in July 1995 at Warwick University arts centre (again, I attended this event in my capacity as a journalist).

A sanctimonious hush came over the conference hall as Frances LeRoy of the NSPCC child witness support project started to speak about child sexual abuse 'through the words of a twelve-year-old child'. LeRoy introduced herself by saying 'My name is Mary', and the play-acting continued as she went on to describe how 'she' was abused by her 'Uncle Bob'. LeRoy broke off to explain that the names in her story had been changed. Delegates were then called upon to accept this melodrama as proof that children's needs should be paramount, for example court officials' handling of children must be 'extra-sensitive', recognizing that 'the video link rooms' (only recently provided so that minors do not have to face their alleged abusers) are 'claustrophobic' and unfortunately do not 'protect children from hostile cross-questioning'.

LeRoy's contribution derived its dramatic effect from her claim to represent the authentic voice of an abused child. But this claim was disingenuous. Conference delegates were listening to an interpretation of the reported experiences of abused children as relayed to them through the medium of a middle-class professional woman. The call for the anonymity of vulnerable witnesses suggests that a similar situation might soon be reproduced in court, with intermediaries such as LeRoy speaking on behalf of children and other victims in order to save them from further trauma.

The basic assumption behind the idea of victims' rights is that those against whom crimes have been committed are so enfeebled by the experience that they need someone else to speak for them. The assumption is redoubled if the victim happens to be a child. This self-appointed spokesperson is then invited to decide what the victim needs, and to influence what should happen to the criminal. The authority vested in such spokespersons is ultimately derived from the state. The extension of their professional discretion, and the expansion of state control in the form of their increased discretionary power, are the inevitable results of championing victim's rights and 'children's rights'.

The extension of state control can only mean the degradation of adulthood and the rights traditionally attendant upon it. Demanding new rights for victims and children sets up a spurious counterposition between 'victims' rights' and defendants' rights (increasingly referred to as 'privileges'), and between 'children's rights' and the rights of adults, with the state in an increasingly privileged position as the final arbiter between them. In fact defendants' rights ('privileges') are the legal expression of universal, democratic rights which have traditionally provided adults with a measure of protection from the state. Notions of 'victims' rights' and 'children's rights' are characteristic of the recent redefinition of right. Instead of protection *from* the state, the term 'rights' has been twisted to mean protection by the state. This is a form of 'protection' and dependency which, as independent adults, we could well do without.

Excommunication

In frustration at the perceived epidemic of child sexual abuse, the London *Evening Standard* columnist Victor Lewis-Smith joked that he alone appears not to have been the victim of it: 'Despite the nationwide search I launched several months ago in this very paper, it appears that I am *still* the only person in Britain who wasn't sexually abused as a child.'[20]

Lewis-Smith's remark was facetious, but it nevertheless illustrates a serious problem, namely that the consensus around the paramountcy of the child and the victim is such that very few individuals have dared to question it. In this respect the entire realm of public debate may be said to have been infantilized.

The childish character of public life today has been amply demonstrated in the response to the tragedy at Dunblane in March 1996, when gun fanatic Thomas Hamilton walked into the town's primary school and killed sixteen pupils and their teacher before shooting himself. Within eighteen months successive Tory and New Labour governments brought about a blanket ban on handguns in Britain (except those in the possession of the state itself). During this period only a tiny minority of commentators dared to criticize the rush to legislate for our whole society on the basis of the actions of a solitary lunatic, and those who did were shouted down immediately. Even royalty, in the form of HRH Prince Philip, came in for a roasting, after declaring that it made no more sense to ban shooting than to outlaw cricket bats. Indeed it seems that the royal writ counts for little these days, compared to the holy seal of approval for any measure, no matter how authoritarian, which promises to ensure the safety of children.

Furthermore, the discussion of Dunblane occurred entirely on the level of childlike emotionalism. Standing back and appraising what really happened, as one might expect an adult to do, was frowned upon and immediately interpreted as a slur on the memory of Dunblane's holy innocents. Thus when a *Guardian* music critic, Emma Forrest, dared to suggest that the Dunblane Christmas single was by no means a great record,[21] she was vilified in the tabloid press. It was as if she had excommunicated herself from a culture created in the image of the child and the victim.

Beyond left and right

If politics today has gone beyond left and right, then the transcendent motifs of the new politics are the victim and the child. These motifs are now as significant throughout pop culture and mainstream politics as they were in the minority counterculture of thirty or forty years ago.

The authoritarian consequences of the transfer of such icons from the counterculture to the new political order has attracted the attention of a handful of commentators. Andrew Sinclair, for example, observed the 'trend' of the 1960s being 'stood on its head', and becoming 'the thought-police of the politically correct academics and politicians who would rise to govern America'.[22] Jeff Nuttall noted that 'Political Correctness comes straight out of the old sixties Underground'.[23] At the beginning of the 1980s Bernice Martin sensed that the sensibility of the 1960s would outlive the left-wing politics with which it was originally associated, and that it would give shape to the times to come: 'Underneath the red clothing was a beast of a different colour, or perhaps a chameleon able to take on *any* political colouring ... a specialist and exaggerated form of a phenomenon which is affecting all spheres of society.'[24]

The radical sociologist Stanley Cohen recognized that the 1960s notion that 'the personal is political' has come to unexpected fruition in victim culture, where it also has the effect of undermining democratic rights:

> For victims, if not for deviants (as we thought in the sixties), the personal has indeed become political. This culture of victimisation emerges from identity politics: groups defining themselves only in terms of their claims to special identity and suffering. And this trend is given a spurious epistemological dignity by the ethic of multiculturalism. The result of all this is to actually subvert the ... politics based on such old fashioned Enlightenment meta-narratives as common citizenship and universal rights.[25]

Cohen seems to be suggesting that, by coming down to the level of the personal, politics has been reduced in scale. But instead of thereby expanding the scope of the individual, as was the hope in the 1960s, this has served only to reduce the range of humanity.

Arrested Development

In *Cynicism and Postmodernity*, his first book, Timothy Bewes points out that the individual in this new context is not only diminished but also heavily moralized. Bewes sees Blair as a politician without a political programme, who uses the notion of individual moral responsibility as a poor substitute:

> Political responsibility is abrogated to the individual, whereby it is stripped of its essentially political character. The 'Blair Revolution' is a programme not of structural change, but of change in a way that individuals live their lives. Socialism, for Tony Blair, has no particularly economic or even political significance, but constitutes rather a 'moral purpose to life'.[26]

The reconstitution of politics, and life itself, as 'moral purpose' was something that the counterculture dreamed of repeatedly. Martin mentioned its 'new, purified rituals',[27] and she also cited Frank Parkin's account of the Campaign for Nuclear Disarmament in which the latter is described as inextricably linked to the 'expressive politics' of middle-class moral purification.[28] It seems that in the 1990s the new politics exists on the same narrow terrain of individual behaviour which was previously the preserve of the counterculture and its anti-politics.

Back in the 1960s Richard Alpert, an associate of Timothy Leary, was wont to 'imagine what it would be like to have anybody in high political office with our understanding of the universe'.[29] When Blair, on the stump in Stevenage towards the end of April 1997, declared himself 'part of the rock'n'roll generation',[30] he brought Alpert's dream to life, although not in the way it was originally intended. Blair was announcing more than his penchant for Bruce Springsteen. He wanted us to know that he is familiar with the themes and motifs that were generated by the counterculture and its music. Moreover, he was inviting the electorate to contextualize the New Labour strain of middle-class moral purification within the tradition of the counter-culture. Thus New Labour's authoritarianism is rendered not only more palatable but also true to our times.

After the gap

June 1997 was the wettest June this century, and the pop festival at Glastonbury almost sank in a sea of mud. In previous years the Glastonbury festival had symbolized the notion of a radical counter-culture in opposition to the authorities and the mass circulation media.

In 1997, however, the festival line-up included a short speech from the newly appointed Arts Minister, Old Etonian Mark Fisher, and the national press looked favourably on the mud-bathers and even commended festival goers for braving the elements and showing the 'Dunkirk spirit'. With this description the counterculture was finally embraced within the mainstream.

The gap between them may never have been as large as was originally supposed. A useful illustration of their proximity is to be found in an inappropriately titled book, *The Gap*, which was co-written in 1968 by an American hippie student and his uncle, an advertising executive. At the end of this slim volume the former withdraws his attack on 'commercialism', the latter has been 'turned on' to smoking 'pot', and, in the words of the nephew, the adman uncle 'learned to refuse to condemn'.[31]

Only a few years after the publication of *The Gap* Jerry Brown, governor of California, began the incorporation of the counterculture into government. According to Theodore Roszak, 'Brown had the knack of associating himself, if only obliquely and ambiguously, with a range of offbeat values and countercultural types ... He was known to keep company with Zen Buddhists, rock stars and Schumacher-style economists.'[32] But the convergence between counterculture and government should come as no great surprise, given that the hippies were only an exaggerated representation of the alienation from corporate America which was first expressed by their parents. In this respect the burning of draft cards and the refusal to fight in Vietnam was the natural heir to the earlier disillusionment and disengagement on the part of many of those who *had* fought in the Second World War.

As well as giving voice to the alienation which had been experienced almost silently by the previous generation, the counterculture – as John Clarke, Stuart Hall, Tony Jefferson and Brian Roberts realized in the mid-1970s – also acted as a test-bed for the next generation of mainstream society: 'The counter-cultures performed an important task on behalf of the system by pioneering and experimenting with new social forms which ultimately gave it greater flexibility.'[33]

This process was not just a one-way street, however, with the counterculture feeding into a more flexible but largely unchanged mainstream. It would be more accurate to suggest that the anti-politics of the 1960s counterculture was the flowering of the anti-society seeds planted by the previous generation. In the 1990s, furthermore, this crop is now the mainstay of our entire way of life, to the point where politics is being re-defined as a subset of pop culture.

Politics as subculture

In their essay 'Subcultures, cultures and class: a theoretical overview', Clarke *et al.* discussed the role of youth-oriented subcultures and concluded that 'they "solve" but in an imaginary way, problems which at the concrete, material level remain unresolved'.[34] This definition seems to have been based on an earlier statement by Phil Cohen in his seminal work on Mods and subcultures in London's East End. Cohen described the 'latent function of subculture' as follows: 'to express and resolve, albeit "magically" the contradictions hidden, or unresolved, in the parent culture'.[35]

The function of resolving 'magically' problems which remain unresolved at the 'concrete, material level' has now been taken on by politics, just as the politicians' capacity really to resolve problems, concretely and materially, has receded. Thus, instead of an economic programme which would create real jobs and eradicate unemployment, New Labour has offered out-of-work single mothers the opportunity to come into a government office and have their lives reviewed, with a view to going back into the world of work. This back-to-work scheme contains an element of coercion, but it is unclear whether large numbers of single mothers will really be driven to take unwanted jobs because of it. If such a situation does not in fact arise, this does not mean that the scheme will have failed in its own terms, however; the primary role of such schemes and the discussion surrounding them is not to get things done but to provide an arena where difficulties can be solved 'magically' or 'in an imaginary way', as if the problems of society really were reducible to personal behaviour and its remoralization.

New-time religion

Neither is this to say that such 'imaginary' solutions have no effect, but rather that their effects are not what they seem; instead of being primarily a measure to deal specifically with unemployed single mothers, the real effect of the single mothers initiative, as with many others like it, is to help build a new relationship between individuals generally and the state, in which the onus is increasingly on the former to prove their intentions and verify their behaviour with reference to a representative of the latter.

In this respect politics now operates in a way which is broadly similar to the Cohen/Clarke definition of a subculture; that is to say it is not expected to provide real solutions, only 'imaginary' ones. Politics, in other words, is no longer political. Instead, politics and pop have fused into a new social phenomenon which is as significant and as mystical as religion, although without the sense of purposeful activity which the latter has occasionally encapsulated.

It is hardly surprising, therefore, that politics should now be redolent with the iconography of powerlessness. This has come about not least because politics, as the implementation, 'magically', of 'imaginary' solutions, is at one and the same time the fantastic and the fetishized expression of powerlessness at the programmatic level. If politics today focuses on the image of the child, that is entirely in keeping with the advent of a new generation of politicians who in the face of adversity, and their own programmatic bankruptcy, liken themselves to children in their powerlessness and vulnerability. Nor are they alone in their self-image. The sense of powerlessness is widely shared throughout society; and it is through the common language of pop culture (née counter-culture) that the elite and the rest of society are able to communicate their shared sense of powerlessness and victimization.

New adulthood?

From this it can be seen that the erosion of adulthood, and the absence of a plausible image of history-making activity, cannot be remedied merely by the invention of a new self-image or the re-presentation of an old one. Indeed, when the outward form of adulthood is re-presented in today's context, its content is usually turned inside out. Thus the donning of suits and bow ties by followers of the black separatist leader Louis Farrakhan does not express the progressive but by no means perfect culture of universalism and democracy which was originally presented in the anonymity of the man's dark suit; rather it is a loud demonstration of particularism, in this case on the part of blacks – a response to the failure of bourgeois universalism which re-presents that failure all the more intensely.

In short there are no cultural solutions to the problems posed by victim culture. The latter can be addressed, not by the desire to look like adults but only by our attempts to act as adults. How can we succeed in our attempts? Firstly, by resisting any further incursion into what little adult autonomy we have left. For example, if Jack Straw, the

Arrested Development

Home Secretary, proceeds to act *in loco parentis* by imposing a curfew on under-sixteens, parents should resist any such measure on the grounds that it makes children out of them too, and inform the relevant authorities that they are perfectly capable of fixing their own children's bedtimes, thank you very much.

Generally speaking, if those in authority insist on issuing lists of instructions on how we should bring up our children, we can make it clear that we have no need of such 'advice' (for to accept it, and hence to become dependent on it, is the equivalent of wearing L plates for the rest of our lives). Furthermore, we should encourage those around us to reject the self-image of victims. On different occasions, the rejection of this self-image might mean issuing a challenge to the current pre-eminence of identity politics, or it might involve campaigning for free speech, and opposing the authorities' patronizing assumption that the rest of us are not adult enough to cope with offensive remarks.

However, resisting the new power generation in our day-to-day lives will make sense only if it is connected to a broader critique of society and its current impasse – otherwise the new mode of infantilized existence will never be revealed as the creature of authoritarianism and the obstacle to human development which it most certainly is. When such a critique becomes something like common knowledge, the absence of history-making subjectivity will have been recognized as a consequence of the essential but none the less not immovable character of today's society; and, having demystified the dearth of subjectivity, we will once more be able to envisage ourselves making history. It is this last which is the ultimate rejoinder to the insidious process of infantilization.

Notes

1. Janet Reno, quoted by Bruce Shapiro, *The Nation*, 10 February 1997.

2. James Hillman, *The Soul's Code* (New York: Random House, 1997), quoted in *Utne Reader*, January–February 1997, pp. 53–5.

3. Christopher Lasch, *The Minimal Self* (London: Picador, 1985), p. 67.

4. C. J. Sykes, *A Nation of Victims: The Decay of the American Character* (New York: St Martin's Press, 1992), pp. 16–17.

5. Nicci Gerrard, 'The monster inside us all', *Observer*, 16 June 1996.

6. Damon Albarn, 'End of a century', *The Face*, January 1997, p. 169.

7. Peter Bradshaw, 'That tired old body politic', *Evening Standard*, 14 April 1997, p. 11.

8. Richey Edwards's lyrics, quoted by Andy Beckett, 'Missing Street Preacher', *Independent on Sunday*, 2 March 1997, p. 21.

9. William Eccleshare, quoted by Alasdair Palmer, *Sunday Telegraph*, 2 February 1997.

10. *Ibid.*

11. Jon Snow, 'Still not grown up at 50', *Daily Telegraph*, 8 April 1997.

12. Ted Polhemus, quoted in *Observer*, 15 September 1996.

13. Frank Furedi, *The Culture of Fear* (London: Cassell, 1997).

14. James Heartfield, 'Why children's rights are wrong', *Living Marxism*, October 1993, pp. 13–14.

15. *Ibid.*, p. 14.

16. Patricia Hewitt speaking at 'Men and Their Children', a conference convened by the Institute for Public Policy Research at Church House, Westminster, on 30 April 1996.

17. David Blunkett, quoted by Liz Lightfoot, education correspondent, 'Child-rearing lessons promised by Labour', *Daily Telegraph*, 23 January 1997, p. 23.

18. Tony Farsides, 'Isn't it ironic?', *The Face*, January 1997, p. 174.

19. Bruce Anderson, *Spectator*, 28 June 1997, p. 8.

20. Victor Lewis-Smith, 'Pained by the psycho-babble', *Evening Standard*, 19 October 1995.

21. Emma Forrest, 'In tune with tragedy', *Guardian*, 5 December 1996.

22. Andrew Sinclair, *In Love and Anger* (London: Sinclair Stevenson, 1994), p. 168.

23. Jeff Nuttall, interviewed by Roger Hutchinson, in *High Sixties* (Edinburgh: Mainstream, 1992), p. 192.

24. Bernice Martin, *A Sociology of Contemporary Cultural Change* (Oxford: Blackwell, 1981), p. 21.

25. Stanley Cohen, 'Crime and politics', *British Journal of Sociology*, vol. 47, no. 1 (March 1996), p. 15.

26. Timothy Bewes, *Cynicism and Postmodernity* (London: Verso, 1997), p. 186.

27. Martin, *op. cit.*, p. 25.

28. *Ibid.*, p. 21.

29. Richard Alpert, quoted in Jay Stevens, *Storming Heaven: LSD and the American Dream* (London: Paladin, 1989), p. 446.

30. Tony Blair, quoted in *Daily Telegraph*, 23 April 1997.

31. Richard Lorber and Ernest Fladell, *The Gap* (New York: Signet, New American Library, 1968), pp. 126–7.

32. Theodore Roszak, *The Cult of Information* (Cambridge: Lutterworth Press, 1986), p. 143.

Arrested Development

33. John Clarke *et al.*, 'Subcultures, cultures and class: a theoretical overview', in Stuart Hall and Tony Jefferson (eds), *Resistance through Rituals* (London: Hutchinson, 1975), p. 47.

34. *Ibid.*

35. Phil Cohen, *Subcultural Conflict and Working-class Community*. Working Paper in Cultural Studies 2. University of Birmingham, 1972.

Index

Adamov, Arthur 51
Adams, Bryan 7
Aitken, Jonathan 171
Albarn, Damon 88, 234
Albee, Edward 51
Aldridge, John W. 7
Algren, Nelson 25
alienation 19, 23–6, 29, 30, 32–6,
    38, 40, 41, 44–5, 100–1, 135, 137,
    153–4
Allen, Walter 40
Allen, Woody 140
Alpert, Richard 70, 248
Alvarez, Al 132
Amis, Kingsley 33, 34, 40
Amis, Martin 186
Anders, Gunther 210
Anderson, Brett 42
Anderson, Lindsay 213
Antonioni, Michelangelo 11
Appleyard, Bryan 5, 19, 30
Arendt, Hannah 31
Aron, Raymond 8
Artaud, Antonin 9, 130, 131, 136,
    137

Baez, Joan 81, 112, 139
Baker, Chet 43
Baldwin, James 199
Ballard, J.G. 50
Bambi 119
Bane, Michael 194, 195, 202

Barbusse, Henri 27
Barker, Paul 160
Barnes, Richard 54
Barrett, Ed 183–4
Basquiat 107
Bateson, Gregory 53
Beatles, the 12, 14, 28, 49, 54, 60,
    95, 114, 133, 153, 192, 211
Beck 11, 61, 92
Becker, Howard 26, 27, 135
Beckett, Samuel 51, 169
Beefheart, Captain 140
Bell, Daniel 8, 9, 35, 95
Bellos, Alex 226
Bellow, Saul 132
Benello, George 37
Bennett, Catherine 163
Berger, Peter 227
Bettleheim, Bruno 69
Betts, Leah 1, 16–18
Bewes, Timothy 248
Bird, Caroline 93
Bjelland, Kat 42, 116
Bjork 19, 88
Blair, Cherie 99
Blair, Tony 14, 15, 91, 99, 119,
    120, 186, 187, 226, 234, 236, 248
Blake, William 149
Bloom, Allan 54, 60, 67, 95, 96
Blues Brothers, The 203
Blunkett, David 243
Bly, Robert 98, 99

Index

Bolt, Robert 97
Bono 58
Booker, Christopher 52, 68, 94
Boulez, Pierre 51
Bowie, David 10, 51, 140, 223
Bracewell, Michael 209
Bradbury, Malcolm 52, 97, 175, 179, 180
Braden, William 65, 68
Bradshaw, Peter 235
Brake, Mike 84, 219
Brando, Marlon 33, 40, 43, 60, 79, 109, 211
Brecht, Bertolt 51, 161
Brooks, Cleanth 186
Broom, Leonard 101
Brown, Jerry 249
Brown, Norman O. 54, 81
Bruce, Lenny 111, 210
Burchill, Julie 57, 181, 183, 184, 209, 223
Burroughs, William 9, 10, 43, 51, 70–1, 110, 161, 180–2, 227

Cage, John 51, 140
camp 170–2, 174–5
Campbell, Alistair 15
Camus, Albert 8, 19, 25, 30, 67–9, 109, 168–70, 192, 208, 209, 211, 214, 215
Carr, Roy 43, 176
Carter, Angela 29, 134, 139
Casey, John 11
Cashmore, E. Ellis 30
Cassady, Neal 43, 179
Caulfield, Holden 109
Cave, Nick 141
Chapman, Roger 10
Charles, Prince of Wales 133
Charters, Ann 80, 93, 152, 153
Christagu, Robert 61
Clapton, Eric 28, 81, 133, 199
Clarke, John 249–51
Clash, The 20, 57, 193
Clift, Montgomery 40, 79, 80, 109–11, 117, 119, 211

Clinton, Bill 12, 14, 15, 42, 99, 116, 118, 119, 162, 233
Cobain, Kurt 11, 30, 42, 116, 142, 211
Cocker, Jarvis 18, 19, 78, 79
Cohen, Leonard 110, 112
Cohen, Phil 250–1
Cohen, Stanley 176, 247
Cohn, Nik 161, 175
Cohn-Bendit, Daniel 62
Coleman, Ornette 51
Collin, Matthew 2, 89
Cook, Chris 217
Cook, Peter 177
Cooper, David 136, 137
Coupland, Douglas 87–8, 162, 177
Cream (band) 139
Cream (club) 3
Cronenberg, David 43
Crumb, Robert 132

Davis, John 85
Davis, Miles 210
Dean, James 30, 33, 39, 40, 43, 79, 87, 94, 109, 126, 209, 211
Debord, Guy 38
Debussy, Claude 51
Deleuze, Gilles 130
Deneslow, Robin 174
Deverson, Jane 123, 193
Diana, Princess of Wales 11
Dirke, Sabine Von 139
Doren, Charles Van 32
Dostoyevsky, Fyodor 86, 132
Dryden, Spencer 219
Dubuffet, Jean 10, 51, 131
Dunson, Josh 39
Dylan, Bob 53, 59, 80, 112, 114, 139, 155, 183, 216, 217

Easton Ellis, Brett 169
Eccleshare, William 235
Edwards, Mark 184
Edwards, Richey 235
ego-death 70
Eisenhower, Dwight D. 82

Eisner, Bruce 1
Ellison, Ralph 65, 125, 177, 198
Ellul, Jacques 124
Elms, Robert 226
Erikson, Erik 128
Esslin, Martin 51, 113, 130–1, 156–7
Evans, Chris 20
Evans, Gil 210

Face, The 3, 90, 116, 162, 234, 243
Farrakhan, Louis 251
Farren, Mick 25
Farsides, Tony 243
Feldman, Gene 58, 66–8, 110, 124, 130, 136
Fellini, Federico 11
Feuer, Lewis S. 39, 62, 95, 224
Fiedler, Leslie 93, 94, 110, 111, 175, 180, 181
Fiennes, Ralph 30–1
Finkelstein, Sidney 37
Fisher, Mark 249
Fitzgerald, F. Scott 110
Flacks, Richard 29
Fletcher, Joseph 60
Flugel, J.C. 25
Fonda, Jane 109
Forrest, Emma 246
Foss, Daniel 139
Foucault, Michel 136
Franklin, Aretha 12
Friedman, Maurice 132
Frith, Simon 59, 60, 82
Fromm, Erich 32
Frye, Northrop 187
Fuller, Peter 21, 65–6
Future Sound of London, The 8

Gallagher, Noel 14–17, 120
Garratt, Sheryl 4
Gartenberg, Max 58, 66–8, 110, 124, 130, 136
Genet, Jean 172, 204
Gerrard, Nicci 234, 235
Ginsberg, Allen 9–10, 20, 28, 43, 110, 129, 132, 143, 149–52, 154, 158, 160, 213
Goethe, Johann Wolfgang von 108, 109, 111
Gogh, Vincent van 130
Gold, Herb 125
Goldman, Albert 111, 199
Goodman, Paul 34, 36, 161, 210, 220, 221
Gosling, Ray 114
Gould, Tony 192, 199
Gouldner, Alvin 197
Grant, Linda 208
Greenfield, Jeff 32, 54, 82, 83, 200
Grogan, Emmett 139
Grossman, Lloyd 54
Guattari, Felix 130
Guevara, Che 113, 115
Guiffre, Jimmy 51
Gysin, Brion 51

Haley, Alex 193
Hall, Stuart 62, 249
Hamblett, Charles 123, 193
Hamilton, Thomas 246
Harrison, Charles 131
Harron, Mary 86
Harvey, Brian 1, 15–18, 43
Harvey, Polly Jean 19
Hayden, Tom 209
Haynes, Jim 84, 218
Heartfield, James 242, 243
Hebdige, Dick 29, 175, 193, 194, 218, 223
Hegel, Georg Wilhelm Friedrich 96, 107
Heidegger, Martin 50, 63
Helfgott, David 11
Heller, Joseph 168, 179
Hendrix, Jimi 5, 92, 200
Hentoff, Nat 112, 113
Herman, Gary 114
Hernton, Calvin C. 201
Hersh, Kristin 115
Hewitt, Paolo 2, 89
Hewitt, Patricia 243

Index

Hicks, Granville   212
Himes, Chester   172
Hinton, S.E.   29
Hockney, David   171
Hoffman, Abbie   61, 63, 139
Holmes, John Clellon   60, 151
Holzer, Baby Jane   82
Hopkins, John   217
Horovitz, Michael   153
Hoskyns, Barney   110
Howden, David   240–1
Hughes, Dorothy   25
Hughes, Robert   98, 107, 108, 111
Huizinga, Johan   83
Huncke, Herbert   151
Hutchinson, Roger   218
Huxley, Aldous   35, 150, 151, 159, 214, 215

Ice-T   194
instantaneity   50, 62, 64
Ionesco, Eugene   51
irony   167, 175–86

Jackson, Michael   78, 199
Jaspers, Karl   32
Jezer, Marty   59
Johnson, Paul   94
Jones, Dylan   181
Joplin, Janis   114, 193
Josephson, Eric   32
Josephson, Mary   32

Kafka, Franz   112
Kantner, Paul   219
Keats, John   183
Kelly, Kevin   212
Keniston, Kenneth   24, 34, 35, 37, 39, 58, 92, 95, 124, 125, 176
Kennan, George   211, 212, 215
Kennedy, Robert   34
Kerouac, Jack   8, 9, 28, 43, 60, 80, 93, 110, 125, 129, 143, 151–3, 179, 191, 199, 213
Kesey, Ken   10, 70, 134, 152, 214
Kidd, Jodie   115

Kohn, Marek   4
Konig, René   25
Konigsberg, Eric   19, 99
Kramer, Gary   41

Laing, Dave   217
Laing, R.D.   23, 45, 134–7, 139, 140
Landesman, Cosmo   98, 184
Landesman, Jay   126, 184
Larkin, Ralph   139, 221
Lasch, Christopher   68, 181, 227, 228, 234
Lawrence, D.H.   158
Lawson, Nigella   155
Leary, Timothy   4, 55, 69, 70, 139, 160, 214, 248
Legg, Barry   18
Legman, G.   126, 213
Leiber, Mike   172
Lenin, V.I.   83
Lennon, John   81, 92, 94, 95, 114, 193, 217, 219
Leonard, Neil   190
LeRoy, Frances   244, 245
Levin, Bernard   96–7
Lewis-Smith, Victor   246
Lhamon, W.T.   61
limitation   207–9, 214–16, 220, 227
Lindner, Robert M.   125, 126, 128, 209
Lipton, Lawrence   54
Little Richard   53
Loach, Ken   140
losers   8, 9, 11, 15, 110, 119
Love, Courtney   88, 99, 116
Lukács, Georg   167
Lyttleton, Humphrey   88

McCann, Graham   40, 79, 94, 109, 211
McCartney, Paul   114
McClellan, Jim   91
MacDonald, Ian   49, 55, 62, 63, 65, 94, 95
McGee, Alan   15

McGrath, Tom 65
MacInnes, Colin 80, 192, 193, 199, 213
MacIver, Robert 67
McKenna, Terence 159, 160
McKie, David 217
McLaren, Malcolm 86
McLuhan, Marshall 64
McLure, Michael 213
Mad (magazine) 132
madness 10, 13, 123–4, 128–9, 131–6, 139–44, 174
Madonna 43
Mael, Ron and Russell 140
Mailer, Norman 25, 54, 80, 127, 128, 192, 198, 209
Mairowitz, David Zane 214
Major, John 15
Mandelson, Peter 15
Manic Street Preachers, The 142, 235
Manners, Elizabeth 140
Mannheim, Karl 23–4, 163
Manson, Charles 12
Marat/Sade 143
Marcel, Gabriel 50
Marcus, Greil 211
Marcuse, Herbert 21, 35, 63, 71, 83, 95, 124, 134
Martin, Bernice 84, 114, 181, 247–8
Marx, Harpo 133
Marx, Karl 24, 107
Maxwell-Davies, Peter (Sir) 51, 140
Mellers, Wilfrid 51, 81
Melly, George 65, 94, 170, 209
Mezzrow, Mezz 195
Miles, Barry 149, 150
Milligan, Spike 81, 133, 143, 174
Milosz, Czeslaw 181
Monk, Thelonius 177
Moore, Charles 138
Moore, Suzanne 90
Morden, Ethan 34
Morrison, Jim 58, 61
Morrissey 19, 115

Morse, Mary 28
Mort, Frank 207
Moss, Kate 115
Mulligan, Gerry 210
Murdoch, Iris 131
Musgrove, Frank 92, 93, 124
Myrdal, Gunnar 196, 203

negrophilia 195
negrophobia 195
Neurotica 126–7
Neville, Richard 55, 61, 84, 226
Newfield, Jack 219
Newton, Francis 37, 38, 126, 197
Nichols, Jack 53
Nicholson, Jack 10, 119, 134
Nicosia, Gerald 80, 110, 129, 152, 153
Norman, Philip 92
Nuttall, Jeff 37–8, 53, 57, 60, 66, 70–2, 96, 111, 114, 133, 135, 158, 167, 168, 210, 223, 247

O'Connor, Sinead 115
O'Hagan, Sean 143
O'Shea, Suzanne 90
Oasis 14, 15, 49, 90
Oglesby, Carl 113, 134
Okonogi, Keigo 97
Oldman, Gary 12, 13
Orbach, Susie 160
Orff, Carl 81
Orridge, Genesis P. 142
Osborne, John 33

Packard, Vance 125
Palmer, Patsy 162
Parker, Charlie 33, 50, 57, 64
Parkin, Frank 221, 248
Parkinson, Michael 117
Parsons, Tony 57, 223
Pearson, Geoffrey 135, 138
Peel, John 86, 140, 218
Perry, Mark 57
Philip, Duke of Edinburgh 246
Picardie, Ruth 116

Index

Platt, Steve 3
play 83–5, 95
Podhoretz, Norman 64, 101
Polhemus, Ted 207, 208, 236
Pollock, Jackson 21, 56, 57, 65, 66
Polsky, Ned 36, 198
Porter, Henry 31
Prince 201
Pynchon, Thomas 1

Quant, Mary 80
Quotation Generation, The 183–5

Ralske, Kurt 161
Raphael, Amy 42, 116
rationality 10, 50, 52–4, 69, 70, 86, 124, 137, 144, 157, 159, 169
Raven, Charlotte 4, 100
Rawlings, E. Elliot 191
Ray, Nicholas 41, 126–7
Redhead, Steve 86, 87
Reeve, Christopher 118
Reeves, Helen (OBE) 239
Reeves, Keanu 43, 87
Reich, Charles 59, 83, 224
Reno, Janet 233, 235, 243
Revell, Lynn 154–5
Rexroth, Kenneth 25, 35, 64
Reynolds, Simon 72, 115, 141, 161, 203
Richards, Keith 112
Riesman, David 31
Rigley, Francis 125, 128
Rimmel cosmetics 207
Rimmer, Dave 225–6
risk-consciousness 5
Roberts, Ron E. 85
Roddick, Anita 234, 240
Roosevelt, Franklin Delano 118
Rorty, Richard 181, 182
Roszak, Theodore 52, 64, 70, 82, 95, 155, 156, 215–17, 249
Rotten (Lydon), Johnny 86, 141, 225
Rubin, Jerry 83

Rushkoff, Douglas 2, 100
Russell, Ken 140

safety 1–3, 6, 17
Salinger, J.D. 108–9
Sartre, Jean-Paul 25, 50, 170, 192
Saunders, Nicholas 17, 20
Savage, Jon 15, 58, 86
Savio, Mario 39, 40
Sawyer-Luçanno, Christopher 51
Scaduto, Antony 59, 112
Schaar, John H. 200, 210, 218–19, 222
Schlegel, August Wilhelm von 167
Schoenberg, Arnold 51
Schrader, Paul 40
Schwab, Joseph J. 95
Schwarzenegger, Arnold 176
Searle, John 59, 158, 159
Shaw, George Bernard 51
Sheehy, Gail 98
Shertser, Pete 170
Shils, Edward 95
Simpson, Mark 98–9
simultaneity 49, 50
Sinclair, Andrew 28, 247
Slack, Charles 139
Slater, Philip 32
Smith, Joan 1
Snoop Doggy Dog 203
Snyder, Gary 153
Solomon, Carl 9, 129, 130, 132
Sontag, Susan 171, 172
Sophocles 118
Spencer, Neil 14
Springsteen, Bruce 248
Stevens, Jay 2, 33, 54, 69, 70, 100, 128, 139, 213
Stewart, Dave 142
Stoller, Mike 172
Straw, Jack 14, 252
Stuart Hughes, H. 52
subjectivity 111, 137, 153, 173, 177, 179–80, 182, 185, 195, 197, 198, 209, 252
Sutherland, Mark 91

Tate, Sharon 12
Taylor, Laurie 176
Terkel, Studs 216
Thatcher, Margaret 216
therapy 13, 113, 139, 142, 160, 161, 226, 228
Thomas, Dylan 64, 112
Thompson, Richard 41
Tommy 86, 113, 114, 118
Tosches, Nick 68
Townshend, Pete 7, 54, 114, 118
Trench, Richard 218
Trilling, Diana 70
Trilling, Lionel 136, 137
Trocchi, Alexander 26, 68, 83
Truman, Harry S 32
Twiggy 115

Utne Reader 90

victim support 236, 237, 239, 240, 244
victims 2, 11–12, 14–18, 21, 72, 107, 111–12, 116, 119, 138, 187, 233–41, 244–5, 247, 251
Vonnegut, Kurt 97, 179
vulnerability 108–20, 235, 240–1, 251

Walden, George 11
Warhol, Andy 109, 140

Watt, Ben 116, 142
Watts, Alan 52, 157, 159
Waymouth, Nigel 170
Weber, Bruce 43
Wells, H.G. 50
Wenner, Jann 34, 219
Werther, Young 111
Weschler, James 213
Who, The 28, 54, 114
Wicks, Joe 143
Williams, John L. 87
Williams, Liza 37
Williams, Richard 210
Williams, William Carlos 9
Wilson, Colin 19, 27, 59, 132
Wilson, Morris 201
Wolfe, Tom 2, 31, 56, 81, 82, 195–7, 199, 200, 203
Wolfenstein, Martha 83
Wolin, Sheldon S. 210, 218, 219, 222
Wood, Paul 131
work 20, 83–5, 88, 95
Wright Brothers, the 152
Wright Mills, C. 31, 224

Yablonsky, Lewis 113
York, Peter 97, 207
Yorke, Thom 97, 101
Young, Hugo 217
Young, Jock 37, 55, 60
Young, Toby 183–6